The Last Utopia

The Last Utopia

Human Rights in History

Samuel Moyn

The Belknap Press of Harvard University Press

Cambridge, Massachusetts, and London, England

First Belknap Press of Harvard University Press paperback edition, 2012

Library of Congress Cataloging-in-Publication Data

Moyn, Samuel.
The last utopia : human rights in history / Samuel Moyn.
p. cm.
Includes bibliographical references and index.
ISBN 978-0-674-04872-0 (cloth : alk. paper)
ISBN 978-0-674-06434-8 (pbk.)
1. Human rights—History.   I. Title.

JC571.M88 2010
323.09—dc22   2010012998

Contents

The Last Utopia

When people hear the phrase "human rights," they think of the highest moral precepts and political ideals. And they are right to do so. They have in mind a familiar set of indispensable liberal freedoms, and sometimes more expansive principles of social protection. But they also mean something more. The phrase implies an agenda for improving the world, and bringing about a new one in which the dignity of each individual will enjoy secure international protection. It is a recognizably utopian program: for the political standards it champions and the emotional passion it inspires, this program draws on the image of a place that has not yet been called into being. It promises to penetrate the impregnability of state borders, slowly replacing them with the authority of international law. It prides itself on offering victims the world over the possibility of a better life. It pledges to do so by working in alliance with states when possible, but naming and shaming them when they violate the most basic norms. Human rights in this sense have come to define the most elevated aspirations of both social movements and political entities—state and interstate. They evoke hope and provoke action.

It is striking to register how recently this program became widespread. Over the course of the 1970s, the moral world of Westerners shifted, opening a space for the sort of utopianism that coalesced in an international human rights movement that had never existed before. The eternal rights of man were proclaimed in the era of Enlightenment, but they were so profoundly different in their practical outcomes—up to and including bloody revolution—as to constitute another conception altogether. In 1948, in the aftermath of World War II, a Universal Declaration of Human Rights was proclaimed. But it was less the annunciation of a new age than a funeral wreath laid on the grave of wartime hopes. The world looked up for a moment. Then it resumed its postwar agendas, which had crystallized in the same years that the United Nations—which sponsored the declaration—emerged. The priority fell on victory of one or the other of the two global Cold War visions for America, the Soviet Union, and the European continent they were dividing between them. And the struggle for the decolonization of empire made the Cold War competition global, even if some new states strove to find some exit from the Cold War rivalry to chart their own course. The United States, which had driven the inflation of global hopes during World War II for a new order after it, and introduced the idea of "human rights" into minor circulation, soon dropped the phrase. And both the Soviet Union and anticolonialist forces were more committed to collective ideals of emancipation—communism and nationalism—as the path into the future, not individual rights directly, or their enshrinement in international law.

Even in 1968, which the UN declared "International Human Rights Year," such rights remained peripheral as an organizing concept and almost nonexistent as a movement. The UN organized a twentieth-anniversary conference in Tehran, Iran, to remember and revive stillborn principles. It was an extraordinary scene. The dictatorial shah, Mohammad Reza Pahlavi, opened the spring conference by crediting his ancient countrymen with the discovery of human rights: the tradition of the great Persian emperor Cyrus of more than a millennium before, the shah asserted, had now found fulfillment in his own dynasty's respect for moral principle. The meetings that followed, chaired by his sister Princess Ashraf, brought to the fore an interpretation of human rights altogether unrecognizable now: the liberation of nations formerly under imperial rule was presented as the most significant achievement so far, the outcome of the long march of human rights, and the model for what had yet to be accomplished—not least in Israel, which received withering attention in the proceedings, due to its acquisitions after the Six Day War against its Arab neighbors. Yet outside the UN in 1968, human rights had not yet become a powerful set of ideals, and this fact is more crucial than anything that went on at the shah's staged event.[1] As the conference went through its scripted motions, the real world was exploding in revolt. May 1968 brought to Paris its greatest postwar upheaval, with students and workers shutting the country down and demanding an end to middle-class compromises. In far-flung spots around the globe, from Eastern Europe to China, and across the United States, from Berkeley to New York, people—especially young people—demanded change. But outside Tehran, no one in the global disruption of 1968 thought of the better world they demanded as a world to be governed by "human rights."

The drama of human rights, then, is that they emerged in the 1970s seemingly from nowhere. If the Soviet Union had generally lost credibility (and America's Vietnamese adventure invited so much international outrage), human rights were not the immediate beneficiaries. During the 1960s crisis of superpower order, other utopian visions prospered. They called for community at home, redeeming the United States from hollow consumerism, or "socialism with a human face" in the Soviet empire, or further liberation from a so-called neocolonialism in the third world. At the time, there were next to no nongovernmental organizations that pursued human rights; Amnesty International, a fledging group, remained practically unknown. From the 1940s until 1968, the few NGOs that did view human rights as part of their mission struggled for them within the UN's framework, but the conference in Tehran confirmed the agonizing fruitlessness of this project. One longtime NGO chief, Moses Moskowitz, observed bitterly in the aftermath of the conference that the human rights idea had "yet to arouse the curiosity of the intellectual, to stir the imagination of the social and political reformer and to evoke the emotional response of the moralist."[2] He was right.

Yet, within one decade, human rights would begin to be invoked across the developed world and by many more ordinary people than ever before. Instead of implying colonial liberation and the creation of emancipated nations, human rights most often now meant individual protection against the state. Amnesty International became newly visible and, as a beacon of new ideals, won the Nobel Peace Prize in 1977 for its work. The popularity of its new mode of advocacy forever transformed what it meant to agitate for humane causes, and spawned a new brand and age of internationalist citizen advocacy. Westerners left the dream of revolution behind—both for themselves and for the third world they had once ruled—and adopted other tactics, envisioning an international law of human rights as the steward of utopian norms, and as the mechanism of their fulfillment. Even politicians, most notably American president Jimmy Carter, started to invoke human rights as the guiding rationale of the foreign policy of states. And most visibly of all, the public relevance of human rights skyrocketed, as measured by the simple presence of the phrase in the newspaper, ushering in the current supremacy of human rights. Having been almost never used in English prior to the 1940s, when they experienced only a modest increase, the words "human rights" were printed in 1977 in the *New York Times* nearly five times as often as in any prior year in that publication's history. The moral world had changed. "People think of history in the long term," Philip Roth says in one of his novels, "but history, in fact, is a very sudden thing."[3] Never has this been truer than when it comes to the history of human rights.

There is no way to reckon with the recent emergence and contemporary power of human rights without focusing on their utopian dimension: the image of another, better world of dignity and respect that underlies their appeal, even when human rights seem to be about slow and piecemeal reform. But far from being the sole idealism that has inspired faith and activism in the course of human events, human rights emerged historically as the last utopia—one that became powerful and prominent because other visions imploded. Human rights are only a particular modern version of the ancient commitment by Plato and Deuteronomy—and Cyrus—to the cause of justice. Even among modern schemes of freedom and equality, they are only one among others; they were far from the first to make humanity's global aspirations the central focus. Nor are human rights the only imaginable rallying cry around which to build a grassroots popular movement. As Moses Moskowitz so well understood on the brink of their ascendancy, human rights would have to win or lose on the terrain of the imagination, first and foremost. And for them to win, others would have to lose. In the realm of thinking, as in that of social action, human rights are best understood as survivors: the god that did not fail while other political ideologies did. If they avoided failure, it was most of all because they were widely understood as a moral alternative to bankrupt political utopias.

Historians in the United States started writing the history of human rights a decade ago. Since that time, a new field has crystallized and burgeoned. Almost unanimously, contemporary historians have adopted a celebratory attitude toward the emergence and progress of human rights, providing recent enthusiasms with uplifting backstories, and differing primarily about whether to locate the true breakthrough with the Greeks or the Jews, medieval Christians or early modern philosophers, democratic revolutionaries or abolitionist heroes, American internationalists or antiracist visionaries. In recasting world history as raw material for the progressive ascent of international human rights, they have rarely conceded that earlier history left open diverse paths into the future, rather than paving a single road toward current ways of thinking and acting. And in studying human rights more recently, once they did come on the scene, historians have been loathe to regard them as only one appealing ideology among others. Instead, they have used history to confirm their inevitable rise rather than register the choices that were made and the accidents that happen. A different approach is needed to reveal the true origins of this most recent utopian program.

Historians of human rights approach their subject, in spite of its novelty, the way church historians once approached theirs. They regard the basic cause—much as the church historian treated the Christian religion—as a saving truth, discovered rather than made in history. If a historical phenomenon can be made to seem like an anticipation of human rights, it is interpreted as leading to them in much the way church history famously treated Judaism for so long, as a proto-Christian movement simply confused about its true destiny. Meanwhile, the heroes who are viewed as advancing human rights in the world—much like the church historian's apostles and saints—are generally treated with uncritical wonderment. Hagiography, for the sake of moral imitation of those who chase the flame, becomes the main genre. And the organizations that finally appear to institutionalize human rights are treated like the early church: a fledgling, but hopefully universal, community of believers struggling for good in a vale of tears. If the cause fails, it is because of evil; if it succeeds, it is not by accident but because the cause is just. These approaches provide the myths that the new movement wants or needs.

They match a public and politically consequential consensus about the sources of human rights. Human rights commonly appear in journalistic commentary and in political speeches as a cause both age-old and obvious. At the latest, both historians and pundits focus on the 1940s as the crucial era of breakthrough and triumph. High-profile observers—Michael Ignatieff, for example—see human rights as an old ideal that finally came into its own as a response to the Holocaust, which might be the most universally repeated myth about their origins. In the 1990s, an era of ethnic cleansing in southeastern Europe and beyond during which human rights took on literally millennial appeal in the public discourse of the West, it became common to assume that, ever since their birth in a moment of post-Holocaust wisdom, human rights embedded themselves slowly but steadily in humane consciousness in what amounted to a revolution of moral concern. In a euphoric mood, many people believed that secure moral guidance, born out of shock about the Holocaust and nearly incontestable in its premises, was on the verge of displacing

clash between law & politics

interest and power as the foundation of international society. All this fails to register that, without the transformative impact of events in the 1970s, human rights would not have become today's utopia, and there would be no movement around it.

An alternative history of human rights, with a much more recent timeline, looks very different than conventional approaches. Rather than attributing their sources to Greek philosophy and monotheistic religion, European natural law and early modern revolutions, horror against American slavery and Adolf Hitler's Jew-killing, it shows that human rights as a powerful transnational ideal and movement have distinctive origins of a much more recent date. True, rights have long existed, but they were from the beginning part of the authority of the state, not invoked to transcend it. They were most visible in revolutionary nationalism through modern history—until "human rights" displaced revolutionary nationalism. The 1940s later turned out to be crucial, not least for the Universal Declaration they left behind, but it is essential to ask why human rights failed to interest many people— *not in Germany* including international lawyers—at the time or for decades. In real history, human rights were peripheral to both wartime rhetoric and postwar reconstruction, not central to their outcome. Contrary to conventional assumptions, there was no widespread Holocaust consciousness in the postwar era, so human rights could not have been a response to it. More important, no international rights movement emerged at the time. This alternative history is forced, therefore, to take as its main challenge understanding why it was not in the middle of the 1940s but in the middle of the 1970s that human rights came to define people's hopes for the future as the foundation of an international movement and a utopia of international law.

The ideological ascendancy of human rights in living memory came out of a combination of separate histories that interacted in an unforeseeable explosion. Accident played a role, as it does in all human events, but what mattered most of all was the collapse of prior universalistic schemes, and the construction of human rights as a persuasive alternative to them. On the threshold is the United Nations, which introduced human rights but had to be bypassed as the concept's essential institution for it to matter. In the 1940s, the UN arose as a concert of great powers that refused to break in principle with either sovereignty or empire. From the beginning, it was as responsible for the irrelevance of human rights as for their itemization as a list of entitlements. And the emergence of new states through decolonization, earth-shattering in other respects for the organization, changed the meaning of the very concept of human rights but left them peripheral on the world stage. It was, instead, only in the 1970s that a genuine social movement around human rights made its appearance, seizing the foreground by transcending official government institutions, especially international ones.

To be sure, there were a number of catalysts for the explosion: the search for a European identity outside Cold War terms; the reception of Soviet and later East European dissidents by politicians, journalists, and intellectuals; and the American liberal shift in foreign policy in new, moralized terms, after the Vietnamese disaster. Equally significant, but more neglected, were the end of formal colonialism and the crisis of the postcolonial state, certainly in the eyes of Western observers. The best general explanation for the origins of this social movement and common discourse around rights remains the collapse of other, prior utopias, both state-based and internationalist. These were belief systems that promised a free way of life, but led into bloody morass, or offered emancipation from empire and capital, but suddenly came to seem like dark tragedies rather than bright hopes. In this atmosphere, an internationalism revolving around individual rights surged, and it did so because it was defined as a pure alternative in an age of ideological betrayal and political collapse. It was then that the phrase "human rights" entered common parlance in the English language. And it is from that recent moment that human rights have come to define the present day.

To give up church history is not to celebrate a black mass instead. I wrote this book out of intense interest in—even admiration for—the contemporary human rights movement, the most inspiring mass utopianism Westerners have had before them in recent decades. For today's utopians, it is surely the place to start. But especially for those who feel their powerful appeal, human rights have to be treated as a human cause, rather than one with the long-term inevitability and moral self-evidence that common sense assumes. Understanding better how human rights came to the world in the midst of a crisis of utopianism reveals not simply their historical origins but their contemporary situation much more thoroughly than other approaches. For their emergence in an age when other, previously more appealing utopias died came at a very high price.

The true history of human rights matters most of all, then, in order to confront their prospects today and in the future. If they do capture many longstanding values, it is equally critical to understand more honestly how and when human rights took shape as a widespread and powerful set of aspirations for a better and more humane world. After all, they have done far more to transform the terrain of idealism than they have the world itself. In and through their emergence as the last utopia after predecessors and rivals collapsed, the movement's most difficult quandaries were already set. Though they were born as an alternative to grand political missions—or even as a moral criticism of politics—human rights were forced to take on the grand political mission of providing a global framework for the achievement of freedom, identity, and prosperity. They were forced, slowly but surely, to assume the very maximalism they triumphed by avoiding.

This contemporary dilemma is what has to be faced squarely, yet history as celebration of origins will not help in doing so. Few things that are powerful today turn out on inspection to be longstanding and inevitable. And the human rights movement is certainly not one of them. But this also means that human rights are not so much an inheritance to preserve as an invention to remake—or even leave behind—if their program is to be vital and relevant in what is already a very different world than the one into which it came so recently. No one knows yet for sure, in light of the inspiration they provide and the challenges they face, what kind of better world human rights can bring about. And no one knows whether, if they are found wanting, another utopia can arise in the future, just as human rights once emerged on the ruins of their predecessors. Human rights were born as the last utopia—but one day another may appear.

It did get rid of torture in the west
Outsourcing?

1

"Each writer *creates* his precursors," Jorge Luis Borges writes in a wonderful meditation on Franz Kafka's relationship to literary history. "His work modifies our conception of the past, just as it will modify the future."[1] From the Greek philosopher Zeno on, through obscure and famous sources over the centuries, Borges presents a collection of Kafka's stylistic devices and even some of his seemingly unique personal obsessions—all in place before Kafka was born. Borges explains: "If I am not mistaken, the heterogeneous pieces I have assembled resemble Kafka; if I am not mistaken, not all of them resemble each other." How, then, to interpret these early texts? The earlier writers were trying to be not Kafka but themselves. And the "sources" were not sufficient to make Kafka possible on their own: no one would even have seen them as anticipating Kafka had he never emerged. Borges's point about "Kafka's precursors," then, is that there are no such things. If the past is read as preparation for a surprising recent event, both are distorted. The past is treated as if it were simply the future waiting to happen. And the surprising recent event is treated as less surprising than it really is.

The same is true of contemporary human rights as a set of global political norms providing the creed of a transnational social movement. Since the phrase was consecrated in English in the 1940s, and with increasing frequency in the last few decades, there have been many attempts to lay out the deep sources of human rights— but without Borges's awareness that surprising discontinuity as much leaves the past behind as consummates it. The classic case begins with the Stoic thinkers of Greek and Roman philosophy and proceeds through medieval natural law and early modern natural rights, culminating in the Atlantic revolutions of America and France, with their Declaration of Independence of 1776 and Declaration of the Rights of Man and Citizen of 1789. By that point at the very latest, it is assumed, the die was cast. These are usable pasts: the construction of precursors after the fact. The worst consequence of the myth of deep roots they provide is that they distract from the real conditions for the historical developments they claim to explain. If human rights are treated as inborn, or long in preparation, people will not confront the true reasons they have become so powerful today and examine whether those reasons are still persuasive.

Of all the glaring confusions in the search for the "precursors" of human rights, one must have pride of place. Far from being sources of appeal that transcended state and nation, the rights asserted in early modern political revolutions and championed thereafter were central to the construction of state and nation, and led nowhere beyond until very recently. Hannah Arendt saw this most clearly, though she did not spell out the consequences for the history of rights. In a famous chapter of *The Origins of Totalitarianism,* Arendt contended that the so-called "right to have rights" accorded by collective membership remained the key to the values the new Universal Declaration of Human Rights listed: without communal inclusion, the assertion of rights by itself made no sense.[2] Rights had been born as the first prerogatives of citizens; now, she felt, they risked becoming the last chance of "humans," without membership and therefore without protection. She was correct: there is a clear and fundamental difference between earlier rights, all predicated on belonging to a political community, and eventual "human rights." If so, the *droits de l'homme* that powered early modern revolution and nineteenth-century politics need to be rigorously distinguished from the "human rights" coined in the 1940s that have grown so appealing in the last few decades. The one implied a politics of citizenship at home, the other a politics of suffering abroad. If the move from the one to the other involved a revolution in meanings and practices, then it is wrong at the start to present the one as the source of the other.[3]

True, the conceptual foundation of rights even before the Universal Declaration may have been natural or even "human" for some thinkers, especially at the high tide of Enlightenment rationalism. But even then, it was universally agreed that those rights were to be achieved through the construction of spaces of citizenship in which rights were accorded and protected. These spaces not only provided ways to contest the denial of already established rights; just as crucially, they were also zones of struggle over the meaning of that citizenship, and the place where defenses of old rights, like campaigns for new ones, were fought. In contrast, human rights after 1945 established no comparable citizenship space, certainly not at the time of their invention—and perhaps not since. If so, the central event in human rights history is the recasting of rights as entitlements that might contradict the sovereign nation-state from above and outside rather than serve as its foundation. *natwal rghts?*

Establishing the essential connection between rights and the state is important because it also casts the common association of rights with human universalism in a very different light. For many, human rights today are simply a modern version of a longstanding universalistic or "cosmopolitan" faith. If the Greeks or the Bible announced that mankind is one, it is often thought, then they must have their place in the history of human rights. But the fact is that there have been many different and opposed universalisms in history, with each equally committed to the belief that humans are all part of the same moral group or—as the 1948 declaration was to put it—the same "family." From there, they diverged about what humans shared, what goods they should acknowledge, and what rules they must follow.

A universalism based on international rights, therefore, could count as only one among others in world history. And in fact, the long-term entanglement of rights and states helps identify rights talk as a very precarious kind of cosmopolitanism that historically abetted the proliferation and competition of different states and nations more than it has helped imagine a world without moral borders. After the Enlightenment era, the search for rights through state and nation meant that it became hard to sustain the very universalism with which rights were sometimes invoked. If the state was necessary to create a politics of rights, many nineteenth-century observers wondered, could they have any other real source than its own authority and any other basis than its local meanings?

Finally, the creation of the concept of rights did not mean the immediate end of the rivalry of universalisms. Distinctive globalisms and internationalisms existed all along in modern history that would have to be ruled out in order for a utopia based on individual rights to become the singular watchword of hopes for a better world. Just as the doctrine of rights comprised a late universalism in world history, its contemporary reinvention as "human rights" is best understood as following from its survival in a difficult struggle against internationalist rivals old and new. It was in those recent developments that the source of contemporary beliefs and practices is largely to be found; the rest is ancient history.

With some regularity since they came onto the political stage, human rights have been proclaimed "the birthright of man."[4] The bare assumption that humans are part of the same group may have been available as far back as the distinction of people from gods and animals, long before recorded history, though the boundaries between these groups was permeable ever after.[5] Yet human universalism alone—including the versions of universalism in Greek philosophy and monotheistic religion—is of no real relevance to a history of human rights, for two main reasons. One is that these sources offered raw ingredients for a huge array of doctrines and movements over the millennia; the other is that they did so only in connection with other elements that would have to be eliminated in order to achieve "human rights" later. Greeks and Jews both demanded "justice," albeit rooting it in the very different sources of nature and theology. Since then, numerous successor universalisms have arisen.[6] But their alien conceptions, no less than the diversity of their legacies, makes crediting them with the origins of contemporary morals simply unbelievable. What matters is not any of the many breakthroughs to universalism in world history, but what happened for human rights to seem like the only viable kind of universalism there is now.[7]

In conventional stories, it is the "cosmopolitanism" of the Stoics that always is presented as the major leap toward modern conceptions.[8] For these Greek and Roman philosophers and poets, reason rules the world; since all humans share in reason, they form part of the same polity. Indeed, it was Romans—several of whose leading thinkers were deeply influenced by Stoic notions—who coined the very concept of "humanity" *(humanitas).*[9] Yet neither the cosmopolitanism of the Stoics nor the original concept of humanity were remotely similar in their implications to current versions. The sorts of exclusionary social practices encouraged or tolerated in Roman culture, including by the Stoics on principle, make this point easily, because of attitudes toward or treatment of foreigners, women, or slaves. The Stoic "cosmopolis" united all men, but not in a reformist political project; instead, it drew them into an otherworldly sphere of reason divorced from social improvement. As for "humanity," it typically connoted an ideal of personal educational distinction, not global moral reform, and only in modern times would coinages like "humane" and "humanitarian" become thinkable. Indeed, according to Arendt, if simple humanity in Rome had moral associations beyond the realm of educational formation, it implied unimportance rather than ultimate value. "A human being or *homo* in the original meaning of the word," she observed, "indicat[ed] someone outside the range of the law and the body politic of the citizens, as for instance a slave—but certainly a politically irrelevant being."[10]

Like Stoicism, Christianity is self-evidently universalistic. But if it is one thing to be for cosmopolitanism of one form or another, another to be for human rights specifically, then the mere fact of Christian universalism is no argument for awarding credit to the religion for the conceptual or political possibility of human rights. On the basis of prior universalisms, notably those of Hebrew prophets, Christianity inspired a number of its own over the centuries. Its founders, Jesus and Paul, offered apocalyptic visions of the imminent kingdom of God on Earth. Soon, the religion offered a hopeful message to the meek around the Mediterranean and, after the emperor Constantine's conversion, it helped Roman concepts of political belonging travel from cities into the countryside. A thousand years later, it undergirded medieval natural law. And though its egalitarianism is famous, the cultural and political implications of Christianity from age to age and place to place were simply too different, in need of too much drastic transformation, to approach modern conceptions on their own.

The premise of accounts that try to claim more, after all, is that there is only one move from particular cultures to universal morality to be made—and Christianity is it. But once it is acknowledged that there were, are, and could be many universalisms, the fact that one or another movement or culture is universalistic—even floridly so, as Christianity is—lends it no necessary role in the prehistory of human rights. Similarly, when Europeans left their own territory behind, and most especially in the encounter with the disconcerting novelty of American native peoples, they were forced to confront the limits of their assumptions. But, because they relied on the categories of classical philosophy and medieval religion to interpret the radical difference of indigenous cultures abroad, they could make no simple breakthrough to "humanity." Contemporary human rights still awaited their own Christopher Columbus.[11]

Another, more promising approach to the "precursors" of human rights focuses not on the achievement of their universalistic scope but on when societies began to protect the values named by specific items in revolutionary declarations and current lists. But this history, too, forces the stress onto accident and discontinuity. Instead of dating universalisms, this approach tracks the social concern each current right singles out, one at a time, sometimes before those protections were integrated in the language of rights. It is a fascinating exercise, and numerous sources have been proposed. Given this multiplicity, the basic lesson is that the concerns now addressed through a unified package of "human rights" have their own histories, with different chronologies and geographies, incubated as they were in separate traditions and for different reasons. They eventually figured in the Universal Declaration and other canonical lists. But much as in retrospect Kafka could seem the outcome of a disparate literary past only once Kafka made his innovations, the emergence of specific rights by no means explains how they were reinterpreted as part of a fused list, and then made into "human rights" later still. Nothing of what came together in modern declarations was originally pursued to reach them.

A few examples make this clear. Not surprisingly, it is probably the right of possession that has been the most frequently asserted and doggedly fortified right in world history, albeit typically within legal systems that made no real claim to base entitlement on humanity. After Roman law, old feudal agreements securing what were variously called liberties, franchises, immunities, and privileges underwrote the sanctity of possession; and newer legal protection of the preconditions of early capitalism put special weight behind the definition and defense of the property right.[12] But the very antiquity of this protection, and the successive languages developed to carry it out, are pieces of distant background for the history of modern rights.

Ironically, the values incorporated in what are occasionally dismissed as newfangled social protections are probably at least as old as the defense of property; both are earlier than the value of things like immunity from bodily invasion or now familiar rights of the criminal process (including rights against torture). Because when human rights exploded in the 1970s they were focused so centrally on political and civil rights, their social and economic cousins have come to be regarded as "second-generation" principles. But unlike most civil and political protections, concern for inequality and socioeconomic deprivation appears in the Bible and other antique expressions of human culture around the world. In the European Middle Ages, there were even interesting defenses of "rights"—not yet personal and legally secured modern citizenship entitlements, of course—to steal in case of need.[13] And as much as it made a central place for the protection of private property, the history of rights during and after the French Revolution made room for social concern from the beginning.

To choose another item from the list, the notion of freedom of conscience inviolable by the state, is to turn to a different, newer set of sources that also made their bequest to the modern human rights canon by accident. The originally Protestant conscience drove a wedge between the external body and the "free" internal forum of belief. The innovation, not uncontroversial in the Reformation's bloody aftermath, led to proposals to unify states under the religion of the prince and not just acceptance of plural denominations. Revealingly, the original natural rights thinkers of the seventeenth century—like the Dutchman Hugo Grotius and the Englishman Thomas Hobbes—ranked preservation of the self through the state as paramount and regarded the acceptance of religious pluralism as risky in the extreme. Instead, the value of toleration was pioneered within religious debates that were at first completely separate from the elaboration of "rights." It was forged in the name of the coexistence of factional Christians, rather than as a secular proposal to make religion a private entitlement. But eventually, the political isolation of conscience as a protected interior forum became the source of the assertion of rights of belief, opinion, and perhaps even speech and press. In its Lutheran and Calvinist guises emphasizing spiritual freedom, Protestantism had intended to return to Christian fundamentals, not destroy religious hold over state and society. But the calling of a halt to inter-Christian competition for state rule over the soul ended up shaping the specifically modern commitment to a zone beyond justifiable state intervention.[14]

Yet another—and also essentially distinct—source of specific values that rights were to protect was the longstanding and untheoretical legal traditions of the common and civil law, which by the revolutionary era had provided now mundane protections of person, not just property, for centuries. Common-law developments, later together with Enlightenment reformism, were responsible mainly for promoting the safeguards of criminal procedure: immunity from intrusive search, the rule against *ex post facto* laws, the availability of the writ of *habeas corpus,* the ability to confront one's accuser, a jury of one's peers, and so on. Originally, however, all were attached to "freemen" rather than all Englishmen (let alone man as such). They were totally independent in origins and meaning from later natural and universal rights. In other words, they could have remained simple legal rights for all time, embedded in the so-called "ancient constitution" and famously listed in the English Bill of Rights of 1689, without elevation from English tradition to natural precepts.[15] John Wilkes, defender of "liberty" against the crown, agitated for them in these terms, and so did Edmund Burke when he founded the conservative intellectual tradition on the distinction between such inherited rights and the new, natural ones. "Far am I from denying in theory, full as far is my heart from withholding in practice," Burke intoned in his critique of French abstractions, "the *real* rights of men. In denying their false claims of [natural] right, I do not mean to injure those which are real, and are such as their pretended rights would totally destroy."[16] Burke considered reinventing the motley list of historically accreted rights as "the rights of man" a simple mistake—not just as a political matter, but because their universalization disguised their true origins.

The tangled history of how the political values today protected as "human rights" arose shows they bear no essential relationship either to each other or to the universalistic belief that all men (and, more recently, women) are part of the same group. This remained true even during the Enlightenment, when a new secular version of the old Christian imperative of pity made more familiar appeals to "humanity" possible, first by shifting the meaning of the term so that it now typically implied feeling others' pain. Though this new culture of sympathy had its own boundaries, it clearly did help construct new norms opposed to depredations against the body like enslavement and violence in punishment.[17] All the same, the real story of how the values protected by "rights" crystallized is one about warring tendencies and dead projects, whose contributions to the package of modern rights were incidental and not intentional. Rather than originating all at once as a set and then merely awaiting later internationalization, the history of the core values subject to protection by rights is one of construction rather than discovery and contingency rather than necessity.

The universalism of the Enlightenment and revolutionary eras clearly does bear some affinity to contemporary forms of cosmopolitanism. Yet what it put forward as "the immortal rights of man" was nevertheless part of a political project strikingly distinct from contemporary human rights (which, in fact, were born out of a criticism of revolution). The rights of man were utopian, and evoked emotion: "Who will dare to avow that his heart was not lifted up," Johann Wolfgang von Goethe exclaimed in 1797, "when the new sun first rose in its splendor; when we heard of the rights of man, of inspiring liberty, and of universal equality!"[18] Unlike later human rights, however, they were deeply bound up with the construction, through revolution if necessary, of state and nation. It is now the order of the day to transcend that state forum for rights, but until recently the state was their essential crucible.

From a very early date, legal systems have afforded "rights," notably the Roman legal system of which most branches of Western law are tributaries. It may have been due to Stoic influence that occasionally the rights of the Roman legal system could be conceptualized as rooted partly in nature.[19] Before the rise of the modern state, empires from Rome onward provided citizenship, or lesser forms for subjecthood, as well as the rights premised on that inclusion; indeed, they were to do so long into the twentieth century.[20] The rights of these imperial spaces were in this sense more like the rights of state inclusion, which premised entitlements on membership, than contemporary human rights. Some Roman language aside, however, thoroughgoing *natural* rights approaches were no older than the seventeenth century and were a byproduct of the origins of the modern state. The first natural rights doctrines were the children of the absolutist and expansionist state of early modern European history, not attempts to step outside and beyond the state. Their emergence was a spectacularly pivotal moment, given that it was to be for so long that rights were closely identified and bound up with the state—until this alliance was recently seen as insufficient.

The concept of "natural rights" did not come out of nowhere. When Hobbes first referred to the right of nature, he used the same word *ius* that once referred to the law of nature. This earlier doctrine, which arose from a combination of Stoic universalism and Christian values, had its heyday in the medieval period; its most famous version is found in St. Thomas Aquinas's thought. Yet if the idea of natural rights first emerged in the old language of natural law, it was so different in its intentions and implications as to be a different concept. In modern times most revivalists of natural law, usually Catholics, have regarded it as a disaster for their creed that it gave way to an apostate rights-based successor. They are at least right that natural law, derived most often from God's will and thought to be embedded in the fabric of the cosmos, was the classic Christian version of universalism. For it to be displaced by natural rights it had to be made plural, subjective, and possessive. Natural law was originally one rule given from above, where natural rights came to be a list of separate items. Natural law was something objective, which individuals must obey because God made them part of the natural order he ordained: illegitimate practices were deemed *contra naturam* or "against nature." But natural rights were subjective entities "owned" by humanity as prerogatives. The timing and causes of the transition between natural law and natural rights have received massive attention in recent decades, in part because of an overestimation of how critical they were in the origins of today's human rights. The founding natural rights figures were, however, anything but humanitarians; on theoretical principle, they endorsed an austere doctrine that refused an expansive list of basic entitlements. If their invention of natural rights mattered as any sort of precursor, it is because natural rights were bound up with a new kind of powerful state taking off in the era. In many ways, the history of natural rights, like that of the rights of man after, is the history of the very state that "human rights" would later attempt to transcend.

The case for the link revolves around the fact that the autarkic or freestanding individual of natural rights—the person whom Grotius and Hobbes saw as the bearer of the new concept—was explicitly modeled on the assertive new state of early modern international affairs.[21] That individual, like the state, tolerated no superordinate authority. It was for this reason that, as in the contest of states, natural individuals were imagined as in or close to a war to the death, qualified only by cooled hostilities, but never universal norms. Of moral precepts every man would acknowledge, Grotius and Hobbes argued, there was indeed only one: the legitimacy of self-preservation. It was self-preservation that Hobbes declared the first "right of nature," and the only such right that he saw. "The Right of Nature," Hobbes wrote, "is the Liberty each man hath, to use his own power, as he will himselfe, for the preservation of his own Nature; that is to say, of his own Life; and consequently, of doing any thing, which in his own Judgement, and Reason, hee shall conceive to be the aptest means thereunto."[22] Just as the early modern state answered to no higher authority than its core need to preserve itself, so natural individuals had only one right, to fight—with a license to kill if necessary. Yet while states in competition in international affairs could do no more than postpone their standoff, Hobbes famously argued that domestic politics could only achieve peace if their feuding citizens empowered the state to rule. The argumentative goal of the first right—the motivation for introducing it into political thought—was to empower the state, not to limit it. And one clear motivation for this act of empowerment was that states of the era were, aside from providing disci-

plinary pacification in a time of civil war at home, pursuing unprecedented colonization of worlds elsewhere.[23]

The century that followed witnessed a wide variety of more generous visions of natural rights and duties that were not to be so
strictly focused on self-preservation, and the construction of a state
that might provide more than the blessings of discipline and security. But to the extent that appeals to nature became more expansive,
it was often because they refused to revolve around individualized
rights alone.[24] The possibility of inventing rights beyond self-
preservation depended, according to eighteenth-century natural lawyers like Swiss thinker J.-J. Burlamaqui and his American followers,
on the deeper foundation of all entitlements in a robust doctrine of
God-given duties.[25] It was in part through this process that some of
the values incubated in diverse traditions were made natural rights—
the right to private property in John Locke's famous theory, and
many other items later. Notwithstanding the crafting of these more
full-bodied lists of natural rights, however, the age of democratic
revolution only furthered the very alliance between rights and the
state through which rights had emerged. Now, even the first right of
self-preservation meant the prince needed continuing consent—for
Locke at least—and it was joined by a series of other natural entitlements. But even these momentous shifts did not change the fact that
the answer to abridged rights was a move to a new sovereign or a new
state rather than a move beyond sovereignty and state altogether.
Further, in the revolutionary era, not just states but now nations became the formative crucible of rights, and their indispensable ally
and forum—in other words, exactly what human rights as an idea
and a practice would later have to set itself against.

The actual significance of the era of democratic revolution in
America and France, in other words, is as much in negating the possibility of twentieth-century human rights doctrines as in making
them available. Properly told, the history of democratic republicanism, or the narrower history of liberalism, is more about how human

rights did not arise rather than how they did. One unintentional proof is how deeply nationalism has defined, not simply the rights of man, but partisan interpretations of their trajectory in the age of revolution. A century ago, the German scholar Georg Jellinek caused an intellectual contretemps by arguing for the priority of American rights talk (which he in turn rooted in earlier German Reformation–era breakthroughs) as a source for the French Declaration of the Rights of Man and Citizen of 1789; the French were predictably unhappy with this attempt to steal their birthrights. Such tawdry disputes have cropped up, from time to time, ever since: When the French were commemorating their achievements on the revolution's bicentennial in 1989, the mischievous Margaret Thatcher provoked a diplomatic sensation when she mordantly observed on French television that the French had not invented human rights but had taken them from elsewhere (and had then gone on to throw the debt overboard by descending into revolutionary terror).[26]

In fact, the Americans—not so much in the Declaration of Independence of July 1776 as in the even earlier and much fuller-bodied Virginia Declaration of Rights of the month before and its successors in other states—did steal a march on the French by founding their polities on enumerated rights, even if they declined to do so within their national confederation.[27] Thomas Jefferson, in Paris in 1789, helped the Marquis de Lafayette draft the first proposed version of a French declaration. Even so, the sources for both American state and French revolutionary documents have remained hard to isolate. Whatever the answer, the French declaration arguably did move the politics of rights in a brand new direction in the eventful summer of 1789. The French abbé Emmanuel-Joseph Sieyès—whose proposed draft superseded Lafayette's in Parisian debates—claimed as he and other revolutionaries moved toward constitutional monarchy in 1789 that the American commitment to rights remained too dependent on an antique tradition of aristocratic rights talk stretching back to the Magna Carta, which merely reserved prerogatives "negatively" from the king rather than actually founding the polity "positively" on rights principles. In the *Federalist Papers* of the same period—written before a bill of rights for the new national government had been forced on him—Alexander Hamilton even took this antiquarian aspect of bills or declarations of rights as a reason for *not* including one in the new American Constitution: "It has been several times truly remarked," Hamilton noted, "that bills of rights are, in their origin, stipulations between kings and their subjects, abridgements of prerogative in favor of privilege, reservations of rights not surrendered to the prince."[28] If there were no prince, in other words, no enumeration of rights would be necessary.

In the event, of course, Frenchmen decided that a list of rights had to become the first principles of a constitution, and the American framers were forced to append one to their handiwork to gain public support for it. These events surely did document the meteoric rise of the notion of "the rights of man" across the second half of the eighteenth century, however it is to be explained, and whether it was self-evident to many at the time or not.[29] Americans had typically invoked natural rights in their earlier revolution, and even by 1789 the naturalistic framing of their assertion had faded. After Thomas Paine's defense of the French Revolution for Anglo-American republicans in *The Rights of Man* (1791), the fortunes of that new phrase were cemented across the Atlantic world and beyond. Paine's accidental variation of his translation of *droits de l'homme* as "human rights" once in his book did not, however, catch on, as it would a century and a half later.

The detailed history of rights in this turbulent period is no doubt fascinating, especially when the original French canon gave way, during the Terror of 1793, to a new declaration introducing social concern as rights for the first time. The overwhelmingly important point, however, is that the rights of the revolutionary era were very much embodied in the politics of the state, crystallizing in a scheme worlds away from the political meaning human rights would have later. In a sense, every declaration of rights at the time (and until recently) was implicitly what the French openly labeled theirs: a

declaration of the rights of man *and citizen*. Rights were neither independent arguments nor countervailing forces, and were always announced at the moment of founding the polity, and justifying its
erection and often its violence.[30] The "rights of man" were about a
whole people incorporating itself in a state, not a few foreign people
criticizing another state for its wrongdoings. Thereafter, they were
about the meaning of citizenship. This profound relationship between the annunciation of rights and the fast-moving "contagion of
sovereignty" of the century that followed cannot be left out of the
history of rights: indeed it is the central feature of that history until
very recently. If so, it is far more fruitful to examine how human
rights arose mainly because of the collapse of the model of revolutionary rights rather than through its continuation or revival. Not
least, revolution with its nonreformist radicalism and potentially violent techniques framed the rights of man as the era of democracy
began. In glib terms, revolutionary-era rights were revolutionary: the
justification for the creation or renovation of a citizenship space, not
the protection of "humanity."

As principles to which positive law was supposed to conform,
the rights invoked by many Enlightenment thinkers and then in the
revolutionary moment were in some sense above the state. But they
only appeared through the state, and there was no forum above it, or
at times even in it, in which to indict the state's transgression. Indeed,
once they were declared, it was not self-evident that rights would
have many purposes independent of the emergence of the state. For
example, they did not give rise directly to mechanisms of judicial
protection against sovereign authority—even though this may seem
like their obvious function today. In the United States, the now familiar practice of judicial review of legislation in the name of fundamental rights was not a foregone conclusion in 1789, when the first
ten amendments were framed. And even when judicial review appeared it did not spark a rich tradition of litigation, given the initially
restricted purposes of the national government. In England, it was
assumed that wise opinion and tradition would protect unwritten

rights, making it unnecessary to announce them, much less provide a high court to protect them. In France, meanwhile, it took more than 150 years, until after World War II, for the constitutional rights on which successive republics were always based at the outset to become the grounds for judicial indictment of the state.[31] What now seems like a natural assumption, that the very point of asserting rights is to restrict the activities of the state by providing a courtroom forum for their protection, was not what revolutionary rights were about. Instead, the main remedy for the abrogation of revolutionary rights remained democratic action up to and including another revolution. And while no nongovernmental organizations now contemplate that extreme recourse, it was the only response imaginable at the time in the name of the rights of man.

If abstract principles were called upon in the era mainly as grounds for creating new states, they were just as important in the justification of the erection of their insurmountable external borders. Where the American states based on natural rights entered a weak confederation, while retaining local autonomy, France set the model for the modern nation-state in its achievement of centralized sovereign independence for a democratic people. Far from providing rationale for foreign or "human" claims against states, assertions of rights were at root—and for at least a century—a justification for states to come about. Unlike the founding documents of the American states, the Declaration of Independence had no real list of entitlements in it, since it aimed primarily to achieve sovereignty externally against European encroachment.[32] As a matter of fact, rights were subordinate features of the creation of both state and nation beginning in this era, for few took the trouble to distinguish them.[33] A mere decade after the Americans declared the autonomy of their new state to the world, the French in their own revolutionary declaration of rights insisted "the principle of all sovereignty resides essentially in the Nation," adding for good measure that "no body and no individual may exercise authority which does not emanate expressly from it" (Art. 3). In an era in which American popular unity coalesced thanks as much to bloody Indian wars as to high principles, it may have been simply true to stereotype for the French to identify their own national identity with universal morality; they saw no conflict in proclaiming the emergence of a sovereign nation of Frenchmen and announcing the rights of man as man at one and the same time. As a result, rights announced in the constitution of the sovereign nation-state—not "human rights" in the contemporary sense—were the great and fateful bequest of the French Revolution to world politics.

No doubt, the transition to the world of potentially republican states did not simply reproduce the international affairs of a world in which empire and monarchy set the standard. The French Revolution did have profound implications for the global order, immediately making several Enlightenment visions of "perpetual peace" seem within reach to a few. Yet aside from the memorably outlandish German baron Anacharsis Cloots—who joined the revolutionary National Assembly as the representative of non-French humanity and supported aggressive warfare as a step toward truly world government—utopian visions took a form wholly compatible with the spread of national sovereignty, rather than imagining rules or rights above it.[34] In practice, when the encirclement of the revolutionary state by the armies of its European enemies forced it to spread its fire abroad in the closing decade of the eighteenth century, the republic did not move toward global law but set up "sisters" (as they were called) and toyed with some sort of concert of new republics.[35] In theory, Immanuel Kant consciously rejected Cloots's radicalism, instead holding out a wholly minimal *Weltbürgerrecht* or "world citizen law" that envisaged no more than an asylum right for individuals out of place in a world of national states. True, Kant, like the Stoics, was a cosmopolitan thinker. But he was not for today's human rights, in the full-bodied protection they promise even when they rest content with an international order composed of nations.[36]

As a result, in the nineteenth century the often heartfelt appeal to the rights of man always went along with the propagation of national sovereignty as indispensable means, entailed precondition, and enduring accompaniment. If there was a rights of man *movement* in the nineteenth century, it was liberal nationalism, which sought to secure the rights of citizens resolutely in the national framework. By the end of his career, Lafayette found himself bringing the rights of man to Poland, where he assumed, like so many adherents of modern revolution, that "the universal and particular rights of any people . . . were best protected by sovereign nation-states."[37] To take the most emblematic figure, Italian Giuseppe Mazzini, the revolutionary rights of man were high ideals. "The individual is sacred," Mazzini maintained. He had "Liberty, Equality, Humanity" written on one side of the banner of his movement, Young Italy. But on the other, he emblazoned "Unity, Independence," in perfect conformity with the spreading conviction across the continent that liberty and nationality were mutually implied. Indeed, the full dependence of rights on national autonomy meant that "the epoch of *individuality* is concluded," as Mazzini firmly announced. Now, "collective man is omnipotent on the earth he treads." Without placing the nation-state first among aims, through whatever means, "you will have no name, token voice, nor rights," as he put it to his fellow Italians, "no admission to the fellowship of the peoples."[38]

Mazzini very much caught the spirit of the rights bequeathed by revolution. As a result, rights were impossible to free from the apotheosis of the state even for those who worried about revolutionary excess. French liberal thinkers like Benjamin Constant, François Guizot, and Alexis de Tocqueville, anxious about popular despotism, treated rights as only one element on a long list of tools liberal civilization had afforded to ensure freedom in the state. Elsewhere on the political spectrum in France, the one-time epicenter of the rights of man, the political language was strikingly abandoned in the nineteenth century, and the same thing happened everywhere.[39] For premier German philosopher G. W. F. Hegel, rights were worthwhile only "in context," in a state reconciling freedom and community.[40] In German lands before and after their unification, the partisans of liberalism were deeply statist and nationalist in their thinking and strategy of mass appeal; even when they were motivated by universal principles, they first allied themselves with the *Rechtsstaat* ideal of princely bureaucracy, and later shared in the conviction that the mild cosmopolitanism of Kant's era had passed in favor of the absolute supremacy of the national project. The rights that Germans argued over in the revolutionary year of 1848 were for this reason civil rights linked to citizenship boundaries; and their paeans to the coming of liberty were bound up with outbursts of nationalist chauvinism.[41] In this, they were unique only in details. Their "national liberalism" fit with that of all who invoked rights everywhere else.

The alliance with state and nation was not some accident that tragically befell the rights of man: it was their very essence, for the vast bulk of their history. After the era of revolution, the right of collective self-determination, as it would come to be called in the twentieth century, would offer the obvious framework for citizen entitlements. And this framework was to resonate until living memory, notably during the post–World War II decolonization of the world. If the promise of self-rule of the Atlantic revolutions inspired so many during the nineteenth century and after, it was thus not because their examples had secured "universal human rights" directly. Rather, their appeal lay in emancipation from monarchical despotism and backward tradition in the French case and postcolonial liberation from empire and the creation of state independence in the American one. As Arendt understood, the centrality of the nation-state as the crucible for rights is of understandable appeal, if the first order of business is to construct spaces of meaningful citizenship even at the price of political borders.

Indeed, the subordination of rights to the nation-state may have been the main historical reason that rights became less salient the more the nineteenth century passed. Put another way, the shift in the direction of statism and nationalism in the nineteenth century occurred on the basis of congenital features of rights talk. It must have become clearer and clearer as time passed that not the assertion of abstract principles but the achievement of specific citizenship is what truly mattered. Once justified as given by God or nature, rights talk more and more acquired a statist or "positivist" rationale everywhere it percolated. The rights of man, as Arendt phrased it, were "treated as a sort of stepchild by nineteenth-century political thought and . . . no liberal or radical party in the twentieth century . . . saw fit to include them in its program. . . . If the laws of their country did not live up to the demands of the Rights of Man, they were expected to change them, by legislation . . . or through revolutionary action."[42] However human in basis, rights were national political achievements first and foremost.

There were, obviously, many other sources of and reasons for a slow but sure "decline of natural rights" in the nineteenth century, as rights were less and less envisioned as natural authority for the state and more and more acknowledged as its creatures. Today, Jeremy Bentham's very early utilitarian critique of rights as "nonsense on stilts," along with Burke's acid rejection of their abstraction, is always easiest to remember in Anglo-American circles.[43] And it is certainly true that—as Elie Halévy vividly observed—the force of the utilitarian critique meant that if the rights of man remained in public circulation, it was only "in the same way we still make our exchanges under a republican régime with coins bearing the effigy of fallen monarchs, without noticing it and without thinking it important."[44] But even in Britain, the centrality of the state as the forum for rights was if anything even more relevant, as positivist John Austin and later communitarian and Hegelian T. H. Green insisted. The modern pattern, therefore, is clear: notwithstanding a decline of naturalism, in many ways the collective—even nationalist—context for rights simply extended the alliance with the politics of the state to which even the most naturalistic of rights assertions were closely tethered from the beginning.

In spite of the remarkable decline of appeals to nature's authority, rights—including the rights of man—were the watchword of extraordinary citizen movements in modern history. Women proclaimed them immediately, and workers soon after. Jews were granted them in the French Revolution, and pursued them more slowly across the European continent. Enslaved blacks claimed them, most vividly in the once barely remembered Haitian Revolution. Given the necessary boundaries of states, immigrants raised thorny questions all along, and advocates for both including them in and excluding them from citizenship did battle. Even animals were said, by a few, to deserve rights.

As tempting as it is to reclaim these campaigns because they won victories, honed methods, and made preparations for later struggles beyond the nation, to do so leaves out so much, and reshapes what is left, as to be more obfuscating than illuminating. After all, the main consequence of the availability of rights in domestic politics was not to point outside the state but to enable various constituencies within it to claim their authority. Citizenship contests always had sides, with interpretations on each about the boundaries and meaning of citizenship. This structural role for rights—which mainly provided for citizen mobilization not judicial action—was long their historically essential one.[45] And however else they differed in programmatic goals, conservative, liberal, and radical appeals to rights were unified by the fact that they were struggles over the form of the nation-state and the meaning of citizenship in it. The Haitian revolt, to remember that one example, as much sought black inclusion in citizenship through slave emancipation as rights by themselves, which is why until recently it was regarded as the precursor of the revolutionary nationalism of decolonization, not the precursor of the universal human rights movement of the present.

It remains possible, of course, to revisit modern history selectively to identify causes that look more like contemporary human rights—the campaign against the slave trade and slavery at home and abroad, or calls for intervention that popped up frequently as the decline of the Ottoman Empire in the east and Spanish empire in the west encouraged nibbling at their borders, sometimes in the name of the oppressed.[46] But startlingly, these causes were almost never framed as rights issues. The transnational solidarity of Christians for their co-religionists, and organized Jewry's for theirs, surely did offer universalistic rhetoric.[47] Yet a more hierarchical (and frequently religious) language of humanitarianism served better to justify the deployment of compassionate aid without undermining the imperialist attitudes and projects with which it was normally entangled. As for primitive but interesting treaty-based protection of minorities across borders beginning in the later nineteenth century, it was pioneered to afford protection for Jews in Eastern Europe, with Great Powers conditioning the sovereignty of weaker powers on sufficiently enlightened rule. Revealingly, such protection was conceived as group based, even when set up with ramshackle international supervision. It was the search for guarantees of subnational citizenship, rather than the direct international assurance of individual rights, and restricted to states presumed unreliable in affording the civic entitlements. A similar model would become the main form of rights protection under the interwar League of Nations too. If it was an attempt to protect the rights of others, it also presupposed the nations of others, not simply in the groups targeted for supervision but also for those protected.[48]

In contrast to all these examples, throughout the period before World War II, battles at home were enormously more likely to involve invocations of individual rights, precisely because—unlike calls for "humanity" abroad and minority protection in backward states —they were able to take for granted an existing space of inclusive citizenship in which such claims could be given meaning. Massachusetts senator and leader of the Radical Republicans Charles Sumner remarked shortly after the Civil War in the United States, in one of the very rare invocations of the phrase in English prior to the 1940s, "Our war [means] the institutions of our country are dedicated forevermore to Human Rights, and the Declaration of Independence is made a living letter instead of a promise."[49] Domestic struggles reinforced rather than ruptured the connection between rights principles and sovereign foundings, and like revolution could still take violent form.

All struggles for rights for new groups, or struggles for new rights, illustrate the point just as clearly. Revolutionary-era claims for women's inclusion in humanity—and the polity—like Olympe de Gouges's Declaration of the Rights of Woman and Citizen and Mary Wollstonecraft's *Vindication of the Rights of Woman* are classic examples. And the women's movement, which took a half century thereafter to coalesce, did make rights central to its activism. The first right on the agenda was the suffrage right of citizenship. From Wollstonecraft on, feminist advocacy had more generous aims, to be sure; and after the acquisition of the vote in the Anglo-American sphere after World War I, social rights and deeper conditions of women's citizenship defined the movement. Given women's unique roles in reproduction and childrearing, pioneering critics insisted that the state must go beyond inclusion in the form of electoral participation to address endemic structures of dependency. This deepening of the premises of citizenship, however, did not automatically imply the expansion of its boundaries.

The same connection of the uses of rights to the definition of citizenship held just as much for all campaigns for all kinds of "social rights" since they were first articulated as rights during the French Revolution and after. For a long time, such protections were understood to mean workers' rights in particular, and were sought through domestic struggle. In the French Revolution, social rights—following various Old Regime projects for putting the needy to work—were considered from the first, and featured prominently in the second Declaration of the Rights of Man and Citizen of 1793 (Year I of the Revolution).[50] This political radicalism changed the debate so as to incorporate "the beginnings of a language of social security based on citizenship," and thus presupposing communal inclusion as much as universal rights from the first.[51]

After the Revolution, Charles Fourier in France and John Thelwall in Great Britain tried to extend natural rights to work and income. "Our social compacts," Fourier wrote circa 1806, "cannot provide the first of the natural rights, the RIGHT TO WORK. By these words 'natural rights,' I do not mean the chimeras known as 'liberty' and 'equality.' . . . Why does philosophy jest with these poor creatures by offering them the rights of sovereignty when they demand only the rights of servitude, and the right to work for the pleasure of the idle?"[52] A generation later, when the idea of the right to work returned, it did so in a similar guise. "We will do much more for the happiness of the lower classes," utopian socialist Victor Considérant wrote, "for their real emancipation and true progress, in guaranteeing these classes well-remunerated work, than in winning political rights and a meaningless sovereignty for them. The most important of the people's rights is the *right to work*." In the 1848 revolution in France, organizing government to provide useful activity, as in the famous national workshops, was a major goal.[53] In all cases, as T. H. Marshall classically emphasized, the achievements of social rights were first and foremost revisions of citizenship in the state—not the state's transcendence.[54] In different terms, the choice was between the early ideal of the *Rechtsstaat* and the generally later one of the *Sozialstaat*, as Germans called them: a move from the state based on the rule of law to the state based on welfare, each sharing a common premise of inclusion.

Despite all of these initiatives, property protections remained by far the most persistent and important rights claim in theory and law (including constitutional law) throughout the nineteenth century and modern history. In response, social movements in search of new terms of inclusion were often forced to set themselves against rights rather than simply propose new ones. Free-market conservatism, after all, could and did make the rights of man its own powerful battle cry. That concepts like "natural rights" and indeed the "rights of man" became the best arguments that conservatives could find through the interwar economic crisis to support the freedom of contract and the immunity of property from social regulation—and that these concepts were besieged for more than half a century prior to the invention of human rights—is an essential chapter of modern ideological history.[55] In America, a conservative jurist like Stephen Field could constantly invoke the rights of nature and nature's God as a kind of talismanic magic, even as he more and more identified the promotion of these rights with the defense of capitalism from state intrusion.[56] This severe interruption in the historical trajectory of the rights of man between the age of revolution and the founding of the United Nations is always omitted from attempts to reconstruct their history as one of uplift because it is an episode that simply will not fit. But because the main role of rights was to establish a space of citizenship for rival claimants to its meaning, rights were an equal-opportunity tool.

The competitive success of proponents of *laissez-faire* in appealing to the "rights of man" meant that their critics often chose the route of targeting rights as abstractions in the name of concrete social goods. The progressive assault against *laissez-faire* was very far from being always or simply the championship of new rights, which left the concept of rights itself intact. In this sense, it would be hard to say for sure whether the long modern struggle for social protections counted as an advancement or retreat for rights language. Indeed, already Fourier and Considérant signaled at the outset that the assertion of a right to work is a significant challenge to the formalism of rights and not just a new item in the list. Philosophers like Green supplemented negative liberty against the state with positive freedom of state inclusion, institutionalists like Robert Hale pioneeringly demystified natural rights as social products, while realists like Wesley Hohfeld showed them to be bundled and systemically granted sets of claims and liabilities rather than sacrosanct metaphysical entities. However different in their particulars, all of these views began by departing self-consciously from the self-sufficiency or even believability of "individual rights."

These various critiques, associated with British New Liberalism, followed by American pragmatism and realism, all undercut the concept of individual rights so revered by defenders of freedom of contract, in a far larger progressive move from outdated individualist abstractions to concrete social goods. And they were distinctively Anglo-American only insofar as they typically took a liberal guise. Kindred attacks on individualist metaphysics outside the Anglo-American sphere went far further. As the nineteenth century waned, and as the sovereignty of the abstract state came in for new criticism, a powerful new revolt against the formalistic "metaphysics of rights" targeted the abstract individual too in the name of social integration and welfare. The most interesting arguments in this regard came from the French solidarist theoretician Léon Duguit, who contended that the ideas of the personality of the state and the personality of the individual were bound up with each other and ought to fall together.[57] Given the long-term linkage between individual rights and sovereign state, it was not an unreasonable conclusion; it did not yet occur to anyone to assert the one over or against the other. And even calls for new rights for new people often gave way before the trend to criticize atomistic individualism in the name of social unity. For example, in the later nineteenth century, French feminists articulated demands for women's equality in the name of collective social betterment rather than rights-based entitlement.[58] Similarly, the history of labor movements shows that there is no way to credit workers for advancing rights without failing to mention that their claims, like those of so many others, often required criticizing the very concept of rights.

There was another rights tradition between revolutionary rights and human rights that was as different from each of them as they were from one another: civil liberties. The fact that it was bounded citizenship that gave political rights meaning also affected the origins of this new concept. While icons like John Wilkes, who protested state trampling of cherished prerogatives of speech and press, were active in the eighteenth century—and some of his friends even founded a Society of the Supporters of the Bill of Rights to pay his debts—the *institutionalization* of activism around civil liberties occurred only in the late nineteenth century in France, and then in the

World War I era in Britain, America, and Germany. The permanent organizations founded then, like the Ligue des Droits de l'Homme or the American Civil Liberties Union, certainly did invoke the liberties of speech, press, and association primarily against the state that betrayed them. And they helped develop novel mechanisms for the restraint of the state—in the United States through the constitutional judiciary—as alternatives to its revolutionary toppling or drastic renovation. But like revolutionary-era rights, civil liberties drew their ideological authority and cultural premises from the nation-state. All of these groups rooted their claims not in universal law but in allegedly deep national traditions of freedom. Civil libertarians were part of a common phenomenon that sprouted in different places around the same time, and they were frequently internationalist in their sentiments. But they were enough the inheritors of revolutionary-era rights to overwhelmingly restrict not simply their rhetorical appeals to national values but their activism to the domestic forum (sometimes including, in European cases, the imperial spaces of their states).[59] For many years, civil libertarians mostly gazed within, rather than toward suffering around the world. And so they did not spark the creation of international human rights as an idea or as a movement.

If the umbilical connection between rights and citizenship is the central feature of the history of rights, then the natural question is when and why rights incorporated any sort of impulse beyond the nation-state as the forum that once gave them meaning so exclusively. What is perhaps most startling to record is that the rise of the international forum in the second half of the nineteenth century had no effect on the national framework in which rights—to the extent they were invoked at all—were valued. Although Bentham had coined the term "international" as early as 1780, the rise of internationalization in the form of economic and regulatory integration, together with a variety of other internationalist projects, largely awaited the communications and transportation revolution after 1850. This process covered the banal and the sublime—from postal unions to police enforcement, from famous international exhibitions (dating from 1855) to the Olympic games (dating from 1896). Almost never implying the wholesale abolition of the state, internationalization often simply provided it a grander stage for its self-expression. Indeed, in the later nineteenth century, the rise of the new international space occurred in tandem with the burgeoning of a more chauvinistic brand of nationalism that, after Mazzini's era, predominated everywhere. (Later, there was even such a thing as fascist internationalism.)[60]

The new international sphere of the later nineteenth century did make international activism, unthinkable before, possible. Since that era, this "internationalism" has been the dominant modern universalism, presupposing nations but seeking their interdependence. After about 1870, international organizations and leagues began to sprout, some of which prioritized the promotion of a new global consciousness. Beginning in the 1870s, one or two were founded each year, then as many as five each year in the decades before 1914 and about ten each year between the world wars.[61] At times it seems as if internationalism could serve anyone—from aristocrats to bureaucrats, from workers to lawyers—yet none of them moved the notion of rights to the international level, let alone pursued their legalization above the state.[62] Insofar as a generally rights-based movement like the women's movement took on international form, its internationalism was about sharing techniques and building confidence for national agitation, not making the global forum itself a scene of invention or reform, participation in the quest for international peace aside.

But international socialism remains perhaps the most crucial case for coming to grips with why the expansion of internationalism and the explosion of rights did not and need not connect. While it had long since been possible to articulate social concerns as rights claims, it was neither inevitable nor even usual to do so. Beginning with the origins of organized socialism as a political project in the early nineteenth century, the various movements typically verged much more in the direction of utopian transformation. And whatever the invocation of rights by the Marxist movements that followed, Karl Marx himself pioneered what became a prevailing and longstanding way of arguing for a better world in which the rights of man remained the problem, not the solution. He took the general skepticism of rights involved in the advancement of workers' concerns so far as to lead to complete repudiation of them. His early text, "On the Jewish Question," offered a critique of the modern capitalist state as a forum for freedom, in which the abstraction of rights is alleged to obviate "real" freedom. Like other, later critics of formalism, Marx attacked states and rights alike in recognition of their umbilical linkage; and if he appealed beyond to a global order, it was in the name of a communism that required the transcendence of individual rights.

While one might be tempted to depict the rise of Marx's "scientific" socialism as a disaster for the possibility of a liberal, rights-based socialism, the latter movement proved a tiny competitor.[63] And even the reformist socialisms of the later nineteenth century, which resolved to play by the rules of parliamentary democracy rather than seek violent revolution, dreamed of other long-range utopias that did not appeal to the rights of man. The careers of "revisionist" Eduard Bernstein in Germany, the Fabians in Britain, and even Jean Jaurès in France—the extraordinary socialist who worshipped the French Revolution and argued, like so many others, for its anticipation of socialist utopianism not legal internationalism—illustrate this clearly.[64] "*Le droit du pauvre est un mot creux*," the workingman's and later communist anthem significantly entitled the "Internationale" says. "The right of the poor is a hollow phrase."[65] Even as it neglected to place rights center stage, however, socialism did do more than any other movement to promote internationalism as a political cause, beginning with the International Workingmen's Association (1864–1876) and proceeding through the Second International (1889–1914).[66] Current histories of internationalism in the later nineteenth century are still radically incomplete. But it does seem clear that even the word internationalism (particularly when capitalized) became associated most often with international socialism, and that liberal forms of internationalism—like the new international law, with its comparatively respectful attitudes toward state sovereignty—developed largely in open ideological competition with their terrifying socialist rival.[67]

Though they tried more than many, even the most internationalist late-nineteenth-century socialists were not able in the end to escape the gravitation of state and nation, as the road to 1914—when European socialist parties rallied to war—would make so graphically clear. But their example shows that for cosmopolitanism to be defined as the supremacy and internationalization of rights, other utopias would have to be left behind. Just like the premodern diversity of universalisms, later history would show that a wide variety of internationalisms were available; their crisis was to create the conditions for international human rights. But if human rights now so thoroughly define cosmopolitanism as to seem its only possible form, it is precisely not because of their ancient vintage. Even during the birth of internationalism in the nineteenth century, human rights were not on the horizon. And this followed not from some intellectual failure or inexplicable opposition—certainly not in the long era of the rights of man in which they were the creature of the state, and remained unaffected even by new patterns of relationship with other states that internationalization began to bring about. People living in the past were not blind or confused, simply because they did not hold later beliefs, or embark on current projects.[68] Rather, human rights were the creation of later and unanticipated events that upended previous assumptions. Those events occurred only a generation ago.

In criticizing what he called the "idol of origins," famed historian Marc Bloch put the essential point best.[69] It is tempting to assume that the trickle of melted snow in the mountains is the source of all the water in a great downstream flood, when, in fact, the flood depends on new sources where the river swells. They may be unseen and underground; and they come from somewhere else. History, Bloch concluded, is not about tracing antecedents. Even what continuity there is depends on novelty, and persistence of old things is due to new causes as time passes. And when it comes to human rights, it is not a persistent stream but a shocking groundswell that has to be explained. Tempting myths aside, they are something new in the world that transformed old currents—and not least the idea of rights before—beyond recognition in unprecedented circumstances and as a result of unsuspected causes.

In fact, long into the twentieth century, the overall link between rights and the nation-state remained relatively untroubled, in spite of some early voices to the contrary. The state and its projects now are understandably regarded with suspicion. Yet in the long view, the search for rights beyond it may have been at a considerable price: the loss of the inclusive space of membership that the concrete state, and even empire, had long provided in some form or other. After World War II, Arendt worried pioneeringly that the new concept of "human rights" presupposed nothing comparable, and would therefore provide nothing comparable—that as in prior history, there would continue to be "nothing sacred" in "the abstract nakedness of being human."[70] If human rights did not reckon with their departure from rights before, they would remain meaningless or even counterproductive.

That Arendt wrote at all does show that there really were some who hoped to place rights above the nation-state in World War II's aftermath. The trouble is that it was an unpropitious time to do so, not least because most of the world—especially the colonial world—still wanted the very nation-states whose ill-advised contests had led the European inventors of the political form to ruin. Though the phrase was elevated to new potential significance in English then, the 1940s were not to be the hour for "human rights." And when they entered popular consciousness decades later, it was not through the sort of political utopianism that so long fired the modern quest for the nation-state, but through the moral displacement of politics. The true key to the broken history of rights, then, is the move from the politics of the state to the morality of the globe, which now defines contemporary aspirations.

2

When "human rights" entered the English language in the 1940s, it was unceremoniously, even accidentally. They began as a subsidiary part of a hopeful alternative vision to set against Adolf Hitler's vicious and tyrannical new order. In the heat of battle and shortly after, that vision of a postwar collective life—in which personal freedoms would fit with more widely circulating promises for some sort of social democracy—offered the main reason to fight. Only rarely, however, were human rights understood as a departure from the persistent framework of nation-states that would provide that better life. And whether as one way to express the principles for all postwar societies, or even as an aspiration to transcend the nation-state, the concept never did percolate in public and around the world with anything like the currency it acquired later, even as the Universal Declaration of Human Rights of 1948 was negotiated. Why not?

From a global perspective, the rise of human rights displaced an earlier wartime promise in the Atlantic Charter of 1941 of self-determination of peoples. Soon, however, it became clear that the Allies meant for the basic principles of postwar international organization to be perfectly compatible with empire. But even in their north Atlantic birthplace, and in second-tier Latin American and Australasian states outside it, human rights failed to take. In the beginning, as a vague synonym for some sort of social democracy, human rights did not address the genuinely pressing question of which kind of social democracy to bring about: a version of welfarist capitalism or a full-blown socialism. Then, by 1947–48 and the crystallization of the Cold War, the West succeeded in capturing the language of human rights for the crusade against the Soviet Union; the language's main promoters ended up being conservatives on the European continent. Having failed to carve out a new option in the mid-1940s, human rights proved soon after to be just another way of arguing for one side in the Cold War struggle. Never at any point were they primarily understood as breaking fundamentally with the world of states that the United Nations brought together.

What would the 1940s look like if freed from the widespread myth that the era represented a kind of dry run for the post–Cold War world, in which human rights did begin to afford a glimpse of the rule of law above the nation-state? What if the history of the 1940s were written with credit for later events given where it is due, and a radically different set of causes for the current meaning and centrality of human rights reconstructed? The central conclusion would have to be that rereading World War II and its aftermath as the essential source of human rights as they are now understood is misleading, however tempting. Human rights turned out to be a substitute for what many around the world wanted, a collective entitlement to self-determination. For the subjects of empire were not wrong to view human rights as a kind of consolation prize. But even for the Anglo-American, Continental European, and second-tier states where they had at least some minor publicity, the origins of human rights need to be viewed within a framework explaining not their grand annunciation but their general marginality throughout the era.

The formation of the United Nations must occupy the focus since through the 1970s "human rights" were a project of its machinery only, along with regionalist initiatives, and had no independent meaning. Yet the founding of the United Nations—the emerging institution responsible for the originally peripheral existence of human rights—actually presents a very different face than its recent chroniclers have been willing to portray. In the startling 1944 Allied outlines of the prospective international organization for the postwar era, the so-called Dumbarton Oaks documents, it was already clear that the wartime rhetoric that included the new concept of human rights masked other agendas. And the campaign by various individuals and groups climaxing at the epoch-making San Francisco conference in mid-1945 to alter this result failed quite spectacularly, despite the symbolic concession of the reintroduction of human rights into the United Nations Charter written there. Given the great-power realism of wartime decisions, the postwar history of human rights, from its earliest days, would have to be as much one of reanimation as it was one of definition of the phrase, and the catastrophic failure of the former cannot be dropped to magnify the importance of the latter.[1]

If a different view is familiar, it is because of two understandable but unworkable strategies. The first is to overstate—often drastically—the effects of the campaign against the Dumbarton settlement. The second is to isolate the path toward the Universal Declaration as a road people travel still, even if the Cold War temporarily erected a barrier on it. But this deeply selective history needs to be replaced by one in which those events, though not without their place, are demoted to phases in a larger, more complicated, and in many ways far more depressing tale. The now well-understood drafting of the Universal Declaration, the usual focus, cannot be separated from far larger historical forces that doomed it to irrelevance in its time. Indeed, a retrospective focus on human rights in this period risks missing the main point, which is the marginality and miscarriage of the concept in an era in the ferment of debate about prospective global orders. The percolation of the phrase in wartime, the Universal Declaration, and associated developments like the European Convention on Human Rights (1950) were minor byproducts of this era, not main features. Human rights were already on the edge of the stage in the postwar moment, even before they were pushed off entirely by Cold War politics. As an early NGO chief, Moses Moskowitz, aptly observed later, human rights "died in the process of being born."[2]

If there is a pressing reason to concentrate on human rights in the 1940s, it is not because of their importance at the time but because doing so provides precious insight into why they could and did not take off until decades later. It matters what human rights, at the time, were not. They were not a response to the Holocaust, and not indeed focused on the prevention of catastrophic slaughter. Only rarely did they imply principled dissent from modern state sovereignty. And above all, they were not even an especially prominent idea. What they were in this era helps isolate what changes later allowed for their eventually broad popular appeal. Unlike later, they were bound up with international organization rather than a larger popular language. And they inspired no movement. A better way to think about human rights in the 1940s is to come to grips with why they had no function to play then, compared to the ideological circumstances three decades later when they made their true breakthrough.

If, in late wartime and shortly thereafter, rights were simply another way to express a brief social democratic consensus, as time passed they afforded new tools to West European conservatives to signal their distinctive identity. America, which had helped drive the global inflation of wartime hopes, retreated from the language it had helped introduce, leaving Western Europe alone to cultivate it. Even there—especially there—the real debate in domestic politics was about how to create social freedom in the state. Yet European conservatism captured the language of human rights, while few others learned to speak it. After a few years had passed, the meanings the idea of human rights had accreted were so geographically specific and ideologically partisan—and, most often, linked so inseparably to Christian, Cold War identity—as to make the fact that they could return later in some different guise a deep puzzle. Moving into the long postwar period, therefore, human rights were not a promise waiting to be realized but a utopia first too vague then too conservative to matter. To capture the world's imagination, they would need profound redefinition in a new ideological climate.

War is always a contest of words as well as of wounds. Yet human rights were not the first words. They arose because the first ones were inadequate, not specific enough in some ways and too specific in others. The Four Freedoms, which were the original framework in which the principles of possible American intervention emerged, dated to Franklin Delano Roosevelt's State of the Union address of January 1941, with its alternative new-order vision, which joined numerous British wartime statements.[3] Roosevelt's freedoms were the freedom of speech and religion, and the freedom from want and fear—the last defined as disarmed peace. The "kind of world" in which the freedoms would be guaranteed, Roosevelt explained in his speech, "is the very antithesis of the so-called 'new order' of tyranny which the dictators seek to create with the crash of a bomb. To that new order we oppose the greater conception—the moral order. . . . Freedom means the supremacy of human rights everywhere." When he met with Winston Churchill off Newfoundland in August of that year, with Pearl Harbor still months away and American entry into the war still politically unviable, FDR rebuffed internationalist pressure on him by rejecting Churchill's proposal for a revived League of Nations. But he incorporated the freedoms from want and fear in the Atlantic Charter, as the principles that all those who resisted Hitler shared. The stress fell on the domains of armaments and economics as what would need the most attention. The most publicized aspect of the shipboard meeting was the religious service that closed it. Observers thought its anthem for Christian soldiers, not the allusion to human rights, most movingly symbolized the Anglo-American antithesis to Hitler's tyranny. As a public relations exercise, however, the Atlantic Charter failed in its main goal of moving Americans further toward engagement. It was the wounds inflicted by Japanese bombs, not the words Roosevelt hoped would rouse America, that drove the country into battle.[4]

When Churchill sailed west again to spend the winter holidays living in the White House at the so-called Arcadia Conference, human rights made their fateful entry into world history as a politically inspiring phrase. As before in FDR's Four Freedoms speech, the phrase entered not with a bang but in passing. It is astonishing that no evidence has been discovered to explain why and when the phrase appeared as it did; but then, the search is premised on the mistaken assumption that what is now so meaningful could not have emerged by accident. From one draft to the next of the Declaration of the United Nations, issued from the White House on January 1, 1942, the phrase was used in a more detailed rendition of the promises of the Atlantic Charter. And still, the idea appeared subordinate to the Four Freedoms rather than leading or enveloping them. The declaration proclaimed the Allies "convinced that complete victory over their enemies is essential to defend life, liberty, independence and religious freedom, and to preserve human rights and justice in their own lands as well as in other lands." Human rights began first of all as a war slogan, to justify why the Allies had to be "now engaged in a common struggle against savage and brutal forces seeking to subjugate the world."[5] But no one could have said what the slogan implied.

It seems unlikely that FDR—who apparently inserted the sentence in the final revision of the declaration—could have meant to introduce something conceptually new. How, then, to explain the rather undramatic and unjustified entry of human rights into the ideological and rhetorical arsenal of world politics? It is useful, first of all, to know that the phrase was not absolutely new. Early, essentially random uses to one side, the information available makes clear that its first serious circulation in the English language took place in 1933, not only in protest of Hitler's accession to power but in support of New Deal reform. Not one but two "Human Rights Leagues" formed in the United States in those years, one for each cause. But these initial meanings, while they motivated the few overall invocations of the idea, had competitors on both ends of the political spectrum. Updating the transformation of the "rights of man" to mean defense of an unregulated market, Herbert Hoover decried the New Deal for its interference with human rights in 1934, while socialists critical of Roosevelt for siding with and saving capitalism pilloried the nation for trampling on the human rights of workers. The honest conclusion is that the phrase meant different things to different people from the beginning. And therefore, it meant nothing specific as various parties tried to give it sense.[6]

By the later 1930s, however, a dominant understanding began to crystallize in this prewar struggle over the phrase's implications: it came to be antitotalitarian, a meaning codified most clearly by the most prominent world figure ever to use the phrase before FDR, Pope Pius XI, in largely neglected references dating from 1937. "Man, as a person," Pius declared in *Mit brennender Sorge,* his famous encyclical decrying the fate of religion under the Nazis, "possesses rights that he holds from God and which must remain, with regard to the collectivity, beyond the reach of anything that would tend to deny them, to abolish them, or to neglect them." The pope was on his own journey, having discovered only in these years that the "totalitarian" regimes were hostile to Christianity, after a period of judicious waiting and alliance seeking. In the same vein, later in 1937 in another encyclical directed against "reds and pagans," Pius denounced those who "spread snares for the Catholic Faith and the liberty due to the Church, and finally rebel with insane efforts against divine and human rights, to send mankind to ruin and perdition." A year after, not long before his death, Pius wrote Americans celebrating the 100th anniversary of the founding of the Catholic University of America that "Christian teaching alone gives full meaning to the demands of human rights and liberty because it alone gives worth and dignity to human personality."[7]

Thus it was in 1939 that the prominent liberal Catholic John A. Ryan, together with Notre Dame University's Charles Miltner, founded the short-lived Committee of Catholics for Human Rights to oppose the radio priest Charles Coughlin and rampant American Catholic racism, a message they tirelessly propagated in their broadsheet, *The Voice for Human Rights*. In that publication, Amarillo bishop Robert Lucey's complaint rang out in 1940: "Millions of citizens throughout the world are no longer considered as inviolable persons: they are mere things to be juggled at will by gangster governments. . . . The natural law demands that all human rights be afforded to all human beings."[8] By 1941, Anne O'Hare McCormick (a prominent Catholic correspondent on European affairs for the *New York Times*) was frequently describing Hitler and the Nazis as a threat to human rights. "New political concepts are developing," she wrote in her report on Hitler's 1941 address opening the annual *Winterhilfe* campaign. "Subjection has made the victims not only more determined to be free than in careless days before the war but more critical of the leadership that put national rights before human rights and guarding artificial boundaries before guarding real security."[9]

Yet all this said, in January 1942 the concept of "human rights" remained to be clearly defined, especially if it was to signify more than background principles that the state could not transgress. FDR used it, clearly, to also refer to norms that the state could go to war to protect; but in his sloganeering he did not move, either conceptually or politically, to the problem of the role of human rights in the remaking of the international order. There was no assertion in January 1942 that the terrain of application of the idea would be in world governance, as opposed to the temporary interruption of normal interstate relations to put down extreme totalitarianism. Just as important in the long run, there was no hint of how human rights would intervene in the longstanding contest over how to socialize freedom in modern economic circumstances. Human rights entered history as a throwaway line, not a well-considered idea. Instead, the significance of Roosevelt's nonchalant elevation of the phrase to its wartime career is chiefly that, extending earlier trends, it became an empty vessel that could be filled by a wide variety of different conceptions.

The competition over the meaning of human rights drove its wartime itinerary more than anything else. And it is the efflorescence of definitions motivated by vague invocation that has received the attention of historians seeking the prehistory of the postwar moment. Without denying the value of tracking such wartime uses—most of them sparked by FDR's careless phraseology—it is crucial to recall first of all that it proved possible for decades to write about American diplomacy during the conflict without mentioning human rights. Following the percolation of human rights during World War II is something people have begun to do in retrospect, but the focus easily blurs the picture. In the first half of 1942, most high officials, like Vice President Henry Wallace, placed stress on economic reconstruction as the essence of the war promises, and even the main meaning of the Four Freedoms rhetoric.[10] In international view, and especially after William Beveridge's report urging a postwar world of guaranteed work and higher standards of living, human rights were most often simply synonymous with the central wartime promise of Allied leaders for some sort of social democracy. Even then, rhetorical definitions of human rights in government, and among private individuals and groups, amounted to no more than an anarchic cacophony, in which earlier competing ideals were reformulated in new language.[11]

Two of the main groups—in any case essentially overlapping—to give human rights play in 1942–43 were lawyers, including international lawyers, and those members of the peace movement who laid most stress on rethinking the international order to avoid future war. In these groups, definition occurred, but primarily to lay out possible lists of rights, rather than to disrupt the long-term connection of rights and state sovereignty. The American Law Institute produced a draft bill between spring 1942 when planning began and 1944 when it was published.[12] Outside intra-American discussions, there was not comparable activity. Tireless but alone, British international lawyer Hersch Lauterpacht also hit upon the idea of developing an international charter of rights in 1942, and developed it into a book published in 1945. But it can hardly be said that these dogged efforts were that prominent, either among lawyers or in private initiatives like the

Commission to Study the Organization of Peace.[13] The commission, led by Clark Eichelberger and James T. Shotwell, had developed out of the old League of Nations Association, and devoted itself during World War II to proposals for international organization and then unstinting domestic support of the government's own negotiated plans. The fight for an internationalist America during World War II was, in any event, very far from equivalent to the search to define human rights, which was a minor, subsidiary byproduct of that fight rather than its driving force. Indeed, after Wendell Willkie's huge bestseller *One World* appeared in 1943, and prominent Republicans like Senator Arthur Vandenberg rallied to the cause, the internationalist spirit cut across the two major political parties. But while American internationalism, with its longstanding mission of peace and stability, unquestionably enjoyed a nervous triumph, human rights as a prospective governing principle remained on the margins throughout.

In the United States, it was religious groups who were probably the most active in the campaign to raise the profile of the idea, in the midst of the anarchy of other rhetorics. The Federal Council of Churches of Christ in America (FCC)—old-stock Protestants overwhelmingly dominating American internationalism more generally—formed the Commission to Study the Bases of a Just and Durable Peace, which attempted to draw cross-denominational Protestantism away from isolationism and pacifism alike.[14] John Foster Dulles, then a prominent lawyer and Republican foreign policy thinker who had had a religious awakening and worked for Christian ecumenical unity in the name of a just new order, led this wartime "crusade." In his commission's March 1942 guiding principles, the premium fell on "moral order," which the United States had a "great responsibility" to secure. Rights, especially the right of religious observance, did have a place; later, when the group issued its widely circulating *Six Pillars of Peace,* the last made reference to calls for an international bill of rights, which—this group insisted—must prioritize freedom of religion.[15] Though late in coming to human rights,

Jacques Maritain, leading Catholic publicist sojourning in America in wartime, injected them into Catholicism theoretically for a large international audience, and in doing so prepared himself to be the premier philosophical defender of human rights in the postwar decade. Ingeniously breaking with Catholic political thought in modern times, including his own neo-Thomist traditions, Maritain began claiming Catholic natural law as the proper framework for human rights two weeks after the Declaration of the United Nations, and he promoted them tirelessly through the war, especially for clandestine French circulation. Crucially for its postwar European fate, Maritain rallied to rights in communitarian terms, exalting the moralistic "human person" against the atomistic individual as their bearer. Writing in *Fortune* magazine in April 1942, Maritain praised the "concept of, and devotion to, the rights of the human person" as "the most significant political improvement of modern times," even as he warned darkly of the perilous temptation to "claim human rights and dignity—without God." (A secular "ideology" grounded in "a godlike, infinite autonomy of human will," he cautioned, would lead only to catastrophe.)[16] By the end of the war, the American Jewish Committee (AJC) had also incorporated the idea, even if understandably much more concerned with the ignored immediate plight, and specific likely problems in the future, of the Jewish people.[17]

Where were human rights outside these American discussions? The answer is: nowhere yet. The finding is remarkable, since they were to find their lasting homeland not in America but in postwar European politics. The eyes of the rest of the world remained fixed on the Atlantic Charter, given its promise of self-determination, even as behind the scenes Churchill struggled to convince Roosevelt that his interpretation of this promise as applying only to Hitler's empire, not empire generally, should win out.[18] Outside Europe, the reception of the Atlantic Charter and human rights talk is a differential rather than a continuous one, especially insofar as it became clearer and clearer that "human rights" would not imply collective self-determination. But in Europe, the wartime story is slightly different.

It may seem surprising, in light of Nazi ideologue Josef Goebbels's euphoric 1933 proclamation that "the year 1789 is hereby eradicated from history," that the rhetoric of the rights of man were so peripheral in wartime. Yet in Britain, the American activities had no parallel, H. G. Wells's proposals for a new bill of rights as the essential alternative to Nazism aside. Given the pope's rhetoric (continued by his successor, Pius XII), rights talk seems to have been dominated by Catholics, whether in resistance circles or priests in occasional sermons. In spring 1942, some Catholics on the Continent were converging on human rights as a principled Christian language of resistance: German bishops, in a common pastoral letter of Easter 1942, rose in protest of their regime's trampling not just of the church's rights (in disregard of an earlier concordat) but also of human rights—"the general rights divinely guaranteed to men." The extraordinary clandestine resistance group of French Catholics, *Témoignage chrétien,* republished this letter and amplified the call in its summer booklet, "Human and Christian Rights." Of course, what such calls meant differed from place to place; in Hungary, for example, what was at stake for some churchmen and Christian politicians was only "the rights of (Christian) man," chiefly the defense of the right of conversion against racist essentialism, still in the name of an exclusionary vision of a Christianized nation.[19] But in the scheme of things, the wartime attempts to define FDR's tantalizing statement were drowned out by the thunder of events.

The percolation of the phrase got nowhere before the stakes of defining it clearly turned out to be low not high. The very process of the wartime definition of human rights coincided with the reality of their emasculation: birth and death together. FDR's own wartime ideas, though in constant motion on matters of detail, usually revolved around the notion of parceling up the postwar world into zones of influence the Allies would patrol as "four policemen." For FDR, as well as for leading foreign policy wonk Sumner Welles, the Monroe Doctrine and its preservation remained of overriding significance. Only when convinced by his secretary of state Cordell Hull to replace the League—and later, by the need he saw for internationalist voters in the Republican Party in the 1944 presidential elections—did FDR begin to move prior planning of an international organization to the highest diplomatic levels. But along with other Allied leaders, his goal remained a security framework that would balance the Big Three (later Big Four) against each other in postwar circumstances. Formally, the plans moved away from both regionalism and trusteeship; informally, their goal remained in effect to embed great power "dictatorship" (as some critics put it) as the kernel of international governance.[20]

The original idea of great power trusteeship attracted FDR even before Pearl Harbor. It would later coalesce in the concentration of true authority in the UN Security Council.[21] With this proposal approved by Josef Stalin at Tehran in late 1943, the real action in the development of the scheme occurred in the first six months of 1944; it has never since been fundamentally revised. As the Big Three developed their proposals, no diplomat so much as mentioned human rights in the runup to the critical planning meetings that began in late August at the Dumbarton Oaks estate in Washington, D.C. When the main preparatory documents were leaked to James Reston of the *New York Times* by the Chinese (angered at having been invited to the negotiations only to be excluded from main decisions), those with eyes to see understood immediately that the true goal of the prospective United Nations was to balance great powers, not to moralize (let alone legalize) the world.

In the end, the idea of human rights entered the final plans as a negligible line buried in the proposal for an Economic and Social Council and without any serious meaning. The initial American draft, in fact, called for "each *state* . . . to respect the human rights and fundamental freedoms of all its people," while the final text assigned the United Nations itself the task of promoting respect for human rights in a late section of the documents. Its approval occurred in light of potential public backlash: "it would be farcical to give the

public the impression that the delegates could not agree to the need
to safeguard human rights," leading British representative Gladwyn
Jebb commented. But its approval simultaneously neutered the concept in international organization, apparently for good.[22] And while
the fact that it was necessary at all proves that international organization needed to be sold to the people rather than negotiated by elites,
human rights were only one symbolic element in the public rollout:
while human rights had surely risen in prominence in wartime, they
were not yet a general justificatory language of international organization. Even in the popular press, it was obvious that the real dispute
at the conference, and indeed later, revolved around the Security
Council, its voting formula, and the veto, a matter settled first at Yalta
and confirmed at San Francisco with the famous requirement of
unanimity. By this early moment, the foundation stones of the UN
organization had been laid; as Charles Webster, urbane British diplomat, recorded, "later embellishments did not touch the essential
points."[23]

In living memory of Woodrow Wilson's humbling failure to convince his country to accept his grand creation, for American activists
on the ground everything turned on *whether* the U.S. government
and people could be persuaded to enter the international sphere as a
committed participant. It was this question that encouraged these
groups to be full-throated defenders of the United Nations on any
model. "United States membership in the United Nations became
the symbol of United States participation in international society,"
stated Dorothy Robins, a participant who later chronicled private advocacy for the United Nations in these years. For the largest group—
those former isolationists who were converted to internationalism
because they were presented with a model of it poles apart from
transformational idealism—it was less the New Deal than the new
form of international cooperation the United Nations represented
that accounts for the end of American isolationism. As one significant promoter, Vera Micheles Dean, explained at the time, the absence of "fundamental principles" made the basic lines of the new

organization far superior to the League's inflexible and moralistic model. "The Dumbarton Oaks proposals held out no hope of a millennium," she wrote. "This was not the kind of document that could stir after-dinner orators to eloquent speeches about eternal peace. And that was good."[24] More important, the recent memory of the startling Japanese incursion, something with no real equivalent in earlier U.S. history, undermined the country's sense of isolated immunity, making a repetition of its post–World War I attempt to escape embroilment in the world less plausible.

Dissent from a few idealists and pacifists—Oswald Garrison Villard, for example—failed to dominate American discussion, in stark contrast to the post-1919 scene when Wilson had faced not just isolationists but more thoroughgoing internationalists. Insofar as there occurred much reflection on the acceptability of Dumbarton realism, the key consideration remained the apparent lack of alternatives. It was *this* international order or none. "It is quite true that in an ideal international legal order all nations should be equal before the law," Harvard philosophy professor Ralph Barton Perry explained in the *New York Times* in a long letter to the editor in January 1945.

> The Dumbarton Oaks proposals do not create, and are not designed to create, such an ideal political and legal order. It is right and proper to judge them by that standard, and to deem them imperfect when so judged. They carry over many of the objectionable features of the old order, and embody peculiar historical accidents reflecting the present crisis in human affairs. It does not follow, however, that they should be rejected or despised. They should be enthusiastically applauded for the good that they promise, rather than condemned in the name of the perfection they do not reach. . . . Those who refuse to take a step toward their goal because it does not at once reach the goal are likely to stand still or move backward.

Fear that isolationism might rear its head meant that few American pressure groups treated the organizational specifics of the United

Nations as a deal breaker; the repeal in the Dumbarton drafts of the Atlantic Charter's promise of self-determination caused no debate among American internationalists, while the failure to advance wartime promises of human rights, though a concern of some lobbies, did not seriously affect the terms of public discussion. Writing in *The Nation*, Protestant theologian Reinhold Niebuhr praised the strategic acceptance of Dumbarton on the part of American internationalists, going so far as to criticize any proposed injection of human rights on the grounds that to do so would merely confirm rather than abate their meaninglessness: "Nor would the Dumbarton Oaks agreements be substantially improved by the insertion of some international bill of rights which has no relevance, and would have no efficacy, in a world alliance of states."[25]

Understandably gripped by fear that isolationism would have the last laugh, the priorities were American engagement and Soviet participation, not their particular form. Of course, it helped American internationalists that their own country could make a move into an organization that accorded it so disproportionately powerful a role in its structure. Midwar, the old League of Nations Associations retitled itself the United Nations Association, but its agenda remained the same; advocacy for an ornamentalized charter through San Francisco remains a footnote to the deeper support by internationalists of the charter in a form very close to the one designed in secret at Dumbarton. It was—and still is—one based on national sovereignty and great power balance. In this way, American internationalists played an apologetic role, advocating an agenda that scuttled the new concept of human rights rather than making it central. To the extent that they remained in the negotiations, human rights and other idealistic formulations reflected a need for public acceptance and legitimacy, as part of the rhetorical drive to distinguish the organization from prior instances of great power balance. It was a narrow portal to offer morality to enter the world, and a far cry from a utopian multilateralism based on human rights.

The victory of American internationalism thus coincided with the practical marginalization of any idealist language around which activist groups could or did mobilize. Indeed, a mere generation ago, the story of American internationalism during World War II, just like the story of the diplomacy of peacemaking, could be told with no reference to human rights, even while admiring its successful "second chance" to move the country to engagement. No NGOs in the contemporary sense or even of a general character, save the ineffectual International League of the Rights of Man, emerged in the era. The project of nudging the UN processes in new directions both before and after San Francisco prevailed among more familiar groups of Christians, Jews, and women insofar as any model of associational activism did. All of these groups began to reference human rights, but the absolute priority for American internationalists fell on the ratification of the charter, in a form they generally welcomed. "The adherents of international organization," Robins put it inimitably, "conquered the dragons of public indifference and Senate resistance only after intensive labors, and secured the hand of the princess for which they had been fighting. . . . It is a romance of modern times." In *Time* magazine, however, the recognition of what had transpired at San Francisco was more sober. The "charter [was] written for a world of power, tempered by a little reason. It was a document produced by and designed for great concentrations of force, somewhat restrained by a great distrust of force."[26]

It is nonetheless true that, against Niebuhr's advice, advocacy groups kept human rights on the agenda in the winter of 1944–45, a project also adopted by small states powerless to affect the predetermined fundamentals of the organization. It would be an error to underestimate both sorts of agitation, but it would be an equal mistake to unify its opposition and exaggerate its accomplishments up to the great San Francisco conference and beyond. W. E. B. Du Bois, the great African-American thinker and agitator, spent this period directing the failed campaign of the National Association for the Advancement of Colored People (NAACP) to force the United Nations to make good on the Atlantic Charter's promises of self-determination (especially in colonial areas), even as his group collaborated with Jewish and Christian organizations like the AJC and the FCC to return the idea of human rights to more prominence in the prospective charter. Much has been made of diplomacy by Latin American states, but historic fears of conquest and intervention made their first order of business in the Chapultepec Act of 1945 to install the norm of sovereign impregnability as a regional and universal norm.[27] When it comes to the small states more generally, contemporary reflections by Herbert Evatt, Australian participant and important ringleader of the powers intent on revising Dumbarton at San Francisco, show that the best case for additions to what largely remained a "big power peace" could include a number of items, but the expanded role for human rights hardly figured on the list.[28]

After all, the main events of the San Francisco conference were elsewhere. By the end of his life, a mere two weeks before the meetings began, FDR had come to envision the United Nations as a high priority. Most feared the Soviets might pull out, especially as the long period after Yalta had seen disputes over the exact scope of the Security Council's veto. When at the conference the Soviets, in the person of foreign minister Vyacheslav Molotov, acceded to the American interpretation of the formula, the world breathed a sigh of relief, and other issues were secondary. Webster, ever the realistic British diplomat, acknowledged that the "fervour of the speeches concerning justice, human rights and fundamental freedoms . . . represented forces which none of the statesmen could ignore, since in the long run power is a moral as well as a physical entity." The entirety of the 1940s, however, remained the short run. At San Francisco, the main accomplishment where human rights were concerned was symbolic: human rights and fundamental freedoms were mentioned as preambular principles. Ironically, it was South African prime minister Marshal Jan Christian Smuts, who came to the conference insisting on the need for a more uplifting charter (one he did not see as incompatible with the continuation of empire around the world and racial hierarchy in his own country), who achieved this victory of adornment. Otherwise, the advocacy of groups and states resulted in leaving human rights within the ken of the Economic and Social Council, the lowly position to which Dumbarton had first demoted them. Mostly due to the attention of the AJC's Joseph Proskauer and the FCC's O. Frederick Nolde, the charter called for a human rights commission, though one with unclear duties to protect undefined principles. Given the preamble, Arthur Vandenberg, a U.S. delegate in San Francisco, could treat the charter as a major departure: "Dumbarton Oaks has been given a new soul—the Charter names justice as the prime criterion of peace." But according to Virginia Gildersleeve, Barnard College dean and American delegate assigned to handle negotiations on the Economic and Social Council, Vandenberg privately wrote off the "fantastic objectives which are being written into the Economic and Social Council." Like most nations, the United States left that part of the organization to delegates like her as "a suitably feminine field."[29]

The inclusion of references to human rights in the charter was bound to make a difference, both pushing the problem of definition to the fore and opening the path toward the construction of unpredictable agendas in the future by both states and individuals. But the truth is that San Francisco largely repeated Dumbarton, rather than unsettling it. "Neither the Charter nor diplomatic wrangling is reassuring," Belgian Charles de Visscher complained indignantly in the course of encouraging fellow European international lawyers to work for human rights two summers later. His Anglo-American colleagues had long since given up that task. "International organization looks like a mere bureaucracy with neither direction nor soul, unable to open to humanity the horizons of a true international community."[30] Guided tours of the road through the first meetings of what would become the UN Commission on Human Rights in 1946 to the Universal Declaration of December 10, 1948 have been repeatedly led in recent years, but what is striking is how little evidence there is that these diplomatic negotiations, or even the final passage of the

Universal Declaration, captured the imagination of contemporaries. Though the origins of the Universal Declaration are worth some attention, more important is why so few people could muster enthusiasm for it. The space opened by the charter for a mass movement to coalesce around the new concept remained hypothetical only.[31]

Postponed in wartime and at San Francisco, the itemization of human rights finally occurred, even as it was decided that they would be declared first, with the more contentious problem of legal enforcement in a so-called "covenant" saved for later. The American representative on the Commission on Human Rights, Eleanor Roosevelt, led the symbolic campaign. A much admired figure with a background in the peace movement, Roosevelt assumed the role of the commission's "schoolmistress," chairing the proceedings and keeping fractious delegates in line, while also acting as U.S. representative, and generally deferring to State Department direction.[32] The general consensus about the itemization of rights suggests that little was at stake in the proceedings, in spite of a few interesting debates over details. The rights canonized in the Universal Declaration, on the foundation of human dignity, ranged from classical political liberties to promises of work, social security, rest and vacations, education, and an adequate standard of living. (The negotiations over the text of a legal "covenant" were finalized only two decades later, with the treaty split into two as the International Covenant on Civil and Political Rights and the International Covenant on Economic, Social, and Cultural Rights, which both then came into force in 1976.)

That social rights were included at all is sometimes treated as surprising, and they remain striking from the perspective of the present day. But the broad consensus around their presence is more revealing for understanding why the whole notion of human rights had so little uptake at the time. Social rights had already figured in the French Revolution, interwar European history, and FDR's famous proposal of a "Second Bill of Rights" in his State of the Union address in January 1944. There was little conceptually new about them, especially given their prominence in interwar European constitutions (first in the Weimar Constitution of 1919, and most expansively in the new Soviet Constitution of 1936, the same year in which by then centrist French appeals to *droits de l'homme* also reincorporated social rights).[33] After the Beveridge Report, social protections were close to the core of international promises for a better world. It was surely a breakthrough in America for FDR to describe those protections as social "rights" of a potentially constitutional status in his State of the Union address for 1944. But it was also a moment when the transformation and deradicalization of the New Deal promoted an emphasis on individual rights rather than the common good that had been the framework for the government's role in combating economic instability at the New Deal's apex.[34] The powerful welfarist consensus in America and around the world in wartime most of all reflected a brief and unprecedented moment of agreement that unregulated capitalism could not be allowed to bring the world low again. Insofar as any dispute swirled around the very idea of social rights, either in the spate of new constitutions or in early UN processes, it concerned the problem of how much the continuing right of private property would have to be chastened. After the war, however, the general consensus did not help at all in the decisive choice between models, whether of government regulation or of social protection. Human rights were the victims of their own vagueness.

Given the general consensus as to the content of rights, including social and economic rights, there would be no reason to insist on the primacy of any ideology in the original drafting of the Universal Declaration, were it not for the striking prominence of Christian social thought among the framers and even in larger UN debates. Maritain, the main publicist of Christian personalism, had pioneered the introduction of a kind of communitarian liberalism into earlier Catholic traditions. He now undertook to study the philosophical foundations of rights and worked with the UN Educational, Scientific, and Cultural Organization (UNESCO) more generally to promote understanding. In different ways, Christianity primarily defined the worldviews of all three of the main framers of the Universal

Declaration: John Humphrey (the lawyer who directed the UN's Human Rights Division for two decades and assembled the first draft of the list of rights), Charles Malik, and Roosevelt herself.[35]

Though he won the Nobel Peace Prize twenty years later, it is now known that the contribution of the main European party actually involved in the drafting, French-Jewish jurist René Cassin, paled before that of the others.[36] An eminent presence, though not a deep thinker, Cassin had based his advocacy for a humane postwar order on declared rights beginning at the Inter-allied Meeting held at St. James's Palace, London, in fall 1941, where he represented his occupied country as a patriot and humanist; by this point, he hewed to the antitotalitarian denunciation popularized in papal language of the hypertrophic state, to which the rights of the human person were the alternative. In the immediate postwar years, he chaired the Alliance Israélite Universelle, the renowned French-Jewish advocacy organization, and Cassin accepted the quickly established rhetoric of universal victimhood at Nazi hands. In any event, in the tradition of French republicanism, he could generally align with the communitarian focus of his colleagues on the drafting committee.[37]

Malik was perhaps the key figure in the negotiations. A Lebanese Christian who had studied with Martin Heidegger in the Nazi era, he had written his dissertation at Harvard University before becoming a prominent diplomat. After the war Malik hewed to the ideology of Christian personalism, which governed his strong anticommunist leanings and drove his hopes for a Christian future in the Middle East and elsewhere. It was thanks to him, indeed, that Maritain's "human person" became the central protagonist of the Universal Declaration's text. According to his cousin by marriage Edward Said, who sat at his feet in these years (before souring on where his mentor's Christian anticommunism led him), Malik thought devotion to dignity and personhood prompted not incorporation of all worldviews but instead "the clash of civilizations, the war between East and West, communism and freedom, Christianity and all the other, lesser religions."[38]

It is easy to overstate the global and multicultural origins of the Universal Declaration in light of more contemporary pressures and desires. It is, of course, true that the catalogue of items in the declaration drew from domestic constitutions around the world, and notably in Latin America; but these constitutions reflected long since globalized European practices in the first place. Rights talk in the sense of domestic constitutionalism and the citizenship struggles it allows were familiar in many parts of the world, Latin America not least; but no one so far has discovered any additional, popular language of international human rights on the ground in these years anywhere in the world. Similarly, there was non-Christian participation in the small group that produced the rough draft of the declaration (most notably, besides Cassin, P. C. Chang of Kuomintang China, who had earned his Ph.D. in philosophy under John Dewey at Columbia University). And later a long debate occurred in the UN General Assembly that produced light revisions to that draft. The diplomatic agenda of the Latin American states in these debates, especially Cuba, was to bring the new declaration into conformity with the American Declaration of the Rights and Duties of Man, passed in Bogotá, Colombia in spring 1948—a campaign that led Humphrey to complain that the "speeches were laced with Roman Catholic social philosophy, and it seemed at times that the chief protagonists in the conference room were the Roman Catholics and the communists, with the latter a poor second."[39]

Far from demonstrating the multicultural origins of the document, however, these facts mainly show the existence of a global diplomatic elite, often schooled in Western locales, who helped tinker with the declaration at a moment of symbolic unity. To the extent main actors came from outside "the West," like Malik or Filipino delegate to the United Nations Carlos Romulo, the ideology closest to their hearts was a Christian one. Did the canonized items reflect Western values? Not really, for it is only in this era that something called "human rights" could be treated as the heritage or core of anyone's civilization, especially in Christian Europe where the concept played an important role in putting aside illiberal temptations of the recent past. Social rights were possible to affirm from non-Western traditions, like Islam, or by states significantly influenced by both Christian social thought and interwar welfarist ideas, notably Latin American ones. International participation of states in diplomatic negotiations, in any case, is not a useful proxy for the diversity of human culture at this moment or any other. Both the liberal idea of rights and Christian natural law in its oldest forms (as well as newer ones stressing personal dignity) were long since abroad, and the reaffirmation of nationhood by the Universal Declaration implied that it was far from obvious whether the consensus in the document meant to take the principles beyond their state-based relevance in practice.[40]

When Julian Huxley, famed evolutionary theorist and humanist and first director of UNESCO, joined with Maritain to survey intellectuals on the justification for human rights, the results were disappointing. Among philosophers, the exclusion of the most prestigious schools of thought of the day—most obviously, existentialism—means that Maritain's conclusion that everyone concurred on the importance and substance of human rights on condition of not inquiring why is hard to credit. "We agree about the rights but on condition that no one asks us why," Maritain impishly observed; but in fact, the agreement is more interesting for the absence of parties than for the absence of reasoning. Famously, around the same time the American Anthropological Association rejected the concept of human rights as Western and political rather than a polyglot formed at the intersection of all cultures or a metalanguage that unified plural human traditions. It was impossible to affirm "the rights of Man in the Twentieth Century," anthropologists insisted, and to do so in the face of cultural diversity would simply "lead to frustration." Indeed, if these Western students of the non-West affirmed some residual universalism, they did so—rather cannily—by registering clearly the politics of retreat from collective self-determination out of which individual human rights had been born: "The world-wide acclaim accorded to the Atlantic Charter, before its restricted applicability was announced," they acknowledged, "is evidence of the fact that free-dom is understood and sought after by peoples having the most di-verse cultures."[41] The widespread recent belief that human rights were consensually and cross-culturally agreed upon until the Cold War crisis is unsustainable: what universal principles the anthropolo-gists felt they could affirm without straying into partisan ideology had been forsaken in the very move to human rights, rather than proclaimed in their invention.

The passage of the Universal Declaration on December 10, 1948 was undoubtedly a heroic achievement of diplomatic consensus that the global tensions of the moment—besides the origins of the Cold War, the creation of the State of Israel and the South Asian partition come to mind—could easily have excluded. But as important as the Uni-versal Declaration turned out to be in the long run, the story of its diplomatic and ideological origins cannot fail to incorporate what ought in some ways to be the more interesting and important in-quiry: why the language remained so peripheral in its time, in its American birthplace, and even in its subsequent European home-land, to say nothing of the world as a whole. As a plot point in the history of human rights, the mystery of the 1940s is not why human rights emerged, but—given future developments—why they *failed* to do so.

A first if definitely lesser reason is the immediate fate of human rights within UN processes, where they were to be largely restricted for decades both as a matter of the diplomacy of states and the atten-tion of private associations. Even as the Commission on Human Rights moved toward finally itemizing rights, it made clear that the list would be declaratory only, in the first instance; as for the com-mission's function otherwise, the Economic and Social Council an-nounced in a summer 1947 *non possumus* decision that the commis-sion had no competence to investigate, much less act upon, petitions. As Humphrey bitterly recorded, in a frequently repeated comment, this made it "the world's most elaborate wastebasket." The restriction of UN human rights to symbolism is often treated as decisive compared to the road not taken, but in many ways it was the natural corollary of the charter itself, which had so undermined human rights on condition of enshrining them that their activation would have required revisiting organizational fundamentals. The delegate who may have understood this best—the Indian Hansa Mehta, an interesting figure also responsible for revising the declaration's language in the direction of gender neutrality—advocated a failed proposal in favor of human rights as "an integral part of the Charter and . . . fundamental law" that would take many decades to revive even conceptually.[42]

True, the priority accorded to declaratory rather than legal rights, due to American and Soviet predetermination, theoretically promised a subsequent move to legalization. Yet the first draft of a post-declaration covenant—which then took twenty years to finalize—only became possible once the Soviet delegation stopped attending the Commission on Human Rights in early 1950 because the majority at the United Nations refused to unseat the Kuomintang representative in favor of the successful Chinese revolutionaries. Indeed, this bit of spite allowed for the draft to be completed quickly, even as it also identified human rights more and more with Western notions. It was initially restricted to political and civil rights (much like the contemporary European Convention on Human Rights). This moment of progress at one level, however, cemented irrelevance at another, as human rights were revealed as useless in vaulting the distance between the contending ideologies of the world at the time. Charles Malik reported that the apparent "boon" of Soviet absence actually undermined the plausibility of human rights in its bid to become "the highest cause in the world today." Instead, the uncompromising Westernization of human rights meant not inevitable advance but "bashful retirement" from relevance.[43] Postponed in the focus on declaring rights, the prospect of moving to legally enforce human rights across borders that a few observers still considered a live possibility as late as 1949 was dead by 1950.[44] Only in Western Europe did that project survive the origins of the Cold War, in part because the restriction of geographical scope allowed legalization to become a Cold War project.

It had not been a foregone conclusion in 1945 that a Western conception of human rights would prevail. Happy in spite of Marxist ideology to help define human rights in the UN processes, the Soviets had seen neither sham nor threat in the new ideological language; indeed, they could claim on paper what remains the most full-blown declaration of rights yet propounded in world history, in the "Stalin" Constitution of 1936, conceived at a moment when the relevance of communism for the individual personality mattered, both for citizen self-consciousness and Western propagandizing. Writing in 1947, leading Western expert on Soviet law, Columbia University professor John N. Hazard, saw no reason the USSR would need to avoid human rights. Early observers felt that the Soviets, in spite of obvious hypocrisy, identified themselves more consistently as an anticolonial power. The Universal Declaration's emphases on equality and nondiscrimination were largely their contributions. The USSR also pressed for the abandoned promise of self-determination of the Atlantic Charter to be reincorporated, allegedly on the example of the country's own internal self-determination policies. But the Western nations, including the Atlantic powers that had once offered that promise, won out.[45]

In the end, the USSR abstained from the vote on the Universal Declaration itself, but presented itself at home for more than a decade as faithful to the precepts of the documents. Its public justification for the abstention was the Westernization involved in itemization, which also led some Muslim states to dissent during the drafting and abstain in the voting, with special attention to the right of religious observance made increasingly central by Western states.[46] Further, in public debates the Soviets could frequently complain, in recognition of the move away from individualism involved in the notion of the "human person," that the world had simply not moved far enough: according to the Yugoslav delegate speaking just before the vote on December 10, 1948, the Universal Declaration simply "codified" long since secured political and civil rights, while not effectively incorporating the collective interdependence of humanity that modern economics made so glaringly necessary.[47] Ultimately, on theoretical principle, Soviet diplomacy and its international law conceptions stressed sovereign equality in international affairs more than human rights (in tune with its official anticolonialism), balanced by Stalin's explicit insistence that great power unanimity remain the foundation stone of the UN structure.[48]

But it was also the case that human rights became almost immediately associated with anticommunism. Besides an international controversy around discrimination against South Asians in South Africa, the two major *cause célèbres* in which human rights were invoked at the United Nations and in international fora generally were anticommunist in spirit. In one, the Soviet Union was criticized on human rights grounds for prohibiting women who were Soviet citizens from migrating to join their foreign husbands abroad; the second, and most visible of all, revolved around the internment and trial of Cardinal József Mindszenty, the Primate of Hungary, in 1948–1949, and related abuses of Christians in Eastern Europe like the house arrest of Cardinal Josef Beran in Czechoslovakia—both campaigns occurring so quickly after the Universal Declaration as to help define its bearing.[49] The causes prompted UN resolutions and were, together with the occasional denunciation of South Africa, the main cases across decades of Cold War stalemate of what human rights "enforcement" at the United Nations might look like.[50] The Mindszenty case—though forgotten and unstudied since—was by any measure the most prominent and therefore characteristic human rights cause of the era in international politics. In 1947–48, Hungary, Bulgaria, and Romania were excluded from the United Nations on the grounds that the communist takeovers in those countries flouted the provisions of the Paris Peace Treaties, which called for respect for "human rights and fundamental freedoms" as a condition for their UN membership. Together with these events, the controversies over Mindszenty and other clerics cemented the tendency for human rights, with special focus on a privileged right of religious freedom, to be identified more and more with the fate of Christianity in a world in which communism claimed to incarnate secularism.[51] In response, having initially advocated UN attention to South Africa, the Soviets converted to the defense of state sovereignty, and the die was cast for the future.

In its inaugural era, the United Nations did continue earlier humanitarian causes, extending the internationalized campaigns pioneered by the League of Nations against slavery and forced labor, and trafficking in women and children. It also attempted, as the League had before it, to manage refugee displacement, which exploded in war's aftermath. In the League era, these sometimes impressive but always culturally specific and politically selective campaigns had not been conceptualized around notions of universal rights, and were typically philanthropic causes deployed in a hierarchical world to beat back the illicit practices of foreign peoples, religions, and empires cast as brutal and uncivilized.[52] After the war, both at the United Nations and in the popular mind, humanitarian activities remained essentially separate from human rights long into the postwar period. The idea of human rights was occasionally invoked as part of these humanitarian ventures, but it did not succeed in annexing the territory and redefining the meaning of humanitarian action for NGOs like the new Oxfam or for governments, whether national or international. The main exception, the International Labour Organization's campaign against forced labor, which dated from the interwar years but absorbed human rights in the postwar era, did not define the broad public meaning of that language.[53]

A second and more important reason for the irrelevance of the human rights idea to the postwar moment, however, is that it solved no problems. If for different reasons in different Western countries, it would be hard to identify an issue in which an appeal to rights, as such, could or did matter, and this was because there was no debate that they could cut through by themselves. Ironically, the interwar and wartime incorporation of welfarist ideas meant an unprecedented consensus around the availability of social entitlements, though—of course—domestic politics turned on what this common sense meant in practice. On the largest issue, the most promising social model, the language of rights could not determine the choice between a welfarist and a communist scheme—a fact which, more than any other, accounts for the marginalization of human rights as a new ideological paradigm at this moment. Already in 1945, French philosopher Raymond Aron argued that declarations of rights were condemned "to insincerity, because those who subscribe [to them] will despite everything not hesitate to sacrifice either the principle of personal liberties or the principle of the equal division of wealth" in the choice between contending social models. Nothing depends on social rights, E. H. Carr observed skeptically not long after; everything "depends on the nature of the social system prescribed under the category of social rights."[54] The announcement of the Truman Doctrine in March 1947 with its call for decisive choice between "two ways of life" meant that the December 1948 passage of the Universal Declaration must have seemed too much a pretense of unity at a crossroads for humanity to really matter.

That said, insofar as the new slogan of human rights had any visibility, domestically and regionally, it was not among American liberals but European conservatives. Looking back with an understandable desire to identify the upsurge of American internationalism with human rights, it is easy to emphasize that the isolationist conservatives of the era condemned the idea. And there is no doubt that as time passed one American political current—led by Frank Holman of the American Bar Association and Senator John W. Bricker—vilified internationalism in all of its forms as global communism in disguise. They campaigned against it, however, not so much because the minor appeals liberals were making to suprastate norms were genuinely threatening. They did so, rather, because such agitation—identifying internationalism with redistributive socialism—proved an effective partisan rhetoric in populist appeals to the American way.[55] Nevertheless, the emphasis on American conservatives in the end skews the picture as a whole. It misses, most of all, that the story of human rights beginning at the end of World War II was in fact mainly one of their slow association with Cold War conservatism in Europe, to the point that they lost further relevance as a set of potentially common ideals. Indeed, the main survivor of the contest of meanings, against the backdrop of the stillbirth of human rights as a generally inspiring idea, was the conservative Christian interpretation, which had helped to define it from the start, later mummifying it as the Cold War began. In a larger view, in other words, conservatism defined rather than destroyed human rights.

While Christian interpretations of human rights were impressively prominent throughout their minor wartime circulation, the increasing Christianization of human rights after World War II is perhaps the most important one. It helps make sense of why, of all places in the world, they gained their only postwar foothold in West European restabilization. This is not, however, so much because Christian definitions and appropriations faced their hardest struggle in beating back secular ones, as because they were beset for a long time by alternative Christian political aspirations. Briefly, it was the disappearance of Christian reaction and fascism that set the stage for the preeminent role Christianity could play in the postwar framing of human rights; but that role also deeply affected the meaning of those rights as a third-way, personalist, and communitarian alternative to liberal atomism and materialist communism alike. The conversion of religious intellectuals in the course of the war and just after to the cause of human rights, which they then proceeded to interpret as core principles of a continuing antisecularist agenda, is therefore worth some attention.

Most religious figures—especially the Catholics who were to be so significant after the war—had long rejected the whole idea of rights as secularist and solipsistic. The Catholic Church's long-term vilification of this political language is a classic fact. Commenting in 1940, George Bell, the highly influential Anglican bishop of Chichester, commented on H. G. Wells's proposals, "Of course you can dress up the ideas of 1789 and adapt them to the conditions of 1940. But the present situation is the result of secularism. To add a further dose of secularism to what the patient has already absorbed is to add poison to poison. . . . No amount of secular Declarations, no number of claims for human rights, without spiritual sanctions, will save us from destruction." Yet by the postwar period, many prominent Christian intellectuals were championing the new version of the language—on condition that it reflected Christian moral community, whether at the national or international level. These years saw Bell insisting that "the rights of men derive directly from their condition as children of God and not of the State," given "the sacredness of the human personality." When leading Protestant Swiss theologian Emil Brunner addressed the topic in 1947, to take another example, he insisted that "[h]uman rights live wholly from their ground in faith. Either they are *jus divinum* or—a phantom." By contrast, few serious non-Christian intellectuals were theorists or partisans of the new idea of human rights—or even rights generally—until several decades later.[56] There is perhaps no better testament to the fact that human rights died through birth than that they could prompt no more general campaign of thinkers volunteering to defend them, or even define them.

The sheer authenticity and passion with which Christian and conservative championship of "human rights" took place necessarily meant that others could not help but regard it as a deeply partisan idea. The Christian intellectual who made himself in 1948 the first historian of human rights, premier German scholar Gerhard Ritter, provides valuable evidence that the Christian context of human rights in postwar Europe could also embrace a larger West that included—even drew inspiration from—American Christianity. Ritter, a conservative nationalist interned in 1944–45 for his involvement in the aristocratic and military circles that crafted the plot to kill Hitler, awoke in the postwar period to the reality that Christian unity would have to be achieved in order to stave off communism. In this cause, human rights were crucial, as "the essential hallmark of Western civilization in contrast to 'totalitarian' state slavery."[57] After all, Maritain had helped remind Western Christianity that human rights, far from being a dangerous outgrowth of modern secular liberalism, recalled the moral community of Christendom through its emphasis on the "human person." More important, Christian statesmen—John Foster Dulles leading them all—had helped introduce them as a Christian concept. Indeed, Ritter insisted, Dulles's successful wartime campaign for a moralistic but nonpacifistic interpretation of Protestantism showed that human rights were now called to be the last best defense against the communist threat. To be sure, human rights were dangerous too, especially as American history had been the forum not just of godly religion but also of the hedonist materialism of the pursuit of happiness—a promise that wended its way in history from the French Revolution through the Soviet totalitarianism now so prejudicial to the Christian West's traditional identity. But that only meant that human rights had to be saved for spiritualism in the present crisis.

Ritter met Dulles in 1948 when the latter spoke at the epoch-making Amsterdam conference, where long-sought ecumenical Christian unity finally became a reality in the form of the World Council of Churches, which prized human rights in the context of its promotion of peace. But by then, Ritter recognized, Dulles's America and Western unity, not a somewhat unreliable ecumenical formation, represented the true hope of Christendom. For Maritain, Ritter, and many others, human rights, far from originating in 1789, were a Christian bequest to be defended against the legacy of the French Revolution—or even revolution as such—that still threatened. "Geopolitically," Ritter concluded, "there can be no doubt that the future of everything that we customarily regard as the heritage of Christian-Western culture depends on the almost religious zeal with which today's America defends the principle of general human rights against the totalitarian state system."[58] That it was Dulles a few years later who was called upon to announce as Dwight Eisenhower's secretary of state that America would not be party to legally binding human rights covenants should not distract from his role in cementing the Christian interpretation of the language before then, especially abroad. Indeed, America's quick departure from the concept left the European Christian and anticommunist context of human rights even clearer. After glaring wartime absence, they affected early postwar Europeanization, notably the political and cultural origins of the European Convention of 1950.

The so-called federalist agenda had deep roots in interwar European history, and it was intensively discussed in wartime (in spite of the alliance with the Soviets), as when Churchill foresaw the need for "the revival of the glory of Europe, the parent continent of the modern nations and of civilization," to save "ancient Europe" from "Russian barbarism."[59] In wartime negotiations, after the specter of their mutual exclusion had been exorcised, the United Nations and regional arrangements emerged together. The idea of associating the Western European region with rights grew up from almost the first days of associational planning in the immediate postwar years. This is so even though they had not been a fundamental political language in any earlier traditions of imagining and constructing continental European unity. Of course, in most Western European countries, civil liberties unions had been active in the interwar years, however peripherally, but it cannot be said that these parties helped redefine the dominant languages of politics even in the domestic forum. The French *droits de l'homme* tradition, so strongly linked historically to the Radical (left-liberal) Party, entered extreme crisis in the era, not least when prominent members inclined to the appeasement position championed by Paul Faure of the larger Socialist Party, then colluded in scuttling the republic in 1940.[60] Meanwhile, the control by police states of public discourse elsewhere, and in France after 1940, meant that it was only in wartime, when a serious Christian resistance appeared, that rights talk as a set of first principles had any circulation. Even then, in no country was the language the dominant framework for resistance, not least for Free France, where patriotism ruled, or occupation or Vichy France, where the far left figured so significantly in numbers and authority.

Instead, it was other forces that reinvented Europe, most symbolically in the European Convention, as the postwar homeland of rights. After the war, there is little evidence that noncommunist socialist currents in Great Britain, France, and occupied and later West Germany, where powerful parties formed, rehabilitated the language in a serious new way. In part, this must have been because the content of rights catalogues seemed domestically uncontroversial, secured either time out of mind or in recent memory; the novelty in constitutional and parliamentary debate, in the creation of bills of rights for example, was the unprecedented consensus with Christian conservatism (the meaning of the property right, and educational matters, being the main sticking points). Hence the otherwise surprising fact that there was no socialist renaissance of discourse about rights—especially the new international rights—in the postwar moment.[61]

Rather, the main story of postwar rights talk in the Western European region, and especially the Convention, is as a kind of footnote to the reinvention of conservatism in power, notably after the February 1947 communist takeover in Czechoslovakia made the threat elsewhere seem so vivid. Since this "re-recasting of bourgeois Europe" depended for decades on the political hegemony of Christian democracy, it would be surprising if it had no effect on the Europeanization of human rights in the era, to the extent that the idea survived at all. Many of the chief founders of the European project, both in politics generally and in the tradition of European human rights specifically, were avowed Christian personalists (for instance, Robert Schuman, Paul-Henri Spaak, Pierre-Henri Teitgen).[62] From the beginning the energy in the movement to defend and define human rights as the essence of European civilization in the European Convention came from conservatives—Churchill and his allies out of power, anxious about the specter of socialism at home, and opposite numbers on the Continent worried about the impending triumph of "materialism" over spiritual values.[63] In the end, political and civil rights, prioritized as the essence of Western European identity, were alone protected, with social and economic rights dropped. The fact that the convention's negotiation extended later than that of the Universal Declaration meant that the fiction of ideological consensus about basic values could no longer be maintained, and by 1950 European human rights consecrated the basic values of the Western side in Cold War politics. In Britain, the Labour Party, increasingly driven into the negotiations due to Cold War imperatives, and against the backdrop of Churchill's ardent insistence on federalism out of power, acceded to human rights in spite of its confirmed suspicion that they were often not much more than a Conservative attack on its domestic programs. In a larger, regional view, the common Christian basis for unity mattered a great deal—not simply for "Christian personalists," but even for the godless Ernest Bevin, the Labour foreign secretary who cited "spiritual union" as the reason to proclaim Western European rights. Only now that meant the opposition inspired by totalitarian statism on behalf of regional civilization (and religion). From its vague introduction as some sort of social democracy, the idea of human rights had been redeemed only as a concrete Cold War position.

While these local political factors accounted for the existence of the European Convention, and the European Court of Human Rights it set up, it would be a gross error to assume that the language of human rights, let alone the law of human rights, mattered much in the beginning. The European Convention involved much more ideological signaling about the values on which Western European identity depended than it did legally enforceable guarantees. Though the treaty had originated as part of the imperative to give human rights teeth somewhere even as they lost traction everywhere, postwar fundamentals did not immediately make Western European lands a paradise of principle rather than power. Most obviously, there were empires to retain, even for small nations—like

Belgium and the Netherlands—that would much later become associated with human rights advocacy on the world stage. In recognition of the implications of European commitment to human rights, for instance, Martinique poet Aimé Césaire could rage in 1950 that anticolonialism had been adopted by "not one established writer, not one academic, not one crusader for law and religion, not one 'defender of the human person'"—the last an allusion to the dominant European framework for rights. Indeed, it was due not just to the Convention's conservative origins but also to its potential for interference with empire that the French left—including the leader of the Ligue des Droits de l'Homme—kept the nation from signing onto the document for thirty years. Though a small number of jurists worked doggedly over the decades for human rights to mean more within Europe, their victories still awaited a later, global transformation for the close association of European identity and human rights to take.[64]

Within the essentially stillborn European human rights "regime," signs of life awaited the later 1950s and 1960s, and even then the results were to be of little immediate significance. Britain's Cyprus emergency of the late 1950s led to the first use of the system among states, with the original vision of the system as providing a kind of standard-setting within European diplomatic relations taking a strikingly long time even to find a first use; it never became a major feature of intra-European affairs. The path of individual petition, opened in the treaty, was followed to the end only in 1961 in the first Strasbourg court decision in *Lawless v. Ireland*. But even this petition right proved mostly theoretical until the mid-1980s, when both the number of petitions received and—even more startlingly—the number approved for court consideration skyrocketed. (By the mid-1970s, the European Court of Human Rights had decided only seventeen cases.)[65] The "genesis" of the European Convention explains little about its eventual uses. It was to be far more a cultural and ideological victory of human rights in a later era that determined their legal availability and plausibility even in the European zone. The conservative, Cold War origins of the convention were forgotten. Human rights came to mean something different in radically new circumstances—even as the new centrality of Holocaust consciousness to European societies made it powerful to believe that the continent had cleansed its hands of violence and adopted a new credo immediately after its nadir, rather than in very recent times and due to very different events.

Without doubt, conservative ideas can be inspiring too, in this case as an idealistic explanation for the defense of the West in a moment of unprecedented danger. For better or worse, this was the only version in which human rights really survived their bittersweet fate of rhetorical annunciation in wartime. This last fact confirms the wistful anachronism of seeing only one's preferred meaning of human rights as the one that lived long enough into the postwar years to be reactivated later. The real story of the idea is that it had to be appropriated later from the benighted obscurity and ambiguity of its introduction, and from the originally conservative and frequently religious meanings that accreted to it. The "deep freeze" of the Cold War affecting human rights, far from being their death-knell, only extended the original mortification of their birth.

Despite its new international significance, the core meaning of "human rights" in the 1940s remained as compatible with the modern state—background principles of the nations united by them—as the older tradition of the domestic rights of man had been. The itemization of human rights in these years, indeed, went much further than the establishment of a fundamentally new political understanding of their potential global role. Though surely proclaimed by an international organization, the Universal Declaration retains, rather than supersedes, the sanctity of nationhood, as its text makes clear. In this sense if in few others, it more preserved a memory of the rights of man and citizen than it pointed ahead to the utopia of supranational governance through law. The inclusion of social and economic rights in the mid-1940s very much mattered, though they were earlier products of citizenship struggles and have still barely affected the international order. From another view, however, the postwar moment gave the antique idea of declaring rights an altogether new cast: neither genuine limitations of prerogative, as in the Anglo-American tradition, nor first principles, as in the French, the Universal Declaration emerged as an afterthought to the fundamentals of world government it did nothing to affect. (No one registered this fact more clearly than the lone Anglo-American international lawyer still campaigning for human rights by 1948, Lauterpacht, who denounced the Universal Declaration as a humbling defeat of the ideals it grandly proclaimed.)

Later, the postwar moment was to come into a very different retrospective focus that falsified it profoundly even as it allowed revival of some of its contents. Rather than a story of death in birth, the proclamation of human rights became one of birth after death, especially Jewish death. In real time, across weeks of debate around the Universal Declaration in the UN General Assembly, the genocide of the Jews went unmentioned, in spite of the frequent invocation of other dimensions of Nazi barbarity to justify specific items for protection, or to describe the consequences of leaving human dignity without defense. It was far more recent Holocaust memory that encouraged a mystified understanding, too, of the Nuremberg Trials, which in reality had contributed to ignorance of the specific plight of the Jews rather than establishing a morally familiar tradition of responding to mass atrocity. More important, it is not at all obvious that, at the time, Nuremberg and related legal innovations like the genocide convention were conceived as part of the same enterprise as the itemization of human rights, let alone falling under their umbrella—though they are now often treated as if they were a single if multifaceted achievement. The main force behind the genocide convention, Raphael Lemkin, understood his campaign to be at odds with the UN's human rights project; in any case, it was even more marginal and peripheral in the public imagination than the Universal Declaration, passed the day after.[66]

After the 1970s and especially after the Cold War, however, it became usual to regard World War II as a campaign for universal justice, with the shock of the discovery of the camps prompting unprecedented commitment to a humane international order. This inaccurate and depoliticized view of the aftermath of war, which allowed the myth that human rights were a direct response to the worst crimes of the century to take root and prosper, compounds the importance of focusing on the more recent invention of the contemporary utopian imagination. It is true that commitment to human rights crystallized as a result of Holocaust memory, but only decades later, as human rights were called upon to serve brand new purposes. What mattered most of all about the human rights moment of the 1940s, in truth, is not that it happened, but that—like the even deeper past—it had to be reinvented, not merely retrieved, after the fact.

3

In May 1945, Vietnamese anticolonialist Ho Chi Minh
sought some of the first principles of his cause in American history.
In communication with one of his covert handlers from the American Office of Strategic Services, before a common interest in defeat-
ing Japanese imperialism had dissipated, Ho "kept asking . . . if I
could remember the language of our Declaration [of Independence].
I was a normal American, I couldn't. . . . The more we discussed it,
the more he actually seemed to know about it than I did."[1] On September 2, 1945, scant weeks after the Japanese had been brought to
their knees, and before the bitter reimposition of French colonial
rule with British assistance and American connivance, Ho promoted
what is now the most famous premise of 1776 from its originally subsidiary placement to be the opening line of his own Vietnamese Declaration of Independence: "All men are created equal, they are en-
dowed by their Creator with certain inalienable rights; among these
are Life, Liberty, and the pursuit of Happiness."[2]

The encounter captures in miniature the essential historical connection between anticolonialism and rights—but only if it is understood correctly. However reinterpreted with the passage of time, the
American declaration was not really about rights; it had above all
been intended to announce postcolonial sovereignty to the other nations of the world. If it appealed to international law, it was one in
which recognition of states, not the protection of individuals, is what
counted. Like practically all other anticolonialists, Ho placed popular
liberation first, not individual human rights directly. After citing the

declaration's "immortal statement," he immediately continued: "In a broader sense, this now means: All the *peoples* have a right to live, to be happy and free." He could not have been clearer: the utopia that still mattered most was postcolonial, collective liberation from empire, not individual rights canonized in international law.[3]

The surprising fact of the matter is that postwar anticolonialists rarely invoked the phrase "human rights," or appealed to the Universal Declaration of 1948 in particular, though decolonization was exploding precisely in the moment of its passage and after. Apparently aware that the rights of man and the nation-state had long been inseparable, anticolonialists in the post–World War II era proved to be far more interested in the twentieth-century reformulation of that linkage by V. I. Lenin and Woodrow Wilson as "the self-determination of peoples." As a young man in Paris, Ho had boldly sought out Wilson during the Versailles conference to ask why Wilson's grand principle did not apply to his Vietnamese people. Its era of fulfillment, however, awaited the end of World War II, precisely when it is now tempting to argue for a "human rights revolution." Powerfully reanimated and specifically proclaimed by the wartime Atlantic Charter, it was the promise of self-determination rather than any supervening concept of international rights that resounded around the world at that time. The charter inspired anticolonialists, but the same was not to be true of the successor promises of "human rights": the phrase began its career precisely as the Allies stepped back from their apparent promise of self-determination.

Nothing changed after the war to lead anticolonialism to feature human rights more prominently, whether in general or as the United Nations elaborated them. And when decolonization resulted in enough new states to matter at the UN, the phrase "human rights" itself came to be incorporated in the master principle of collective self-determination. If anticolonialism generally spurned human rights, one might say, it was because it was a *rights of man* movement, with all the prior fidelity to the state that concept implied in modern history. And, insofar as anticolonialism gazed beyond the state, it was in the name of alternative internationalisms, in a spirit very different from that of contemporary human rights. Those internationalisms incorporated subaltern national liberation, and focused not on classical liberties, or even "social rights," but collective economic development. But neither is it the case that anticolonialism betrayed or "captured" human rights, destroying their original promise. Given the uncertainty of the meaning and the marginal power of the idea of human rights in the 1940s, it is better to regard the eventual force of anticolonialism at the UN as its own distinctive tradition—one that the rise of human rights in their more contemporary sense would have to displace.

The most general reason to care about the anticolonialist interlude after World War II in thinking about the broad outlines of a history of human rights is because it forces a new perspective on the relationship between Western universalism and global struggle. It is tempting to emphasize how subaltern groups abroad can concern themselves with turning a hypocritical rhetoric into a global reality. This argument about "fulfillment from below" makes a fundamental point about how promises can be moved from paper into politics. Nevertheless, there is no such thing as a necessary "logic of rights," in which they would cascade beyond the intentions of their Western founders, as different groups across the world try to make their universalism more than just words.[4] Indeed, what is so remarkable about the post–World War II moment is that individual privileges potentially protected by international organization and law were not the broken promises that subaltern groups decided to globalize. There was a truncated principle that decolonization universalized. But it was that of collective liberation, not human rights.

There would seem to be few clearer examples than the anticolonialist era, then, that the emergence of human rights as a moral program, and master principle for a new paradigm of global aspiration, has to be written within a larger history of competing ideologies of human betterment. As the agent of the greatest dissemination of sovereignty in world history, not of its qualification, anticolonialism's lesson for the history of human rights is not about the growing relevance of the concept across the postwar era. It is about the ideological conditions in which human rights in their contemporary connotations became a plausible doctrine after the mid-1970s: an era in which collective self-determination, so persuasive before, entered crisis.

Though it achieved almost unbelievable successes then, anticolonialism after World War II did not come out of nowhere. Yet, unlike some first-world movements that appealed to rights language, like the women's movement and (less frequently) the workers' movement, anticolonialists rarely framed their cause in rights language before 1945. Colonial subjects were painfully aware that Western "humanism" had not been kind to them so far.[5] The Ligue des Droits de l'Homme, the French civil liberties union, staged a debate on the topic of the relation of colonization to the rights of man in 1931. The shock of violence on the ground led its members to heartfelt denunciations of existing colonialism, but the task fell on them all the more squarely to reform colonialism in the name of rights. "To bring Science to people who do not have it, to give them roads, canals, railroads, cars, telegraph, telephone, to organize public health services for them, and—last but not least—to communicate the Rights of Man to them," as one speaker proclaimed, "is a task of fraternity."[6]

True, activists sometimes appealed to legal (including judicial) remedies accorded them by the domestic legal systems in which they were working; British and French law, with their hierarchical distinction between the law governing metropole and the law governing the colony, provided legal rights at least on paper to all subjects of their respective empires. And domestic civil liberties traditions—a culture of individual freedoms embedded in different ways in the national traditions of the major colonial powers—had the potential to be transplanted to holdings abroad, and were often appropriated for unexpected use. But there were no international human rights prior to World War II, only the rights of man of membership, and later the civil liberties of patriotic criticism. Early campaigns for citizenship and civil liberties may, indeed, have helped cross the span to the later search for independent statehood better than they prepared the way for appeals to international rights.[7]

But the most critical fact is that their interwar formation left opponents of empire with a range of ideologies, few of which were naturally open to the human rights moment of the mid-1940s. After 1918, only, or mainly, one right was to matter. It was Wilson, along with Lenin, who created the conditions for an anticolonialism in which international human rights—not yet formulated as an idea—were not the goal, with one collective right cherished over others. The "Wilsonian moment," stymied in the immediate aftermath of World War I, had a second, more successful chance after World War II, and it meant that there was no remotely comparable "human rights moment" at that time.[8] The case of the decolonizing world shows clearly that not all universalistic promises spark seizures from below of their unrealized potential. Perhaps more than any seemingly inherent logic, the global history of concepts depends on how rival human actors choose to deploy them, for good or for ill.

The detailed history of wartime promises to the colonial world shows, in fact, that human rights entered global rhetoric in a kind of hydraulic relationship with self-determination: to the extent the one appeared, and progressed, the other declined, or even disappeared. The Atlantic Charter of 1941 had announced self-determination but not human rights as part of the Allied war aims, even if Churchill and Roosevelt differed on what that meant. For Churchill, it applied to the liberation of Hitler's empire, not empire generally, and certainly not his empire. Roosevelt is thought to have been more generous by predisposition: "There are many kinds of Americans, of course," FDR told Churchill at dinner in 1942, "but as a people, as a country, we're opposed to imperialism—we can't stomach it." Yet he came to agree with his ally by the time of his death.[9] The earliest formulations of human rights—up to and including the Universal Declaration—dropped self-determination.

It is clear that the Atlantic Charter, especially, did have great resonance throughout the world. And self-determination continued to apply in Europe, as the Yalta conference's Declaration on Liberated Europe, and later criticism of the communist takeover of Eastern Europe, would show. Elsewhere, to the extent anyone paid attention in an era of galloping struggle, human rights must have seemed like a substitute for self-determination—not least given the latter's glaring absence from the Universal Declaration's text. Ho, who in 1945 initially begged his American interlocutors to live up to the Atlantic Charter's promise of self-determination (and American traditions he celebrated) rather than allow the French to return, stopped asking and never again made even declaratory rights central.[10]

Far more than the stillbirth of human rights in the developed West, such basic but neglected facts are impossible to square with a view of the period after 1941 as a moment when new internationalist traditions were founded in a genuinely universalistic spirit—what one observer calls "a new deal for the world." Going so far to label the Atlantic Charter a "human rights instrument," setting the terms for all the generosity that followed, ignores that it did not include the phrase "human rights"—the consecration of which in the 1940s dropped the concept of self-determination that the charter did, in fact, feature. And from the perspective of much of the world, it may have seemed more revealing than the birth of human rights that the Allies did not feel they were "stuck" with self-determination.[11] If they were really successors of and substitutes for self-determination, it would have been surprising if colonized peoples had been galvanized by the new human rights. And the facts of global reception match this hypothesis well. It is clear that across the globe the Atlantic Charter electrified a great many. But human rights fell on deaf ears. It is tempting to assume that the Universal Declaration "enjoyed enormous global attention."[12] But if little evidence has been found that this in fact occurred, it is not hard to understand why.

To say that self-determination mattered much more than human rights in the global postwar moment and beyond is not to say that the search for the nation-state was the only actual or possible future in the anticolonialist imaginary. Far from it; besides communism, subaltern internationalisms like pan-Arabism and pan-Africanism loomed large. It is simply to say that the specific appeal to supranational values encapsulated in the new human rights failed to affect it. For even the crucial short-term developments after the Atlantic Charter must be set against the background of a long-fermenting anticolonialism: by the time human rights came on the scene, in other words, the train had already left the station.

Interestingly, for instance, Mohandas Gandhi found nothing new to take from the new rhetoric. Starting long before, he could occasionally interpret the theory and practice for nonviolent resistance, *satyagraha*, so as to win the rights of Englishmen for all British subjects (he also insisted on supplementing them with duties). Yet there is no serious record of Gandhi mentioning, much less celebrating, the new idea of human rights in the era after the Atlantic Charter; he responded to a UNESCO request for his version of the idea—the assumption being that he must have one—with puzzlement. His assassination in the beginning of the year whose end would see the Universal Declaration makes the question of what he might have seen in them, and done with them, unanswerable. Similarly, except for his enthusiasm for a UN petition to safeguard Indians living in South Africa, Jawaharlal Nehru—who leavened a healthy internationalist vision with realist pragmatism—did not invoke international rights, even when he addressed the General Assembly in Paris a month before the Universal Declaration's passage.[13]

The anticolonialism of many others was similarly fully formed before the human rights rhetoric after World War II had a chance to impact it seriously. Prominent anticolonialists like Ahmed Sukarno of Indonesia and Gamal Abdel Nasser of Egypt had itineraries that never crossed the terrain of postwar human rights, with the former an alumnus of the interwar League against Imperialism and the latter preoccupied with other things on the road to his 1952 coup, not least fighting in Palestine much of the year the Universal Declaration was being finalized.[14] Often, anticolonialist ideology originated in tiny groups, characteristically on the far left, and in student or immigrant networks in metropoles, forging diverse compromises between nationalism and internationalism. A frequent result was the fateful connection of anticolonialism and communism that so colored twentieth-century history. And while communism had its own culture of invoking rights, especially in 1934–36 and again in the immediate post–World War II moment, those who saw in communism the best choice for liberation from empire were not seriously marked by that culture in any era. The nationalist government of China participated to some extent in early human rights formulation at the UN, but its toppling spelled the end of any ideological association of China with human rights. As for Southeast Asia, the Atlantic Charter had provided renewed grounds for Wilsonian hopes, but these were quickly dashed as the British rushed to re-establish empire throughout the region in the chaotic months after Japanese defeat. The British were eventually failures in many places, but did restore the French Indochinese empire *en passant* and asserted control over Malaysia by conducting a savage counterinsurgency at the very moment the move towards the Universal Declaration was occurring half a world away.[15]

If anything, the continuing course of anticolonial struggles confirmed these trends, not least due to the growing force of Marxism in anticolonialist thought. At the famous Bandung Conference of 1955 and elsewhere, anticolonialists announced their own internationalism, but in a subaltern key that incorporated nationalism and forged ties of idealism across borders based on racial identity and African or "Afro-Oriental" subordination.[16] Kwame Nkrumah, who had not mentioned human rights in his celebrated speech, "Declaration to the Colonial Peoples of the World," given at the Fifth Pan-African Congress held in Manchester, UK in 1945, claimed only the "rights of all people to govern themselves."[17] The effect of Ghana's early independence on the political aspirations of other sub-Saharan Africans was spectacular, and above all in the priority accorded self-determination among all other possible aims: "Seek ye first the political kingdom," in Nkrumah's famous slogan, "and everything else shall be added unto you." When founded in 1963, the Organization of African Unity's charter made reference to human rights but subordinated them to the need "to safeguard and consolidate the hard-won independence as well as the sovereignty and territorial integrity, of our States, and to fight against neo-colonialism in all its forms."[18] It was in this atmosphere that C. L. R. James's revival of the "Black Jacobins" of the French Revolution had such power. He did not think of presenting Toussaint L'Ouverture and his confederates as human rights activists before their time. A Trotskyist, James's view of *droits de l'homme*, instead, seems to have been as the "wordy" promises of "eloquent phrasemakers" who, driven by the true economic motor of history to "perorate," were in the end only willing to give up the aristocracy of the skin at the point of the insurgent's gun. There were exceptions, but most typically, anticolonialists followed him in these views, whether Marxist or not, and there is almost no record of prominent icons taking the human rights of the new United Nations seriously as a core language.[19]

The case of French negritude is perhaps slightly different, as some of its partisans were willing to entertain hopes in the immediate postwar period, after the Brazzaville Conference, for a France that might finally include them as equals. Thus, on occasion the great French tradition of *droits de l'homme* was, even in the angriest texts, held out as perverted rather than false. "That is the great thing I hold against pseudo-humanism," Aimé Césaire, Martinique poet, wrote in his classic *Discourse on Colonialism* of 1950, "that for too long it has diminished rights of man, that its concept of those rights has been— and still is—narrow and fragmentary, incomplete and biased and, all things considered, sordidly racist." The background mattered. This proposal for an alternative and realized humanism had originated in dialogue with the interwar project of colonial reform, and for Césaire, as for Léopold Sédar Senghor, it did not necessarily imply sovereign autonomy in the beginning. The founder of negritude advocated an inspiring vision in which a return to and revival of cultural particularity would contribute to, not interfere with, a universal civilization that deserved the name. Through the 1950s, Senghor hoped France could provide it; yet neither Césaire nor Senghor ever referred to the human rights of the international scene.[20] Later, after Senegalese independence, the focus of Senghor's thought, like that of so many others, was the development of a noncommunist Africanist socialism.[21] The general infiltration of Marxism into anticolonialism, which increased after the mid-1960s, did not change the exclusionary equation, and a self-styled "humanism" tolerant toward violence prevailed. For Frantz Fanon, it was "a question of starting a new history of Man, a history that will have regard for the sometimes prodigious thesis which Europe has put forward." But human rights were not invoked as any part—much less the core principle—of that history.[22]

There was an equally important reason that the human rights figuring in wartime and postwar language failed to restructure the anticolonial imagination: the United Nations, far from being the forum of a new and liberatory set of principles, appeared set at first on colluding in the attempted reimposition of colonial rule after the war. "Remember that Dumbarton Oaks"—the documents of the first plans of the organization—"leaves 750,000,000 human beings outside the organization of humanity," African-American anticolonialist W. E. B. Du Bois commented bitterly in spring 1945.[23] As if the Atlantic Charter had never been, those documents, indeed, did not even mention self-determination. And, in spite of trying, anticolonialists were not to succeed in shaking the organization's complicity in the attempted continuation of colonialism, as its initial formulation occurred.

There was agitation to do so. Especially after the United States concurred by the time of Yalta with the restrictive British interpretation of the Atlantic Charter, however, the high politics did not center on whether to end colonialism outright. Instead, they involved debates on the exact terms of the reinvention of the League of Nations system of mandates, the key question being whether international supervision would cover all dependent areas, or whether its supervision would have teeth.[24] These attempts largely failed, drastically restricting the coverage of the trusteeship system and, within it, largely though not wholly reinstating the weak supervisory authority of the League of Nations–era international community. Only a tenth of colonial subjects at the height of postwar empire were under trusteeship authority; and even then, as outlined in the UN Charter's Chapters XII–XIII, the organization's main aim of preserving the peace trumped the "sacred trust" advanced countries were supposed to have in the interests of subject populations, which did not include any definite obligation to move them toward independence.[25] Compared to the Dumbarton Oaks proposals, the concept of self-determination did enter the UN Charter twice, but only in a rhetorical and subsidiary way. (It was also at this stage that human rights entered, if also ornamentally.) *New Africa*, the monthly bulletin of the Council on African Affairs, led by Paul Robeson, marked the end of the San Francisco meeting at which the UN Charter was signed with resignation: "The hope and faith which the people of Africa had in America when Roosevelt was alive is now at low ebb."[26]

As a result, if the United Nations had a strong impact on decolonization, it was not by design. Decolonization affected it powerfully, however, as the "years of Western domination" of the organization gave way to "the age of decolonization."[27] Without question the first major sign of things to come was India's petition in 1946 to the General Assembly complaining of racial discrimination in South Africa against citizens of Indian origin.[28] Clearly framed as an appeal to the UN human rights principles (before they had yet been precisely formulated), the spirit of the debate in the General Assembly eventually turned around the more specific principle of antiracism and anti-discrimination—so as to narrow the principle of interference with sovereignty to crimes only colonialist nations would commit.[29] Much as at the later Bandung Conference, the dominant version of anticolonialism contemplated interference with sovereignty solely against white men's imperialism.[30] A resolution submitted by France and

Mexico to improve the situation barely passed. It did so over the objections of South African prime minister Jan Smuts, who was shocked to see the liberal internationalism he had long championed, most recently in the preamble to the UN Charter he wrote, turned against his country. It was the first step in the long process that ensued of the marginalization and isolation of South Africa, on the grounds of its postwar apartheid.[31] And these anticipations were all minor ones before the deluge.

If anticolonialism prevailed so quickly and came as a shock, it was not due to the UN processes. It would have been impossible to predict in 1945, or even in the brutal postwar years when the Universal Declaration's framing was a sideshow compared to the world reimposition of empire. The British suppression of insurrection in Malaysia would prove a model for other countries, indeed, down to America in Vietnam, but its success did not become the rule. Anticolonial victory, through force of arms or more negotiated departures, did. The era of the "new states" had begun. It was at the UN, and overwhelmingly there, that an intersection of anticolonialism and human rights occurred. Yet it was in essential fidelity to the modern Western priority of the nation-state as the forum for rights.

By the time of the 1948 vote on the Universal Declaration, fifty-eight states were UN members, a total which would increase within a few short years to the point that an Afro-Asian bloc in the General Assembly could outvote first-world powers with Soviet help. After another few years (most notably, after 1960, when sixteen African nations entered) they could do it with no help at all. In twenty years, the number of humans under some sort of colonial rule declined from 750 million to fewer than 40 million. Though this transition would have been unforeseeable in 1945, ten years later great power observers already understood that anticolonialism would have undoubted effects. After Bandung, at which representatives of so many excluded peoples were in attendance, the likely outcome was clear. One depressed British analyst predicted that the newly independent nations would "use the success of the conference as a means of asserting the Arab/Asian point of view and of claiming that the Bandung countries were entitled to a far bigger share of the world authority (as represented by the UN) than they had when the United Nations was founded."[32]

If that entitlement meant the development of something called human rights, it was subordinate—if not equivalent—to self-determination. It may seem remarkable that at first there was almost no doctrinal or organizational connection at the UN between human rights as a project and dependent areas as a problem. But the pressure—and bit by bit, the continuing accession—of the new nations changed this entirely. In an astonishingly short space of time, the UN could move from seriously considering a proposal to exempt colonial (trust and non–self-governing) territories from coverage by the draft "Covenants on Human Rights" to naming the right to self-determination of peoples as the very first of all human rights in those drafts. These debates, which fundamentally transformed the whole meaning of UN human rights, are worth following in more detail.

In October 1950, the General Assembly's Social, Humanitarian, and Cultural Affairs Committee—the Third Committee—gathered to consider whether colonial powers could bind themselves to human rights in a prospective legal covenant, without fearing that this would increase the basis on which the UN could interfere in their affairs. For the Belgian representative, human rights rules "presupposed a high degree of civilization, [and] were often incompatible with the ideas of peoples who had not yet reached a high degree of development. By imposing those rules on them at once, one ran the risk of destroying the very basis of their society. It would be an attempt to lead them abruptly to the point which the civilized nations of today had only reached after a lengthy period of development."[33] René Cassin and Eleanor Roosevelt—icons of the human rights moment at the early United Nations—agreed, speaking as they normally did for the French and American governments. But this proposal to keep the applicability of human rights law out of empires did not carry the day.

Meanwhile, the same year, the General Assembly approved a resolution from Afghanistan and Saudi Arabia that the Commission on Human Rights explore how self-determination could be taken more seriously after its postwar neglect.[34] The idea that the right of self-determination should be injected into the substance of the covenant, though it had not figured in the Universal Declaration, caused a sensational debate, first in the Third Committee in late 1951 and then in the General Assembly's plenary session in early 1952. The Belgian delegate, Fernand Dehousse, posed his objection as a worry about the "multiplication of frontiers and barriers among nations," with self-determination an artifact of nineteenth-century economic liberalism, now overridden by "the idea of international solidarity."[35] The inclusion of self-determination, he argued, could not be used simply to score points against colonial powers. Abdul Rahman Pazhwak of Afghanistan replied angrily on this point that he and other supporters of self-determination as a right "did not want to teach anyone lessons; it was history that taught them," not least "that under the rule of Powers which regarded themselves as qualified to teach others lessons the world had known oppression, aggression and bloodshed."[36] Self-determination, Kolli Tamba of Liberia insisted, "was an essential right and stood above all other rights."[37] At the plenary session, just before the vote, the Saudi Arabian representative, Jamil Baroody, gave a long and impassioned argument for making it the first right:

A lot of water, so to speak, has flowed under the bridge since a request was made for the insertion of an article on self-determination in the covenant. The anguished cry for freedom and liberation from the foreign yoke in many parts of the world has risen to a very high pitch, so that even those who had been compelled to block their ears with the cotton wool of political expediency can no longer deny that they can hear it. Nor can those who have so far shielded their eyes from the dawn of a new day for those clamouring from freedom pretend that the night is not over and that darkness still prevails. . . . [T]he pressure on the gates of freedom has increased and millions and millions of people trying to break through have been kept at bay with bayonets and with tanks and machine guns. So great has been the pressure that those in the front rows have fallen as martyrs of freedom, while thousands taken into custody languish in prison depths and thousands more live in hiding. . . What we are asking here is that the people living in the Non-Self-Governing Territories should be free. They cannot enjoy any human rights unless they are free, and it is in a document like the covenant that self-determination should be proclaimed.[38]

The General Assembly approved the directive to include in the formulation of human rights covenants the article that "All peoples shall have the right of self-determination." A version of it remains there today; it is the very first right in both the chief international legal document protecting civil and political liberties and the one offering economic and social protections.[39]

Whether one celebrates or rues this momentous day, the restoration of human rights to the principle of self-determination emphasized their necessary basis in collectivity and sovereignty as the first and most important threshold rights. And while treating self-determination as a premise for the exclusion from consideration of other rights at the UN forum did not necessarily follow in theory, it did in practice. Above all, it integrated them in a commitment to collective sovereignty that would later seem the very barrier the concept of human rights was intended to overcome. Thus, in the 1960s Louis Henkin, a Columbia University law professor who would later champion human rights, simply denounced their postwar reinterpretation "as an additional weapon against colonialism."[40] For the time being, however, as another critic put it, self-determination had become "a shibboleth that all must pronounce to identify themselves with the virtuous."[41] As new states joined, a final observer complained, the UN concern with human rights became nothing "but another vehicle for advancing [the] attack on colonialism and associated forms of racial discrimination."[42]

Most obviously, the epoch-making Declaration on the Granting of Independence to Colonial Countries and Peoples of 1960 confirmed the near equivalence of human rights and self-determination. According to its text, "faith in fundamental human rights" means the "inalienable right to complete freedom" of "all peoples." Its essential significance was to make the UN a newly exciting forum for the fight against empire. "The *colonial system* . . . is now an international crime," Amilcar Cabral, Guinean scourge of Portuguese domination, exulted, in response. "Our struggle has lost its strictly national character and has moved to an international level." Dramatically, this elevation of anticolonialism to the level of international institutions coincided with the Sharpeville massacre in South Africa, which amplified the country's stigmatization and led to a number of UN resolutions on human rights grounds.[43]

These resolutions and other kindred events show that human rights were defined by antiracism and anticolonialism more generally, fully reversing the imperialist entanglements of the concept of human rights in the postwar moment. Indeed, even as Portuguese Angola came in for immediate attention, India cited the 1960 declaration explicitly in its own December 1961 invasion of Portuguese Goa. In 1962, explaining how best to honor the fifteenth anniversary of the Universal Declaration, the General Assembly approved a resolution effectively linking the celebration of the advancement of human rights with that of the attainment of independence from colonial rule: it defined the hope for the future realization of human rights as another "decisive step forward for the liberation of all peoples." The Declaration on the Elimination of All Forms of Racial Discrimination was proclaimed in the same spirit the following year, with a convention following two years later—the convention approved the same day as the Declaration on the Inadmissibility of Intervention in the Domestic Affairs of States and the Protection of Their Independence and Sovereignty with its remarkable paean to self-determination.[44]

Such declarations became focal points of—and dominant imaginative rubrics for—human rights activities at the United Nations in a widespread alteration of institutional arrangements. Endless discussion likewise ensued, with South Africa and (later) Israel repeated targets of attention. If typically without obvious consequence beyond the organization, this transformation did break the Cold War deadlock, allowing human rights to proceed as a legal project under UN auspices. Between 1961 and 1966, the Economic and Social Council resolved to almost double the size of the Commission on Human Rights. The finalization of the human rights covenants finally occurred in 1966, thanks to the transformative role of the new states.[45] Of more immediate significance, however, was new machinery for considering "gross" human rights violations developed in the same era, as well as a repeal of the 1947 rule barring the Commission on Human Rights from hearing petitions. Yet as the selective working of this new machinery would instantly show, anticolonialism in its UN forum still prioritized the triumph of sovereignty—linked to subaltern internationalism, and thus abrogable only in an antiracist cause—to the point of defining what human rights could mean.[46] If human rights reached beyond the UN in this era, it was, however, only in this redefined sense: an excellent example is provided by the African-American activist Malcolm X.

If the African-American struggle against subordination is best placed in an internationalist, anticolonialist framework, then the rarity and complexity of its affiliation with human rights has to be acknowledged. It is now known that during the interwar period, left-wing African Americans, often in networks with others abroad, linked their struggles to the general anticolonialist agenda, understanding the fight against Jim Crow to be inextricably related to the emancipation of colored peoples throughout the world. W. E. B. Du Bois's generous imagination of global emancipation stretched back a long time, at least to the early twentieth-century extension of his famous identification of the color line as the era's core problem. Three years after the publication of his *Souls of Black Folk* (1903), he could already assert: "The Color Line Belts the World."[47] Though that expansive solidarity grew slowly in the interwar years, World War II gave it major new relevance and popularity. In particular, African Americans shared in the remarkable enthusiasm the Atlantic Charter sparked across the world; few of them saw how the crusade against Hitler's tyranny could allow for the survival of institutionalized racism elsewhere.[48] Returning to the NAACP in 1944 after a ten-year absence, Du Bois committed himself to reviving pan-Africanism and made it his top agenda item to coax the Americans in charge of the form of the United Nations to take back the great power cynicism (and apparent neo-colonialism) of the Dumbarton documents in light of the original Atlantic Charter promises. And the NAACP as a whole made this a leading priority too.

As a maverick within the NAACP, always tangling with its more moderate leadership (notably his frequent enemy Walter White), Du Bois in these years was fortunate that the goals of the organization he had helped found decades before intersected his own itinerary briefly before the emerging Cold War drove them apart again. Du Bois continued his characteristic activities: angered by Dumbarton into planning a book on colonial problems, he drafted his extraordinary *Color and Democracy* in a few months in late 1944 and early 1945; he also organized a Harlem Colonial Conference that spring and attended the more famous Pan-African Congress in Manchester as the movement's resident elder statesman and historian the following fall.[49]

Of course, Du Bois's annexation of the African-American cause to anticolonial liberation—as well as his tempestuous relationship to his NAACP superiors—was never either obvious or easy. Indeed, it was only when the equation proved irresolvable that human rights emerged in his thought. He at first entertained much more expansive anticolonialist goals in agitating for revision of the Dumbarton documents in the leadup to San Francisco and at the meeting itself. In an article from spring 1945 in the *New York Post*, Du Bois proposed a simple statement of equality of races and an end to colonialism. In *Color and Democracy*, however, he strategically framed his arguments not in terms of human rights (a phrase he had not used in his lengthy prior career) but as a subordinate imperative in the organization of peace, and he moderated his call for colonial liberation to recommend the erection of a mandates commission to supervise all colonial holdings, with the explicit aim of preparing "backwards races of man" for later independence.[50] While the NAACP may have joined with some other groups to encourage the injection of human rights into the UN Charter, after their absence in the Dumbarton drafts, it seems clear that Du Bois himself was at this stage far more concerned about embedding the principle of eventual sovereignty for the world's colonial subjects in the foundational document of the new world organization—which did not come to pass.[51]

It was in a *second* stage, eighteen months later, that Du Bois began to organize and craft an "Appeal to the World" presenting African-American subordination as a human rights violation. The idea to do so had originated with Max Yergan, the communist president of the National Negro Congress, who was struck by the possibilities opened by the example of the UN resolution of 1946 focusing on Indians in South Africa. As the NNC collapsed, Walter White, in spite of the demurral of Roy Wilkins, felt that crafting a similar petition for the NAACP could be more than a "publicity stunt."[52] Thereafter, Du Bois, who had now started to sense the potential uses of the human rights rhetoric for black minorities within states (after losing the earlier battle for UN sponsorship of the liberation of peoples under imperial rule), threw himself into the drafting of this multi-authored appeal. It was never published, and finally submitted to UN official John Humphrey in a private meeting in October 1947.

By then, it had become clear that the Commission on Human Rights—whose first and still incomplete task was to give the vague statements about human rights in the charter meaning, eventually by drafting the Universal Declaration—could not act on complaints. After the appeal was thrown away at the UN, bitterly disappointing White (who had trusted NAACP board member Eleanor Roosevelt to support it), Du Bois sent the appeal to some newspapers, which

accounts for the very minor publicity it received at the time. The Soviet delegation to the Commission on Human Rights made some hay
of it in a (once again private) commission meeting in Geneva. The
following summer, Du Bois attempted a second time to generate attention for the appeal at the UN meetings in the fall, but Roosevelt
responded that American blacks "would be better served in the long
run" by dropping a failed campaign, rather than giving the Soviets
more material for Cold War propaganda. Meanwhile, the NAACP's
support of the domestically cabined and far more prominent President's Committee on Civil Rights submerged the "Appeal to the
World" even within the organization; because of the much noticed
pamphlet "To Secure these Rights" that the committee produced, Du
Bois's campaign had quickly come to seem "crankily obsolete" outside too. White and others concluded that the best way to advance
the interests of African Americans was to align them with America's
Cold War interests, and Du Bois's outrage at these NAACP compromises led to his dismissal. He made no recorded comment on the
Universal Declaration, approved a year after he had been purged
from the NAACP and had gone his own way.[53]

The episode is sometimes treated as a missed opportunity for
both African Americans and the United States, but this view is hard
to sustain. Du Bois turned to the language of human rights when it
was still undefined, and only very briefly: just as he had never used it
before, he never used it again. More important, it represented merely
a tool, not the essence of his thought and his activism, even when
he appealed to it. It is clear that after the defeat of efforts to make
more room for the politics of collective self-determination in the UN
Charter, Du Bois turned to human rights as a second-best strategy
for securing the "human rights of minorities" within larger political
structures. The title of the main article he wrote invoking the concept, "Human Rights for All Minorities," exemplifies this strategy, as
indeed does the subtitle of the appeal, "A Statement on the Denial of
Human Rights to Minorities in the Case of Citizens of Negro De-
scent in the United States of America and an Appeal to the United

Nations for Redress." As he entered the wilderness, Du Bois returned to his most lasting commitments: national self-determination, pan-Africanism, and economic democracy in the communist tradition. The petition got only ephemeral public attention, and the new human rights concept did not then, or ever, seriously impact dominant approaches to African-American subordination.[54]

As the NAACP and others accepted a Cold War strategy, the wartime and immediate postwar anticolonialist spirit of African-American activism disappeared, both enabling a civil rights victory and defining its limited terms.[55] Among internationalist strategies that remained, the more moderate Ralph Bunche ran the UN's trusteeship arm for a time, hoping to link—with little luck, as it turned out—international tutorship of Africans in particular to the slow and orderly transition to self-determination he saw as the reasonable path.[56] It would be mistaken and anachronistic to hold out "human rights" as briefly championed by Du Bois as a true historical alternative to these results, or even to equate human rights as he defined them with their very different current sense. Later, on the rare occasions that the phrase was used during the classic phase of the American civil rights movement, as in Reverend Fred Shuttlesworth's Alabama Christian Movement for Human Rights, they were restricted to domestic meanings. These were, after all, the very years that human rights were playing precious little role in informing the anticolonialist imagination, in spite of the support for Du Bois's campaign that Jomo Kenyatta and Nkrumah voiced privately to him at the time.[57] Finally, even later, when the stigmatized and peripheral tradition of inserting African Americans in a global struggle against colonialism in all its forms staged a spectacular comeback in the mid-1960s, human rights returned only briefly, and in a way that would not survive to define them in their own glory years of the 1970s.

A good illustration of these facts is seen in the career of Malcolm X who, after his break with the Nation of Islam, and especially during his long trip abroad in 1964, flirted with human rights—but in the sense of collective liberation from imperial subordination—for several months. Already in his landmark "The Ballot or the Bullet" speech in Cleveland in April 1964, he explicitly opposed civil to human rights, because the former were confined to domestic struggle and the generosity of a state that had proved unwilling to budge. "As long as it's civil rights," he put it, "this comes under the jurisdiction of Uncle Sam. But the United Nations has what's known as the charter of human rights. . . . Civil rights means you're asking Uncle Sam to treat you right. Human rights are something you were born with."[58] After his emblematic pilgrimage to Mecca, he testified in a May letter that "the Muslim world is forced to concern itself, from the moral point of view in its own religious concepts, with the fact that our plight clearly involves the violation of our *human rights*. The Koran compels the Muslim world to take a stand on the side of those whose human rights are being violated."[59] But it was above all thanks to meeting Nkrumah and other African leaders and speaking at the second meeting of the Organization of African Unity on behalf of his own new group, the Organization of Afro-American Unity, that the strategic uses of human rights struck him as powerful.[60] Along with the new UN declaration against colonialism, Malcolm X was clearly impressed by the post-Sharpeville flurry of activity. He even went so far as to begin to prepare, as Du Bois once had, a UN petition on behalf of African Americans before he was assassinated in February 1965. It was based on an imaginative and rhetorical association of African-American subordination with imperialism, and as part of a pan-Africanist and revolutionary philosophy. Similarly, when Martin Luther King, Jr. turned to place civil rights in a global frame in the last year of his life, at the price of heavy stigmatization, he occasionally invoked human rights as well.[61]

These moves were not without later echo. In 1967, after it had become more militant and associated with black power, the Student Non-Violent Coordinating Committee declared itself a human rights organization. The next year, some African-American runners formed an Olympic Project for Human Rights, which led to one of the most enduring images of the Mexico City games, Tommie Smith's black power salute on the medal stand. This extraordinary and controversial expression of "human rights," occurring in the same year as the Tehran Conference, channeled a wholly different spirit from the one that was to prevail a mere decade later, and in a very different political context. If human rights as championed by Du Bois in the 1940s lost their radicalism—not simply in their international scope but in their content—in their displacement by civil rights championed in the 1950s and 1960s, then a further sort of displacement occurred in the return of human rights to moral consciousness in the late 1970s. Rights did achieve then an unprecedented internationalist relevance. Yet their explosion then did not imply, as Malcolm X and even King hoped at the end of their lives, a revival of a visionary black internationalism suppressed before. Instead, the prominence of international rights spiked only after a more transformational possible trajectory for the American civil rights movement was cut off in the early 1970s (due especially to the election of Richard Nixon and his subsequent Supreme Court appointments), and then after a crucial gap of years.

When human rights exploded on the world stage in the era of their true prominence, in the mid- to late 1970s, they did so in an antitotalitarian, truncated form that Du Bois and his heirs could hardly have recognized. In the rise of human rights in the 1970s, human rights did not mean the campaign for collective liberation against racial inequality or colonial legacies, at home or abroad (except for the escalating engagement with South Africa, especially after the Soweto uprising in 1976). The great irony of postwar African-American engagement with human rights is thus that it was a minor feature of a larger anticolonialism that had to be overcome for the more general ascendancy of human rights to occur. Du Bois had engaged human rights briefly as part of a larger anticolonialism, albeit as a second-best strategy, but human rights were to crystallize as an organizing idealism only on condition of anticolonialism's decline and the general omission of its concerns. Self-determination would have to give way to human rights.

Any attempt, therefore, to place anticolonialism in human rights history must face up to an era when the human rights idea had no movement and anticolonialism, a powerful movement, typically took the new "human rights" in the original, collectivist direction of earlier rights talk. It is true that in a phenomenon as massive and complex as decolonization, the notion of human rights was not entirely absent. Even if the founding of the United Nations meant a palpable deflation of the expectations aroused by wartime sloganeering, the ornamental remainders of original wartime visions remained there for all to read—and to invoke. Together with the importance that the international stage—the United Nations included—assumed as a platform for anticolonialist victory more generally, such invocations have to be taken seriously.

In an early period, however, the relevance of the new idea of human rights mainly struck those few anticolonialists who chose the American side in the emerging Cold War, and hoped to forge a more liberal version of anticolonialism that—unlike many others—clearly refused all truck with communism and rejected neutralism as unviable in the bipolar conflict.[62] By any measure, the two leading examples here were Charles Malik of Lebanon and Carlos Romulo of the Philippines, both deeply involved in human rights at the United Nations and frequent proponents of human rights as a potential Third World political vernacular. Their cases suggest the vanishingly slight prominence of the concept at the time, as exceptions that proved the rule.

Both Malik and Romulo attended the Bandung Conference, though they were minor figures compared to Nasser, Nehru, Sukarno, and Zhou En-lai, pursuing together—whether inspirationally or quixotically—the ideological terms of Afro-Asian and anticolonialist unity. In the major speeches by these icons at Bandung, human rights did not figure significantly. All the same, due to Malik's proposal, the Afro-Asian nations formally "took note" of the Universal Declaration of Human Rights. Even this prominence on paper at Bandung should not be overstated, however, and the causes that led Malik and Romulo to their positions clearly isolated them from the prevailing drift of the conference as well as from anticolonialism generally. Already by 1955, the appeal to UN principles meant an appeal to a concept of human rights that had gone through a conceptual revolution, with self-determination becoming the chief and threshold right—"a prerequisite," as the Bandung Final Communiqué put it, "of the full enjoyment of all fundamental Human Rights."[63] It was thus not obviously inconsistent for those at Bandung to call for human rights even as they gave priority to anticolonial sovereignty, with the conference members contemplating interference with nations only when—as in the emergent UN attention to South Africa of the same era—it was for an antiracist cause.

Malik and Romulo were thus highly unusual. Malik had long worried about separatism and communism in ex-colonies as the Cold War emerged. He was urged to attend Bandung by John Foster Dulles and to isolate China or at least ensure the representation of Western views in an era when the Middle East and Asia had become critical arenas of bipolar struggle. More generally, Malik understood himself then as a defender of the West's spiritual principles, which human rights incarnated, as he illustrated graphically in a contemporaneous testament. Such international meetings, he wrote, compelled "the Western world . . . , faced constantly as it is with the challenge of Communism and the challenge of the East, to fall back upon its own spiritual resources."[64] As for Romulo, the Philippines had just formally joined the Asian version of the Western bloc in the Southeast Asian Treaty Organization, and so he tried to walk a fine line between urging America to change its policies to appeal better to colonial and postcolonial peoples, and underlining the threat of the communist competition for their hearts and minds. (This included a vehement critique of Nehru's neutralism.) Thus, Romulo's basic position was for a liberal, pro-Western nationalism, together with some hope that America might better live up to its antiracist precepts in domestic and diplomatic practice.[65] Like Malik, the moral background that mattered for Romulo was Christianity, as appropriately modernized after World War II in light of the new emphasis on the centrality of the "human person."[66]

In any event, no one at Bandung—including these figures—understood human rights to mean a drive potentially spurred by the Afro-Asian nations to establish international legal protection for individuals. And after Bandung, the Non-Aligned Movement slighted the concept even more, especially after 1960, when the UN General Assembly clarified the role human rights could play in the struggle against colonialism and racism. To the extent they were mentioned, they were treated as one tool among others in a rhetorical arsenal of self-determination campaigns—and by and large simply another way of expressing the drive for sovereignty. "The story of our struggle for basic human rights—self-government leading to national independence and self-determination—has not been very different from so many other struggles," said Kenneth Kaunda, soon to become the first president of Zambia, in a reflection in 1963 on how the UN equation could percolate.[67] Human rights simply *were* the struggle for collective self-government.

Insofar as human rights talk occurred, it presupposed the equation, notably on Kaunda's African continent. The South African Freedom Charter of 1955 mentions the phrase "human rights" in passing as the moral principle Africans deserve, so there is no doubt that the phrase appealed by itself. It may have been due to the fact that the UN trusteeship system focused on Africa that human rights made inroads as a strategic language there more than anywhere else (seven of the original eleven supervised territories were located there). While institutionally separate at the UN, the trusteeship council had been explicitly charged in the charter with "encourag[ing] respect for human rights and for fundamental freedoms for all without distinction as to race, sex, language, or religion" (Art.

76). What this meant is that within the trusteeship activities of the UN in the 1950s and 1960s, both complaint and investigation on human rights grounds were possible, and an excellent means of pursuing anticolonialism in a much more concrete and formalized political venue than the international system otherwise afforded. Little is known about the actual workings of trusteeship, but it is clear that the petition right led to tens of thousands of submitted documents. Evidence from British-supervised Tanganyika suggests that many of these petitions were demands for immediate independence, and few others were framed explicitly in terms of human rights. But it is possible that trusteeship—ironically, the most formalized and institutionalized place that human rights found for decades in the UN architecture—allowed for the idea to be spread abroad.[68]

Given this background, it may not have been accidental that it was Julius Nyerere, later president of Tanganyika and Tanzania, who alluded most frequently of all major anticolonialists to the UN human rights concept, and incorporated it immediately in some of his speeches and writings of the time.[69] Though, in tune with Nkrumah, he prioritized self-determination as the first right, Nyerere could warn journalists in 1959 that they should not trivialize the capacity of Africans to secure sovereignty and human rights at once:

Here we are, building up the sympathy of the outside world on the theme of Human Rights. We are telling the world that we are fighting for our rights as human beings. We gain the sympathy of friends all over the world—in Asia, in Europe, in America—people who recognize the justice of our demand for human rights. Does anybody really believe that we ourselves will trample on human rights? Why do we get so annoyed when we hear of a Little Rock in America? Because we recognize that the American Negro is human. It doesn't matter whether he is black—we get infuriated when we see that he is not being treated as a true and equal American citizen. Are we going to turn round then, after we have achieved independence and say, "To hell with all this nonsense about human rights; we were only using that as a tactic to harness the sympathy of the naive?" Human nature is sometimes depraved I know, but I don't believe it is depraved to that extent that the leaders of a people are going to behave as hypocrites to gain their ends, and then turn round and do exactly the things which they have been fighting against.[70]

Later—again, apparently for external audiences, as in his UN address to mark his country's entrance into the organization—he could make similar statements.[71] And indeed, even when he announced his country's need for a rapid move to socialism in the epoch-making Arusha Declaration of 1967, he justified it as a project of fulfilling the Universal Declaration's promises—though as a second key principle sandwiched between the first plank of self-determination and the actual programmatic aim of socialist modernization.[72] If these examples document minor resonance of the phrase, it is clear that Nyerere invoked it to imply moral principles that states should embody, not superordinate rules to which they must defer.

One might consider whether the wave of rights in the constitutions of the new states—sometimes directly influenced by the Universal Declaration's catalogue—provides much reason to qualify these conclusions. It is surely an example of a trend of constitutional fashion that new states often wanted to secure, at least in their founding documents, the rhetorical power and actual protections of rights. Yet no immediate postwar rights revolution, in which the history of the constitutions and the history of international human rights were deeply intertwined and drew authority from each other, took place.

Bills of rights (which not infrequently included social protections) had already been in fashion in the original new constitutionalism of the interwar European scene; that they continued to be so in the postwar decades around the world is really a continuation of that earlier, state-centered trend.[73] In the Indian case, the Congress Party had declared fundamental rights as far back as 1933, even though there was no accommodation of this demand in the 1935 Government of India Act. After upheaval and repression in the emergency of World War II, the argument was pressed again that circumstances differed sufficiently in India that enumerated rights were needed there even if the genius of the British constitutional tradition had not required them. The result was one of the fullest-fledged bills of rights in human history. It was possible to view it as overlapping more than chronologically with the Universal Declaration, yet it was more typical—as for pivotal figure B. R. Ambedkar, who defended the cause of Dalit or "untouchable" equality—to focus on domestic protection of rights, according to traditions of state citizenship.[74]

Where the British government had an opportunity to control or influence the process of constitution-making, it argued that bills of rights were superfluous, useless, or dangerous, until a 1962 policy change led it to endorse the practice. Indeed, for decades British jurists after A. V. Dicey almost universally assumed that a properly civilized polity had no need to declare rights. Ivor Jennings, a leading legal thinker who also assisted in the drafting of the constitutions of ex-colonies, allowed only that bills of rights might be contemplated at all because "we cannot guarantee that colonies . . . will necessarily acquire the sort of intuition which enables us to react almost by instinct against interference with fundamental liberties." Even so, they were to be avoided unless popular sentiment absolutely required another option. Instead, the turn to bills of rights in the British sphere occurred in the beginning due to local political factors: in Nkrumah's Ghana, for example, a failed proposal to craft one emerged to satisfy an Ashanti minority that feared it would not be represented under the new arrangements.[75]

As a rule, in fact, the main forces at work in the slow shift toward explicit declarations in new constitutions were concerns about ethnic powersharing and settler property rights. Yet there was no straight path. Nyerere, surprisingly, rejected the British proposal of a bill of

rights in 1961—the Colonial Office then being on the way to its explicit policy change—and allowed their inclusion in Tanganyika's
new constitution as preambular principles only. As bills of rights
proliferated elsewhere, the models often remained the French, American, and sometimes Soviet constitutions, though a number of other
African states referenced the Universal Declaration—essentially as
the state of the art—as either partial or general inspiration (Chad,
Dahomey, Gabon, Ivory Coast, Mauritania, Niger, Senegal, and Upper Volta did so along with the French Declaration, while Algeria,
Cameroon, Congo-Brazzaville, Madagascar, Mali, Somalia, and Togo
did so exclusively). American Supreme Court justice Thurgood Marshall, when he acceded to his friend Tom Mboya's request to submit a
draft bill of rights for Kenya in February 1960, obviously used the
Universal Declaration substantially, along with other sources, though
his proposal was not adopted.[76]

Later the breakthrough of international human rights could
seem to draw on the proliferation of formal constitutional rights, but
this does not mean that the way to the former was prepared by the
latter, even when the Universal Declaration was taken as a useful catalogue for domestic lists. The main purpose of these constitutions,
after all, was the constitution of sovereignty. It would be especially
wrong to see in this era "an international human rights movement
with many domestic adherents in particular places work[ing] to
elaborate the international system as well as to bring those international norms into domestic constitutional law"—not even among jurists. The confluence between an earlier tradition of declaring rights
and postcolonial constitution-making more persuasively illustrates
the persisting national framework for rights that defined the modern history of the concept, and that worked as much to ward off as
to prepare the legalization of rights on the international scene. In
particular, there is no sense in which these postcolonial constitutional rights interfered with hard-won sovereignty from without. At
best, in the tradition of the connection of rights and sovereignty in

modern history, they opened a space for democratic contest within the nation-state; at worst, they were trampled in the name of that nation-state's construction.[77]

Given the first-world geography of the birth of human rights in the 1970s, changing patterns of affiliation from outside the zones of direct struggle—where the priority fell on construction of state and nation—may have been the true key to the history of human rights. In the early years, if appeals in international forums and to international norms mattered, they certainly failed to define anticolonialism for sympathizers, including those who were to later define their idealism in terms of human rights. After all, the systematic and total nature of the typical agitation against empire in the postwar era meant—even when human rights were promised as part of a new state—that organizational practices like "naming and shaming" took their place in multifaceted strategies of more extremist agitation. Gandhi's example stood for passive but totalistic resistance, while similarly totalistic revolt and revolution through violent means captured the attention of the world—a far cry from the practices now associated with human rights. It would be hard to conclude that the minor and occasional invocation of human rights by anticolonialist icons was matched by the terms of first-world sympathy and partisanship, whether independently or by influence. The striking fact, indeed, is how little this occurred—apparently, human rights mattered even less there than for the anticolonialists themselves.

If American statesmen cultivated figures like Malik and Romulo to defend their interests in anticolonialist politics, for example, the American public failed to notice that they did so in terms of "human rights." As far as can be told, in Britain, the congeries of movements on the left newly critical of empire, whether associated with communism (including Trotskyism) or the Independent Labour Party, did not invoke the new human rights in their activities, and once the Movement for Colonial Freedom crystallized in 1954, it did not, either. There had been a critique of French counterinsurgency, especially in Algeria, that appealed to the language of rights: Pierre Vidal-Naquet, tireless critic of state torture whose courageous agitation on behalf of mathematician Maurice Audin was featured in early Amnesty International publicity, provides an excellent example here. But even in this case, the reference was almost exclusively to native French traditions and the spirit of republicanism; and it was not the dominant sort of anticolonialist identification.[78]

Meanwhile, the romance of third-world revolution and, where necessary, guerilla warfare provides the starkest counterpoint to later human rights activism—especially since the human rights revolution in the late 1970s not only displaced it but also targeted it for its most passionate criticism. In the era of late colonialism, the third world did not lack its own theorists of armed struggle as the only way to combat empire, and even some of the more moderate figures were not above threatening violence in response to compromise (for example, in Senghor's burst of outrage when the more expansive promises of equality in the imperial community of France's first proposed constitution were dropped). Prefacing Fanon, who saw violence as a "cleansing force," Jean-Paul Sartre explained that "this irrepressible violence is neither sound and fury, nor the resurrection of savage instincts, nor even the effect of resentment: it is man recreating himself." He named rights, but only to argue that their perpetual deferral left natives no choice but blood: "The 'liberals' are stupefied," Sartre wrote, "they admit that we were not polite enough to the natives, that it would have been wiser and fairer to allow them certain rights in so far as this was possible; they ask nothing better than to admit them in batches and without sponsors to that very exclusive club, our species; and now this barbarous, mad outburst doesn't spare them any more than the bad settlers."[79] To date, by contrast, no NGOs organize revolutionary insurgency.

From all parts, third-world pamphlets recommending revolutionary struggle were either imported from abroad, in the case of Ho Chi Minh or Mao Zedong, or developed by intellectuals like Eqbal Ahmad, who roved among countries justifying violent liberation and

theorizing resistance to asymmetrical counterinsurgency. These figures were understood to be offering a youthful alternative to Soviet
communism that could escape the compromises and mistakes of the
first attempt at world revolution. The chief forum of armed struggle—after Fidel Castro's dazzling success, and the iconic ascent of
Che Guevara spreading the Cuban fire through the region—was in
Latin America, and the most famous first-world sympathizer was
Régis Debray, who famously traveled to train as a soldier and to battle in the jungle at Che's side. For theorists of both insurgency and
counterinsurgency, what mattered most of all was the popular and
aspirational character of armed struggle, in which guerrillas were to
the supportive populace (in Mao's famous dictum) as fish in water.
In an era with no human rights movement of note, first-world teen-
agers and young people breathlessly followed Debray's activism, and
digested his theoretical manuals, and worried for his fate when he
was arrested and nearly put to death by "counterrevolutionary" enemies. What captured the imagination of many young Westerners in
this era, by and large, was not human rights but "radical chic." It was
not until the mid-1970s that the romance of leftist armed struggle—
so influenced by the Marxist critique of rights as bourgeois hypocri-
sies—began to be subject to widespread reexamination, first by sympathetic critics like Gérard Chaliand, later by self-appointed revivalists of Western confidence like Pascal Bruckner (not to mention
Debray himself).[80] Human rights thus emerged on the ruins of one
sort of hope for former colonial areas and the search for some alternative.

It is crucial to maintain clarity about the differences between anticolonial forms of idealism and activism and a later and very different idealism and activism—the human rights of recent times. Their
relationship is one of displacement, rather than one of succession
and fulfillment. Anticolonialism's vision of rights remained, both
in principle and practice in the international sphere, so selectively
focused on the threshold right of self-determination, qualified by

subaltern antiracism only, as to count as a wholly different conception. In fidelity to earlier Euro-American conceptions of rights, anticolonialism prioritized the independence and autonomy of the new nation as the forum in which rights had to be won. The dominant thrust internationally emphasized collective sovereignty, not individual prerogative, and the supremacy of the nation-state, rather than its subordination to global law.

Thus, if decolonization advanced human rights, it did so in a distinctive, and for some regressive, sense of the installation of sovereignty across the world, in a period of historically unparalleled triumph for the concept and its practices. Overwhelmingly, the postwar era seemed the scene of a move "from empire to nation." Even at the UN, the main forum in which anticolonialism and human rights intersected, the threshold "right" to self-determination took pride of place, yoked to visions of fair development and—at the high point of third-world power in the organization—calls for a "new international economic order." This agenda profoundly affected the activities of the UN Commission on Human Rights, whether from the point of view of the rights that were given priority, or that of the causes pursued.[81] But even the high tide of UN anticolonialism in the 1970s shows that the ascendancy of human rights in the West in their current sense, and outside the UN structure, has to be ascribed to their *reclamation* from anticolonialism. As it would turn out, human rights spiked even in first-world consciousness only, and perhaps conveniently, once two interlocking events occurred.

First, the sordid nature of colonial rule had to be revealed for all to see, and ultimately ended once and for all. The hard fact to contemplate is that human rights experienced their triumph as a widespread moral vernacular after decolonization not during it—and because of it perhaps only in the sense that the loss of empire allowed for the reclamation of liberalism, including rights talk, shorn of its depressing earlier entanglements with oppression and violence abroad. The last major instances of formal colonialism, in the Portuguese holdings, were finally relinquished in the mid-1970s. The failure around the same time of the bloody, last ditch American attempt to keep southern Vietnam from communism—not simply the moral turpitude or deviation from national traditions of that failure, as Jimmy Carter was to contend—set the stage for the country's promised turn to human rights as a foreign policy ideal. Only once formal empire and direct Cold War intervention fell into disrepute did an internationalism based on rights come to the fore.

Second, the widespread rise of the belief that anticolonialism in its classic forms had shipwrecked as a moral and political project mattered a great deal too—not least because of the sorts of concerns once thought legitimately placed on hold while third-world leaders consolidated power and, if they were not plutocratic new elites uninterested in making good on their promises, attempted the sort of radical social and economic reconstructions that might matter. Even one partisan of the spread of domestic liberties across the world could concede in the mid-1960s that "autocracy, selectively applied, may be necessary in order to create the social requisites for the maintenance of human rights." By a decade later, that bet did not seem worth making. "Is self-determination passé?" one international lawyer could ask in 1973.[82]

The answer started to be affirmative, in the developed West at least. Harvard political scientist Rupert Emerson—long the most visible academic proponent of self-determination—decried in 1975 the emergence of "a double standard which has worked to debase the moral coinage of the Third-World countries and to lessen the appeal of the causes they advocate. . . The wholly legitimate drive against colonialism and apartheid was in some measure called into question when the new countries habitually shrugged off any concern with massive violations of human rights and dignity in their own domain." As Arthur Schlesinger, Jr. put it in 1977, the breakthrough year for human rights, "states may meet all the criteria of national self-determination and still be blots on the planet. Human rights is the way of reaching the deeper principle, which is individual self-determination." In his classic *Rights of Man Today*, Louis Henkin, the international lawyer, surmised that Thomas Paine "would welcome the many new states—the products of revolution and self-determination—[but] would rage at the suggestion that welfare and equality can be achieved only under autocracy, at the cost of liberty, at the sacrifice of the present for an uncertain future." In the postwar era, New York senator Daniel Patrick Moynihan explained, Western policy had failed to stand up for human rights as they were sacrificed on the grim altar of self-determination. The "tremendous investment of hope in what we saw as the small seedlings of our various great oaks" had prompted "a corresponding reluctance to think, much less speak, ill of them," he continued. "Then there was the trauma of Vietnam, which perhaps made it seem even more necessary that we should be approved by nations so very like the one we were despoiling." But now simply too much time had gone by to abstain from criticizing third-world abuses—and Vietnam was over.[83] Only when self-determination entered crisis, for Western observers at least, could there be an opening for a move from the enduring dream of postcolonial liberation to the far more recent utopia, the hope for a world of individual human rights.

4

"One might think that a century rather than a decade separated us from the end of the 1960s," remarked Bronislaw Baczko, a former Polish dissident, at the end of the 1970s. Baczko had emigrated from Warsaw to the West in 1968, when radicals were roiling the world with demands for extraordinary transformation. For young people especially, it was a gust of fresh air: instead of reproducing the old, failed society, they believed the task had fallen to them to invent a new one. "The graffiti on the walls of Paris," Baczko recalled of that recent explosion, "cried for 'power to the imagination' and extolled 'realism that demands the impossible.'" Yet in the ensuing decade, transformative utopianism seemed to have collapsed in the West, as the hope of bringing about the reign of freedom and justice grew faint. Having been proclaimed, it came to be remorselessly scorned, often by its own former partisans. "It is as if utopia were the scapegoat in a collective exorcism of the misnamed and ill-defined demons that haunt our epoch," Baczko concluded. Indeed, by the late 1970s, some sort of expiation for the prior utopian outburst seemed to be underway. Shrewdly, however, Baczko did not think appearances were what they seemed. Rather than the "withering" or "fragmentation" of utopia that others saw, he found it more plausible to see "the transfer of its frontiers," in which it survived in a new form. "Is it not possible," Baczko concluded, "that the disenchantment with utopian 'systems' goes together with the persistence of diffuse utopian hopes and modes of thought which might betray the presence in our times of two contradictory attitudes: the *distrust of utopia* together with the *desire to have one anyway?*"[1]

Baczko's penetrating claim suggests a focus on how human rights emerged in the context of collapsing and transforming idealism. Human rights emerged as a minimalist, hardy utopia that could survive in a harsh climate. These were years of "nightmare" and "nervous breakdown," notably after the oil shock and the global economic downturn of 1973. But the winter of discontent that swept the West also resulted in the mistrust of more maximal plans for transformation—especially revolutions but also programmatic endeavors of any kind. The crucial question is why human rights, which could not have been the focus of global idealism before the 1940s and failed to infiltrate it in that decade, or in the anticolonial struggles or youth activism that followed in the 1950s and 1960s, did so in the 1970s. For the first time in large numbers, people started to use the language of human rights to express and act on their hopes for a better world. But they did not do so in a void. Human rights were discovered only in contest with and through comparison to other schemes. Human rights were a realism that demanded the possible. If so, they were only intelligible in the broad aftermath of other, more grandiose dreams that they both drew on and displaced.

Most of all, social movements adopted human rights as a slogan for the first time. As the 1970s continued, the identification of such causes as human rights struggles snowballed, continuing across the world throughout the decade (indeed through the present). This serial amplification occurred even as states negotiated the Helsinki Final Act, signed in 1975, that inadvertently provided a new forum for North Atlantic rights activists. And then came 1977, a year of shocking and altogether unpredictable prominence of human rights. One of the most fascinating lessons of the period is how little known were the Universal Declaration and the project of international human rights when it began, and how these earlier "sources" were discovered only after the movements that claimed them got going. But human rights allowed diverse actors to make common cause as other alternatives were seen as unviable—a convergence that often began as a strategic retreat from those prior, more grandiose utopianisms.

A general framework for the explosion of human rights activism up to and around the breakthrough year of 1977 depends on capturing this dynamic of the collapse of prior utopias and the search for refuge elsewhere. It is one thing to track the history of citizen advocacy in the international sphere, but another to account for the success of human rights within it and, in the context of many exciting new social movements, its prominence and survival in the harsh ideological climate of the 1970s. It is one thing to record the evolution of supranational human rights mechanisms, for example at the United Nations and in the European region, but another to explain the startling spike in cultural prestige they began to enjoy after decades of irrelevance. It is one thing, finally, to examine the states that claimed to advance the cause of human rights in the midst of the 1970s in an unprecedented new fashion, most especially Jimmy Carter's America, and to canvass those regimes that were stigmatized in a discomforting—though rarely disabling—new manner. But it is another to explain why, at this moment, human rights broke through so substantially on the terrain of idealism, for ordinary people, and in public life. The death of other utopian visions and their transfiguration into a human rights agenda provides the most powerful way to do so.

Moses Moskowitz, one of the very few representatives of dogged old-style NGO advocacy for human rights, was a failure. Born in Stryj, Ukraine, in 1910, Moskowitz emigrated with his family as a teenager to the United States, where he attended City College and Columbia University. An analyst for the American Jewish Committee (AJC) before World War II broke out, Moskowitz served in the European theater in the U.S. Army, playing a special role in occupied Germany after the war as chief of political intelligence in the state of Württemberg-Baden. On his return in 1946, Moskowitz had the idea to represent Jewry at the bar of world organization as the United Nations began its life. With the support of figures like René Cassin, Moskowitz formed the Consultative Council of Jewish Organizations (CCJO), in which the AJC, the Anglo-Jewish Union, and the Alliance

Israélite Universelle participated. Explaining why he worked so doggedly and anonymously for human rights, even after they came to grief in the postwar period, Moskowitz was eloquent: "I wanted to work for something which was permanent, of universal importance, and indestructible," he explained. "I didn't believe it will bring the redemption, but I believed that we could not proceed unless this principle was established solidly in an international treaty."[2]

For this task, Moskowitz felt his best course was to work alone and diplomatically. Indeed, in the end he broke with the AJC, which in the postwar period he saw as moving away from its prewar ethos toward "a so-called mass organization . . . a pressure machine, issued pamphlets, leaflets." "No utopias, etc.," he added. "I mean, that was my saving grace." He even criticized Amnesty International for "invent[ing] all kinds of procedures, all kinds of approaches" and "build[ing] up a Babel, a Tower of Babel which will ultimately destroy the program." Though he was known in New York circles, both Jewish and UN, as "Mr. Human Rights" in the 1950s and 1960s, Moses Moskowitz and his organization remained obscure on principle. This is so even though during the decades of his CCJO work Moskowitz authored the very best studies—true, they were essentially the only ones—of the fate of human rights in United Nations processes. As the years passed, he indefatigably pursued the legalization of human rights and proposed the creation of an "attorney-general" for human rights. (It was only long after Moskowitz's era, in 1993, that this office of the UN high commissioner finally came into being.)[3]

Essentially a one-man show and focused on UN processes, the CCJO was wholly representative of what early human rights advocacy looked like. The first organizations that took up the UN Charter's Article 71 consultation status were nearly all based on group identity. In the postwar moment, numerous NGOs reformulated the earlier terms of their causes—just as Moskowitz did with Jewish advocacy—around the emerging UN bureaucracies and language. After their later nineteenth-century origins, and galloping expansion in the interwar period, NGOs numbered about a thousand in the immediate post–World War II years, with about one hundred soon gaining UN consultative status (including those few concerning themselves with human rights). Yet none, whether they were devoted to trade, standardization, labor, agriculture, social welfare, or peace, succeeded in making the idea of an NGO terribly prominent at the time. Lyman Cromwell White, their first and for a long time leading student, complained in 1951 that "they remain the great unexplored continent in the world of international affairs." And the organizations like Moskowitz's incorporating any reference to the new human rights occupied only a small sector of that landmass, and even those did not do so as a general program. They balanced their preexisting objectives (typically, in the quest for peace or in defense of specific groups) with strategic advancement of the new human rights language. In White's authoritative survey, assembled five years after the UN's founding, he could not yet establish a general category of human rights organization.[4]

Even within the subset of groups that dedicated themselves to human rights at the United Nations, Moskowitz's group was thus typical. Their causes were defined by the borders of religion, ethnicity, or gender on behalf of which they lobbied. And even when they pursued a general agenda, such as peace, their leadership and membership were defined according to group identity. For example, women's internationalism pursued its causes: suffrage, prevention of trafficking or prostitution, higher salaries, and sometimes a larger agenda of bringing a feminist peace to masculinist geopolitics.[5] At most, in the postwar moment, there were groups that had once been devoted to a specific clientele defined by religion, ethnicity, or gender that universalized their rhetoric without shifting the basis of their membership. For the AJC, the truth of the postwar scene was that the cause of Jewish rights was best pursued through the larger cause of human rights.[6] Even then, groups—including Jewish groups—focused on the causes that mattered to their specific constituencies. "Only in procedural matters are the NGOs organized in their relations to the UN," Roger Baldwin, co-founder of the American Civil Liberties Union and, during World War II, the International League of the Rights of Man, remarked. "On substantive issues, they work individually."[7] Humanitarian causes continued to be advanced on a wide variety of bases. There were local, national, and international groups, and they worked through states, international organizations, and on their own. In contrast, human rights advocacy made the United Nations the privileged, indeed exclusive, location of interest, action, and reform.

Some tried to raise the profile of the human rights idea for a broader public. Though many of these early NGOs converged on the quest for legalization and "enforcement," publicity was also attempted—especially after 1953, when John Foster Dulles announced the U.S. government's preference for education rather than law in the field for human rights. Familiar children's author Dorothy Canfield Fisher drafted an education pamphlet, *A Fair World for All: The Meaning of the Universal Declaration*, which various groups distributed in the early 1950s. Similarly, spearheading the efforts of a coalition of church and women's groups, the American Association for the United Nations sponsored radio spots across the country to mark the tenth anniversary of the Universal Declaration, featuring Marian Anderson and Danny Kaye; and on the afternoon of December 7, 1958, in a similar vein, American viewers were treated to a televised play entitled *In Your Hands*, intended to propagate awareness of human rights. However, these hopeful but rudimentary efforts failed to put the concept into general circulation.

Only Baldwin's International League of the Rights of Man emerged as an NGO dedicated to the cause of human rights as such. Apparently founded in late 1941 by European émigrés hoping to transplant the French Ligue des Droits de l'Homme, it was then led by Baldwin beginning in 1942, and with special energy after his ACLU retirement in January 1950. Its civil libertarian commitments on the international stage were emphatic but unique. They were doubly so because of Baldwin's anticolonialism. After some youthful vacillation, Baldwin had long since seen the priority of fighting communism. But unusually, his league understood the pursuit of the rights of man as a commitment to decolonization. Its mode of advocacy, however, failed to raise the profile of the idea, as if its activities were born too soon. Restricted to a tiny membership before an age of new social movements and failing to develop professionalized elites to lead it, the International League did not establish a generally successful model for others to follow. It remained dedicated to UN-based advocacy. Even though, after 1947, the UN Commission on Human Rights neutered itself by deciding it could not consider petitions, Baldwin and John Humphrey, first director of the UN Human Rights Division, were in frequent contact.[8]

Yet by the later 1960s, especially after the founding of Amnesty International, it had become clear that the early strategy of those NGOs that made any reference to human rights—and even of the International League—had borne few fruits. No moment crystallized this conviction more clearly, in fact, than the Tehran Conference marking the Universal Declaration's twentieth anniversary. Though the organization's documents canonized the basic values to pursue, even the leaders of existing NGOs realized then the failure of the UN as a primary forum of human rights activism. After the disastrous April-May meeting and its paeans to anticolonialism (and denunciations of Israel's occupation), Seán MacBride, secretary-general of one group, the International Commission of Jurists, regretted that the event "devoted most of its time to a repetition of current political attitudes in emotive form."[9] In observance of Human Rights Year, private groups tried again to gain a hearing, and the American government even set up a presidential commission, which Averell Harriman chaired.[10] The results, however, were disappointing, given Tehran's embarrassing "acrimony." Moskowitz, too, reported that "no event" had cast "sterner doubt" on the UN human rights program's ability "to support the weight it was intended to carry" than Tehran, which "never came close to what had been expected of it, neither in form nor in content." Moskowitz rued the fact that Tehran's Final Act evoked "no sense of mission, of search, or of discovery. We look in vain to the proceedings and decisions for a center of a great social or political theme that stirs hope and enthusiasm and casts happy auguries for the future. . . . The Conference on Human Rights generated no tidal force to sweep aside all the obstacles that stand in the way of fulfillment of international concern with human rights."[11]

But it was in a collective session in September 1968 that perhaps the most pivotal and revealing lessons were drawn by NGOs themselves from the Tehran catastrophe about human rights strategy. Compared to Tehran, the Conference of NGOs, held in Paris at UNESCO, was a radically different affair. In its composition, the NGOs brought together almost exclusively first-world residents. Most of them were from religious organizations of various kinds, though some of the main speakers—most prominently, Zambian president Kenneth Kaunda—provided new blood. Some of the founding fathers from the 1940s were on hand too. René Cassin, whose Nobel Peace Prize was to be announced a few weeks later, argued that NGO "militants" should continue their pursuit of UN reform, and especially passage of the binding human rights covenants. In view of Tehran, Charles Malik's insistence on the Christian framework of human rights so important in the 1940s could not but have had contemporary resonance: "There is nothing that has been proclaimed about human rights in our age, nothing, for instance, in our Universal Declaration of Human Rights, which cannot be traced to the great Christian religious matrix," he stressed. "Even those in our own day who carry on a non-religious or even on an anti-religious basis the burden of human rights with such evident passion and sincerity . . . owe their impulse, knowingly or unknowingly, to the original inspiration of this tradition." In its current forms, by contrast, Islam had veered from its potential contribution to human rights, with its "remarkable humane tradition which should be revived for our times independently from the transience of politics." But in the aftermath of Tehran and in view of the global upheaval, Malik reserved his greatest complaint for youth activism, which failed to be useful for human rights because it strayed into florid and excessive opposition to existing society, rather than moderating its critique of injustice in view of the substantial achievements of civilization so far. "I wish somebody, preferably a youth himself, would dare stand up before youth and impress on it that there are many things that are also right and that it is their duty to love them," Malik said. "The non-governmental organizations cannot afford to see youth drawn into the pit of nihilism." Others, however, recognized that unlike other aspirations, human rights had failed to become a convincing program for young people. Frederick Nolde, who had also been present at the creation, and without indicting the longtime activities of NGOs like his own Protestant ecumenical group, looked around the room and remarked ironically, "One would have to stretch imagination and memory to locate most participants in the category of youth. The situation can and must be changed."[12]

The Paris event, for those who thought about why human rights had so far failed, reflected above all the unviability of the usual UN-centered approach, and comparison of human rights to the rival social and political causes in the West that had shaken the world. Egerton Richardson, who as Jamaican ambassador to the United Nations had in 1963 first proposed having a human rights year, was most direct. "Tehran was our moment of truth," he exclaimed, "when we came face to face with the nature of our beast—when we saw what it means to be promoting the cause of Human Rights by working mainly through governments." Tehran's "lacunae were many, its achievements few; thus it now seems necessary to rely more on people than on governments for the pursuit, with any enthusiasm, of the promotion of human rights and human dignity."[13] In the face of rival utopias that made no appeal to human rights, the project of human rights would have to find a way to compete.

It would be wrong to completely dismiss the UN human rights processes in these years in accounting for the triumph of the concept the organization both introduced and stymied. It underwent its own slow evolution. Yet in a leading survey, British political scientist H. G.

Nicholas could remain caustic in the mid-1970s about its achievements in the field:

> Nothing has done more harm to the Organization in general and the [UN Economic and Social Council] in particular than the great wild goose chase after human rights. No country is innocent in this matter, neither the United States, which pressed at San Francisco for human rights provisions in the Charter, nor the Soviet bloc, which exploited them with a magnificent indifference to the beams in their own eyes, nor the Latin-Americans, who found here ideal nourishment for their rhetorical appetites, nor the Anglo-Saxons, who, false to their tradition of realism in things liberal and humanitarian, joined with the rest in the collective admiration for the Emperor's new clothes. Thus a cowardly conspiracy developed to gloss over the inherent absurdity of an organization of governments dedicating itself to protect human rights when, in all ages and climes, it is governments which have been their principal violators.[14]

Despite the labors of tiny groups and a small number of bureaucrats in the 1950s and 1960s, human rights exploded in the 1970s in direct relation to the breathtaking marginalization of the UN as the central forum for and singular imaginative custodian of the norms. For this outflanking of the UN, American internationalism during World War II, and its postwar remnants, provided no precedent.[15] It was Amnesty International, above all, which made this move most decisively. Tehran confirmed already the need for some new style of mobilization, for which AI was to provide the model more and more.

Indeed almost alone, Amnesty International invented grassroots human rights advocacy, and through it drove public awareness of human rights generally. Its contribution would reach its highest visibility when it received the Nobel Peace Prize in 1977, the breakthrough year for human rights as a whole, though it began its work years earlier. Unlike the earliest NGOs that invoked human rights occasionally or often, AI opened itself to mass participation through its framework of local chapters, each acting in support of specific, personalized victims of persecution. And unlike the earliest human rights groups, it did not take the UN to be the primary locale of advocacy. Skirting the reform of international governance, it sought a direct and public connection with suffering, through lighting candles in a show of solidarity and writing letters to governments pleading for mercy and release. These practical innovations depended in equal parts on a brilliant reading of the fortunes of idealism in the postwar world and a profound understanding of the importance of symbolic gestures.

Amnesty International's origins in Christian responses to the Cold War had been unpromising, however, and its slow transformation into a celebrated human rights organization makes clear the necessity of distinguishing among the creation, evolution, and reception of such groups. Thanks to its founder Peter Benenson, AI emerged through an interesting and productive improvisation on earlier Christian peace movements. Together with Eric Baker, a Quaker, Benenson intended to provide a new outlet for idealists disappointed by Cold War stalemate, and especially after socialism had been revealed as a failed experiment. After AI's inaugural May 28, 1961 *Observer* spread, "The Forgotten Prisoners," Benenson recorded that "[t]he underlying purpose of this campaign—which I hope those who are closely connected with it will remember, but never publish—is to find a common base upon which the idealists of the world can co-operate. It is designed in particular to absorb the latent enthusiasm of great numbers of such idealists who have, since the eclipse of Socialism, become increasingly frustrated; similarly it is geared to appeal to the young searching for an ideal. . ." Quite strikingly, in private Benenson went so far as to conclude that the outlet AI would provide to idealists made its effects on victims unimportant: "It matters more to harness the enthusiasm of the helpers. . . The real martyrs prefer to suffer, and, as I would add, the real saints are no worse off in prison than anywhere on this earth."[16]

If so, the activist's personal understanding of his activism, not simply the victim who captured his gaze, is what matters. The search for a new venue for idealism presupposed the collapse of Cold War absorption. Amnesty International's origins contain a precious clue to understanding the later explosion of human rights in the mid-1970s when so many were to search for a substitute utopia. The formative context for Benenson's enterprise may have been in a much broader constellation of religious peace movements, like Pax Christi among Catholics (in which Benenson, born of Jewish parents, also participated, after his 1958 conversion), or the World Council of Churches for Protestant ecumenicals. It is very important that, Frederick Nolde notwithstanding, neither group had made human rights a central idea.[17] For that matter, the linkage of AI's own cause to human rights was neither central at first nor even necessary; it seems to have been due not to Benenson but to his barrister colleague Peter Archer, who first suggested alluding to the concept in the campaign on behalf of "prisoners of conscience."[18] Yet however accidental, that allusion, which would become increasingly central in the organization's history, gave AI the vanguard role in the history of human rights advocacy.

Benenson himself at first made the Catholic clerics like Josef Beran and József Mindszenty, whose suffering under communism had defined the meaning of international human rights from December 1948, central to his original *Observer* article. It was an umbilical connection to the immediate postwar shaping of human rights. Similarly, Benenson also insisted on the preeminence of freedom of religious belief along with freedom of conscience generally; Amnesty International was, he wrote in his famous *Persecution 1961*, to be "a non-political, non-sectarian, international movement to guarantee the free exchange of ideas and the free practice of religion." Seán MacBride, also an early AI figure, led its first mission, to Czechoslovakia to investigate Beran's internment.[19] But almost immediately, Amnesty International transcended past causes, severing obvious links to the immediate postwar framework. Compared to earlier and contemporary agitation around political prisoners—a cause over a century old, which had spawned an interwar league as well—AI proceeded "non-politically." It overlapped in its cultural origins with the Campaign for Nuclear Disarmament, but AI much more clearly defined itself against the left, even as it primarily concentrated on the victims of right-wing regimes and the liberal democracies. In this, and its famous early practice of having local chapters or "adoption groups" select prisoners by threes (one each per first, second, and third world), it traded on its powerful claim to be above and beyond politics. This claim to transcendence was, indeed, Benenson's principal innovation.

When Columbia University professor Ivan Morris founded Amnesty International USA a few years later, and the Riverside chapter began to meet in Columbia philosopher Arthur Danto's living room on the Upper West Side, the impulse remained the same: "saving the world one individual at a time."[20] This was to be a recipe of tremendous power: in the face of soiled utopias in politics, a nonpartisan morality existed outside and above them. Yet for a time, and in spite of AI's impressive inroads in Britain, that claim would have only a restricted appeal. The events leading to and away from 1968, and only them, would make the advocacy that Amnesty International pioneered increasingly relevant—not just in redefining NGO advocacy, but also in paving the way for the triumph of human rights as the operative utopia it had never been before.

What mattered most of all, in short, was the competitive forum in which human rights had to win their way in the years straddling 1968. For human rights were only one among other ideologies that could have prospered, and did in fact, as absorption in the Cold War contention of social models entered its 1960s decline. The disintegration of the ideological conditions that had ruled out human rights in the 1940s did not by itself mean they were singled out for new enthusiasm. Benenson and his few early followers were an extreme minority. Most in that decade turned to very different kinds of Cold War dissent. Indeed, the impending collapse of the terms of the Cold War, into which Benenson had so precocious an insight, actually benefited other schemes in the short run. It was nuclear stalemate, above all, that undermined the conditions for stability that partisan Cold War politicians had sought to ensure through nuclear escalation, and the fear and loyalty it inspired. A standoff of contending visions, each insisting it had to win at all costs, also meant that in the West, as in the East, fewer and fewer people could invest themselves in the contest, making it easier to complain of disappointment at home and immorality abroad.[21]

In the 1960s, new visions of social change seeking a way out of Cold War contention flowered everywhere around the world. The human rights movement, including Amnesty International, was extremely peripheral among them. While human rights owes its origins to the "new social movements," for a long time it was one among far more prominent others. If so, it was as much the beneficiary of collapse of the "countercultural" explosion as a set of idealistic causes as it was part of that outburst. The analysis therefore needs to focus on why human rights survived and increased its share among the very different utopias that drew on the massive infusion of energy to social mobilization. The participants in the Paris conference of NGOs, the summer after May 1968 had roiled the city, were only mastering the obvious when they concluded that the spirit of the age had passed to youth, and that so far other ideologies than human rights were winning the competition.

As other causes failed over the next decade, human rights became a novel framework for a series of genuine movements. In the communist bloc, the phenomenon of "dissidence" was a long if slow-developing one. Whatever its deep roots, dissidence emerged only after the de-Stalinization policy of Nikita Khrushchev, marked by his spectacular "secret" speech of 1956, that spurred numerous other critiques of the regime in its name. ("It could be said," human rights advocate Valery Chalidze once remarked, "that this Communist movement for human rights was begun by Nikita Khrushchev.")[22] Within obscure networks or by means of *samizdat* literature—and most especially the famous *Chronicle of Current Events,* beginning in spring 1968—information about friends or spouses in far-flung camps or repressive psychiatric institutions accumulated. Heartrending testimonies of Anatoly Marchenko and, later, Vladimir Bukovsky were especially influential. Most feared in these reports, initially for domestic Soviet networks, was a recrudescence of "Stalinism" after the years of thaw. But it marked an epoch when these minor percolations of dissent in the Soviet Union, increasing among writers and scientists after Yuli Daniel and Andrei Siniavsky stood trial in 1966, were reframed as a human rights cause with the 1969 formation of the Action Group for the Defense of Human Rights. (The next year, an even more significant Human Rights Committee appeared.)

How did this happen? The human rights strategy followed in part from the principle that dissidents argue in terms of socialist law, highlighting the failure of the regime to abide by its own enacted rules. This "legalist" approach—the indigenous creation of Aleksandr Esenin-Volpin—began by alluding to domestic rights that were supposed to be constitutionally guaranteed, not the "human rights" of the international system. Indeed, the origins of dissidence are conventionally dated to the December 5, 1965 *glasnost* demonstration, timed to occur on the holiday celebrating the so-called "Stalin" Constitution of 1936 (rather than international Human Rights Day, five days later). The Action Group of 1969 owed its name to the term that the "Stalin" Constitution uses to describe voluntary citizen organizations for building socialism. Volpin's legalism distinguished the dissident movements even before the concept of human rights did.[23] And from the beginning, dissidence resembled Benenson's Western abandonment of politics, understandably in view of the unviability of actual reform of the Soviet regime.

Puzzlingly, however, there is no clear-cut answer to why the founders of the Action Group chose in 1969 to allude to human rights rather than mainly domestic protections, like the earliest dissidents. The fact that 1968 was the International Year for Human

Rights, and that the Soviet Union went through the motions of celebrating it by signing the human rights covenants, may have been a catalyst. When the *Chronicle of Current Events* began on April 30, 1968 (rather than May Day), it made reference to the abuses the Soviet government was committing against its population in this year intended as a celebration of human rights.[24] Yet the remarkable fact—especially given the homegrown and domestic sources of dissident strategy—is that it might never have become a human rights movement at all. When the Action Group formed in May 1969 after the arrest of former general Piotr Grigorenko and drafted its appeal to the United Nations rather than Soviet leaders, the step proved unintentionally fateful for world history.[25]

There is no way to isolate the rise of human rights protest against the Soviet regime, however, from the larger transformation of hopes for socialism's salvation and redemption. From the beginning, the minuscule group of dissidents was profoundly divided among themselves. They concluded that the regime had failed so catastrophically for different reasons. The group included some heirs of "Old Bolsheviks" (the brothers Roy and Zhores Medvedev most notably) who believed that the regime had simply gone awry and had to return to fundamentals. The disparity between the secular liberal and the religious nationalist positions of the two dissidents who became by far the most famous around the world, physicist Andrei Sakharov and writer Aleksandr Solzhenitsyn, is notorious, but did not stymie their cooperation at first. This coalitional nature of dissidence, which would reappear throughout the Eastern bloc later, allowed for the co-existence of different elements. Most obviously, diverse forms of nationalist resistance could find identification with one another easier thanks to the minimalism of human rights, compared to adherence to a revisionist communism that had little to offer.[26] Yet whatever the sources of internal unity of the movement, the conditions of its escalation at home and celebration abroad certainly lay in the post-1968 collapse of the socialist romance: dissidence of any kind only made significant inroads in the communist world, and became highly visible to the West, as a result of the implausibility of reform communism that the events of the summer of 1968 made so clear.

Even as Paris in May 1968 symbolized the ascendancy of youthful utopia the world over, the Soviet invasion of Czechoslovakia in summer 1968 put an end to Prague Spring, the era of reform communism under popular leader Alexander Dubček. The shocking event set the parameters for a search for a utopia beyond stale communism, in a totalitarian regime that brooked no opposition. When the Soviet tanks rolled into Prague, dissident movements that had once favored "democratization" were both sobered into silence and driven to some alternative strategy. The spectacular collapse of hopes for "Marxist humanism" across the region left new ideological space for the human rights strategy of dissidence to become central in the Soviet Union in the early 1970s and thereafter many other places as well. If Volpin's powerful legalist approach crystallized shortly before, it was only after Prague that parts of dissidence came to conceive of themselves as a "human rights movement," not least in the founding of the Moscow groups. Filling the space left vacant by the implosion of reform communism, dissidence worked by leaving behind political alternatives in the name of moral criticism.

Though it was Czech playwright and dissident Václav Havel who was to formulate the case most prominently, Soviet dissent had begun already in 1972 to oppose morality to a politics that had failed. For one dissident, Anatoly Yakobson, dissent could not offer "a political struggle (for which, be it said, the necessary conditions are absent)." Instead, he explained, it could only take the form of "a *moral* struggle. . . . One must begin by postulating that truth is needed for its own sake and for no other reason." Another high-profile spokesman, physicist Yuri Orlov, referred in 1973 to the basis of the movement as an "ethics common to all humanity." And Pavel Litvinov the next year explained that its "non-political" character was what mattered. In reality, of course, the movement "was political in the sense that it threatened the foundations of Soviet power."[27] But it was based on a politics that worked precisely by claiming to transcend politics—much like Benenson's before.

Sakharov's singular itinerary vividly illustrates the centrality of 1968, and the remarkable contingencies of the years that followed. Sakharov had acted before that date, as when he attended a small Constitution Day rally in 1966 to urge democratization. But he remained disengaged from the trials of literary dissenters. His brief but crucial friendship with Roy Medvedev, whose Leninist history of Stalinism affected him powerfully, mattered most of all, and certainly more than his few other dissident contacts at this stage. Then a courageous act made him a worldwide celebrity overnight. A nuclear scientist who long maintained access to the highest echelons of the Soviet government, Sakharov drafted a plea for coexistence and smuggled it to the *New York Times,* where it was published on July 22, 1968.

Its original context—including for Western reception—was in the cause of détente between the Cold War powers. Sakharov presented a hopeful model in which communism and capitalism alike would be reformed, putting their nuclear standoff behind them, and perhaps even converging someday. Given the timing, the significance of Sakharov's text, entitled "Thoughts on Progress, Coexistence, and Peace," was impossible to interpret separately from the Czechoslovak experiment. (The *Times* reported on it directly below a photograph of a Warsaw Pact convoy in the country.) For its possible contribution to communist democratization, Prague Spring was an experiment that Sakharov warmly endorsed.

At this point, human rights as a dissident language were not yet on the horizon for Sakharov. Remarkably, the Universal Declaration earned a mention in his 1968 plea, but for its value in staving off Western imperialism and "counterrevolution" as much as anything else: "International policy does not aim at exploiting local, specific conditions to widen zones of influence and create difficulties for another country," he wrote, invoking the internationally protected right of collective self-determination, rather than individual rights of speech or religion. "The goal of international policy is to ensure universal fulfillment of the 'Declaration of the Rights of Man' and to prevent a sharpening of international tensions and a strengthening of militarist and nationalist tendencies. Such a set of principles would in no way be a betrayal of the revolutionary and national liberation struggle, the struggle against reaction and counterrevolution."[28] But the collapse of Prague Spring opened the way for a shift.

It was only two years later, however, that Sakharov met Chalidze, who proposed that he join the Human Rights Committee, which, after 1970, became the central dissident group. Even then, Sakharov initially remained aloof. When he decided to join, however, he quickly gave human rights prominence, first of all in his 1970 "Memorandum to Leonid Brezhnev," which boldly took advantage of his high status to invoke the regime's international legal commitments against it. The committee's earliest attention focused on Soviet psychiatry, then, with more controversy, religious freedom. Almost immediately, Sakharov turned to the freedom of movement that Jews but also ethnic Germans were demanding. It was after this shift that Solzhenitsyn, worried that Sakharov had been waylaid by the cause of Jews rather than the redemption of Russia, began to treat him as a simpleton buffeted by winds of influence. Sakharov returned the favor by pointing out that Solzhenitsyn cared less about human rights as such than their use for other, restorationist ends. In the West, however, Solzhenitsyn's public persona, like Sakharov's, crystallized around the idea that an internationally defined morality mattered most of all when revolutionary schemes came to grief. Celebrated the world over already in the 1960s, Solzhenitsyn, too, joined the human rights movement once underway on the basis of his claim in his smuggled Nobel Prize lecture in 1970 that "no such thing as INTERNAL AFFAIRS remains on our crowded Earth!"[29]

That Sakharov could become known abroad as an icon of human rights was due essentially to the destruction of the Czechoslovak experiment and the quick evolution of his career in the early years of the 1970s. Even as late as Hedrick Smith's notable *New York Times Magazine* profile in November 1973, it was possible to present Sakharov as a civil rights activist, on the model of the American movement.[30] But in his work with the committee and on his own, Sakharov shouldered the mantle of human rights more and more. His Nobel Prize lecture, which his wife Elena Bonner read for him in Stockholm in December 1975, was titled "Peace, Progress, and Human Rights." It documented his learning since 1968, when peace and progress had implied democratization and convergence. They now meant something new.[31] Driving it all was a slow drift from the hope for a humanized version of détente to a less transformative but at least untainted form of personal engagement. Sakharov expressed this drift from politics to morality most brilliantly:

> I am convinced that under the conditions obtaining in our country a position based on morality and law is the most correct one, as corresponding to the requirements and possibilities of society. What we need is the systematic defense of human rights and ideals and not a political struggle, which would inevitably incite people to violence, sectarianism, and frenzy. I am convinced that only in this way, provided there is the broadest possible public disclosure, will the West be able to recognize the nature of our society; and that then this struggle will become part of a world-wide movement for the salvation of all mankind. This constitutes a partial answer to the question of why I have (naturally) turned from world-wide problems to the defense of individual people.[32]

For Sakharov, too, human rights were born out of substitution, as a failed political utopia gave way to morality alone.

Initially, the first self-styled "human rights movement" in world history had little resonance internationally. The percolation of dissidence around human rights remained the preserve of tiny and scattered groups: a few monitors of Soviet affairs working with Radio

Liberty in Munich, the British Amnesty International participants who compiled English-language versions of the *Chronicle of Current Events,* or the Brussels-based Comité pour la defense des droits de l'homme en URSS.[33] In New York, a month after Hedrick Smith's article, the International League of the Rights of Man gave Sakharov its annual prize. It joined with the AJC's new Jacob Blaustein Institute to provide early translations of dissident texts, while lawyer Edward Kline made himself a one-man clearinghouse on the subject.[34] The value of freedom of opinion in the Eastern bloc and elsewhere led to other initiatives like Writers and Scholars International, which began to publish its *Index of Censorship* in 1972. As its editor, Michael Scammell, put it in his opening editorial, the cause of freedom of expression was beyond politics: "The thing that all ideologies have in common, . . . to a greater or lesser degree, is intolerance of dissent or opposition." But even as revisionist communism began to die in the East and a few elsewhere noticed the new dissent there, Marxism experienced a huge spike in affiliates in the West in the five years after 1968, whereas human rights did not. (As Sakharov noted, in 1968–69 Mao's *Little Red Book* circulated more broadly around the world than his essay on peace and coexistence did.)[35] Yet just as the Soviet human rights movement coalesced, other, disconnected events occurred, fostering a kind of accidental synergy that ushered in the human rights era.

If socialism with a human face died in Eastern Europe in 1968, it received its deathblow elsewhere with the assassination of Chilean president Salvador Allende in September 1973. "Human rights entered my vocabulary on September 11, 1973," as one activist in Chile put it, alluding to the day of the coup. Following as it did close on the heels of a military seizure of power in Uruguay earlier that summer, the spectacular Chilean events—together, after 1976, with Argentina's own junta regime and its dirty war—did provoke human rights to crystallize as an organizing framework. But why human rights rather than something else, and from where did human rights enter the vocabulary if they had not been there before? There had been similar episodes of repression, including ones making liberal use of violence, as in Alfredo Stroessner's Paraguay after 1954 and military rule in Brazil after 1964. And the American government had provided tacit and financial support before, as it did so notoriously for Chilean strongman Augusto Pinochet before and after the coup in his country.[36]

True, the domino effect of dictatorship in Latin America at this moment seemed breathtaking, especially in the southern cone (previously seen as more stable). But even as a rightist international alliance coalesced in 1975 to destroy the revolutionary left, the infamous Operación Cóndor, crimes in the world alone did not provoke interest in human rights. Their new appeal depended here, too, on the failure of more maximal visions of political transformation and the opening of the avenue of moral criticism in a moment of political closure. Prior coups not only had failed to collapse such maximal visions, but had even helped energize them, so the terroristic regimes mattered in their impact on left-wing hopes as much as in their impressive coincidence. While Prague in 1968 proved that no revisionist socialism would be tolerated in the Soviet sphere, Santiago in 1973 brought home the lesson that no revisionist socialism would be tolerated in the American one. Just as in the escalation of Soviet dissidence, the best explanation for the rise in prominence of human rights in Latin America is that many on the left drew the lesson—at first, a strategic one—that an alteration of plausible hopes had to occur. This is so even though Latin America proved far more hospitable to the persistence of revolutionary and guerilla utopianism even as human rights took root there. While human rights proved more lasting, utopia would remain "armed" in the region through the end of the Cold War, if not beyond.[37]

The turn to human rights as a framework of response happened not rapidly but slowly, as the best-studied case of Uruguayans shows. Initially, leftists often operating in Argentine exile before the 1976 coup there sought like-minded ideological outlets for denouncing the repressive military control of the regime. In these years, the Soviet-led international campaign against what it cast as bourgeois counterrevolution, a campaign focused on interned Chilean communist leader Luis Corvalán but targeting military dictatorship everywhere, provided one forum. Along with Brazilians and Chileans, Zelmar Michelini, prominent Uruguayan leftist, traveled to Rome, where Bertrand Russell's old leftist tribunal—founded to indict the American conduct in Vietnam in the late 1960s—had re-emerged to try new crimes in the southern cone.[38] These versions of internationalism were a world away from the human rights movement soon to form. Indeed, at first, Uruguayan critics of their regime's political imprisonment refused to make "humanitarian laments" or adopt "purely informative activity" but insisted that "prisoners will be freed the day that the revolutionary fight . . . forces the bourgeoisie and its armed tool to do so, or when, sweeping them away together with their exploitative system, those who are exploited open the doors of the jails."[39]

Soon, however, such figures were making alliances with Amnesty International, which began organizing investigations and publicizing torture in single Latin American countries at just this time. Such investigations contributed to American congressional inquiry into U.S. involvement with right-wing dictatorships. In these endeavors, local actors "knew that the success of their denunciations depended on keeping radical claims for social change separated from their human rights activism. . . . Acknowledging that space for radical activism was closing up in the region amidst a wave of unprecedented repression, they looked for new ways of continuing their political involvement. With almost no capacity to perform effectively in their domestic arena, they looked for interlocutors who could press the Uruguayan government to stop repression against their fellow leftist activists." As time wore on, what was at first a strategy became a philosophy, with "many mov[ing] from endorsing a socialist view of rights as only attainable in a revolutionized socioeconomic horizon to accepting the concept of universally held rights."[40] As before and elsewhere, the unviability of political alternatives provided the main rationale for the turn to human rights.

These initiatives did not presuppose the Inter-American Human Rights "system," though the concerns they targeted did give that mechanism a whole new relevance as time passed. Peripheral through this era, the inter-American framework had come about through the Organization of American States (OAS), which had declared rights in Bogotá in the 1940s but left them on paper. But it finally created an Inter-American Human Rights Commission in 1959, revised the larger organization's charter in 1967 to give the commission direction, and drafted an American Convention on Human Rights in 1969. (It would come into force ten years later.) After installing an absolute norm against external intervention—on human rights grounds or any other—in the postwar moment, Latin American states had turned slowly after the Cuban Revolution to the possibility that internal instability threatened "public order" as much as external invasion. With this insight, "human rights" became much more appealing to existing governments. After excluding Cuba from participation in the OAS after 1962, the organization constructed the new human rights commission to target the malfeasance of the communist regime there. But these developments hardly drove public prominence of human rights on their own. Comparative inaction—internationally and within the OAS itself—around torture in Brazil makes this particularly clear.[41]

In this sense, the inter-American system proved to be the beneficiary not the cause of the transformation in the direction of human rights. While it was being built, Fidel Castro's youthful socialism fired the imagination, convincing a great many to join the revolutionary cause, not support human rights. After the regional wave of repression in the 1970s, however, the OAS system—which turned from indicting leftist to indicting rightist regimes—got a second look. Michelini, who had dismissed the OAS as an American tool, and had strenuously defended Cuba from its scrutiny in the name of self-determination and nonintervention, now insisted that self-determination could not mean "a free hand which, within . . . borders, makes possible savage and premeditated attacks upon the most basic standards of human existence."[42]

It was the decision of a sector of the Latin American left to resist the regional repression in human rights terms that helped make the fortune of the concept in that region and beyond. As in the Soviet Union before, it also mattered that the language proved to be highly coalitional and ecumenical in providing a *lingua franca* for diverse voices. In the Soviet sphere, the earliest element of what became the eventual human rights coalition had been a Baptist movement; but in spite of permanent Christian concern about religious freedom behind the Iron Curtain for decades, nothing comparable to the crystallization of an international human rights movement occurred thanks to either indigenous Christian movements or their international partisans. In Latin America, it was Catholics who were crucial partners in the move to human rights. The famous *aggiornamento* of the Catholic Church under John XXIII's papacy had led, notably in his encyclical *Pacem in Terris* (1963), to the sort of explicit linkage of Catholicism and human rights that earlier innovators like Jacques Maritain could only have imagined. The notion that Catholicism stood for something called "human rights" spread rapidly around the world in the 1960s, even if on the ground—not least in Spain and Portugal, with their reactionary clericalism—the politics of the religion remained ambiguous. But as important as it was in accompanying various institutional reforms and individual acts, the reinvention of political Catholicism around human rights failed to spark a human rights movement anywhere in the 1960s, including Latin America. It was simply a condition for a later series of events, notably Cardinal Evaristo Arns's move from case-by-case sympathy for torture victims toward a truly organized human rights movement in Brazil in 1975.[43] The true significance of the creation of Catholic human rights, therefore, was for the coalitions it was to allow around the concept when the time was right.

In Latin America, political Christianity had by and large favored the democratic governments of the 1960s, but typically sided with authoritarianism when the rise of the revolutionary left forced the matter. It also generated important languages of opposition, unthinkable before the Catholic Church's ideological move to human rights. Even as Catholic reforms of the 1960s allowed for the invention of new sorts of "liberation" theologies, more moderate groups appealing to human rights as moral limits also formed immediately after the authoritarian coups, particularly in Chile after 1973. There, in an atmosphere of general Catholic (including episcopal) support for the new regime's restoration of order, an Ecumenical Committee of Cooperation for Peace, mostly led by left-wing Christians with support from the World Council of Churches, quickly emerged. The junta's early success in mastering Christian opposition—in part through the expulsion of many priests—came to grief when Chile's Cardinal Silva Henríquez acceded to its demands to close the committee only to found a Vicariate of Solidarity, an organization based on human rights, in January 1976. Whatever their practical difference, Christian appeals to human rights were ideologically important at a time when the military dictatorship depended on its rhetorical association with Christianity, and the moral framing of this criticism of the regime made it difficult simply to liquidate as a dangerous political threat. By 1978, in spite of generally strong Catholic support for the dictatorship, Cardinal Silva even declared a "year of human rights" with a motto: "every man has the right to be a person."[44]

The Catholic insistence on moral constraints to politics, the explicit framework for human rights activism, allowed critics of the Chilean regime to avoid alienating it, precisely when it drew on much Catholic support, notably in rightist groups. But it also allowed unprecedented collaboration with reforming leftists moving simultaneously toward a strategic, coalitional moral language of opposition. "It is difficult—and fruitless—to view it as somehow having been a 'pure' force, apart from politics," one commentator observes of Catholic moral claims.[45] But just as in the Soviet Union before, the fiction of moral autonomy from politics was a condition of political relevance. It partly insulated Catholic opposition from state repression, and it also provided a minimal language in which what had been radically distinctive agendas could fuse. Through this transcendence of politics in the name of coalitional moral norms, Christians became part of a movement that their own religious innovations had not prompted a decade before.

Meanwhile, foreign sympathy and involvement with such indigenous causes skyrocketed, notably after 1973. In the crucial five years of the creation of the international human rights movement between the early and later 1970s, Amnesty International towered above all other organizations as the focus for observers abroad of new invocations of human rights by Soviet and Latin American local movements. In the late 1960s, AI had been brought to the brink of dissolution by Benenson's foolish insouciance toward his links with British intelligence, ending his leadership of the organization. European sections of Amnesty International were planted soon after its emergence. The American section, founded later, awaited the early 1970s events for expansion from a tiny base. But then it was rapid. From seven local groups in 1972, there were eighty-six by 1976. Membership in the United States languished at a few thousand in the early 1970s, but expanded by thirty times to reach 90,000 by the end of the decade. In spite of the proliferation of sections in continental Europe in the early 1960s, the organization as a whole also experienced its great leap forward in the 1970s, when it grew to roughly 300,000 members. In relation to rival new social movements—most of which were in freefall in precisely the same period—AI experienced galloping growth. Its success depended on the substitute utopia it provided. It

represented a clear break with the predominant political activism of the 1960s. Amnesty's project was a conscious departure from many of its essential elements—its revolutionary aspirations, its search for comprehensive ideological or technocratic solutions to social problems, its lofty ambitions of changing "the system" and its draining in-

ner polarizations. Instead, Amnesty activists turned to a more minimalist and genuinely pragmatic approach—they were "working to
make the world a slightly less wicked place." In this perspective, the
human rights activism of the 1970s reveals itself to be the product of a
post-revolutionary idealism, growing out of a certain disillusionment
about the preceding decade's attempts to bring about political change
and jettisoning some of the highest hopes and most optimistic tones
which had underlain them. Equally far from utopian visions as from
political ingenuity, one group member . . . described the effects of
Amnesty's efforts in utterly realistic terms: "Sending a card . . . will
not change the world very much. But it is surely worth investing a little time and postage to try to help two other individuals to secure justice, or at least to find courage."[46]

For its adherents, the attractions of Amnesty International in its
decisive decades depended on leaving behind political utopias and
turning to smaller and more manageable moral acts.

Amnesty International's novel methods of information gathering went in the 1970s far beyond its original methods of forming
adoption groups to write pleas for individual release. And these methods were also critical to how it came to be (and, soon enough, were
copied by other organizations). Even before the very early translation
of dissident texts provided by AI's London-based research bureau,
the organization had begun to focus its attention on torture in the
later 1960s. It pioneered the gathering of information about depredations under Greek military rule from 1967–1974. Providentially, in
1972 the organization opened a Campaign against Torture, published
a global analysis of the problem, and initiated a petition drive (the
first signatory being Joan Baez, who opened it at an April 1973 concert).[47] Seán MacBride, for his contribution to the campaign, won the
Nobel Peace Prize in 1974, thereby raising the profile of human rights
and broadcasting the very idea that social movements could coalesce
around them. After the political coups in Chile and Uruguay, Amnesty International and other NGOs were active in gathering infor-

mation and raising consciousness about infractions in those two countries. The information they gathered was spread most notably at the United Nations and in Washington, D.C., where AI opened an office in 1976. Such activities prompted some of the first analyses of AI's campaigns for wider publics, both in the academy and at large.[48]

Whether or not such activism made a difference on the ground, or in the larger process of constructing international norms, it succeeded first of all in giving meaning (as Benenson once hoped) to engaged lives. It was engagement of a sort whose minimalism was its enabling condition and source of power when other post-1968 alternatives were dying. Though she would go on to help found Helsinki (later Human Rights) Watch as the decade closed, Jeri Laber recalled that in the early 1970s she had never heard the phrase "human rights." Trained in Russian studies, it was not Soviet activism that hooked her but a searing December 1973 *New Republic* essay written by AI activist Rose Styron on the renaissance of torture around the world. It led Laber to "do something about it." Having been a part-time food writer for the *New York Times* shortly before, Laber placed an op-ed piece in that newspaper based on AI information—the first published—within a year of joining the Riverside Amnesty chapter. "I had found a successful formula," she noted in a memoir. "I began with a detailed description of a horrible form of torture, then explained where it was happening and the political context in which it occurred; I ended with a plea to show the offending government that the world was watching."[49]

The "global concern" of AI activists in America and Western Europe, offering a hearing to Soviet and Latin American voices, set the framework for the unexpected events that were to follow at the diplomatic level—especially unexpected responses to the Helsinki Final Act of 1975. Given the priority of such grassroots movements and their escalating international prominence in the mid-1970s, there is no way to study the human rights revolution of the 1970s primarily from the perspective of either domestic governments or international diplomacy. After all, it was the collapse of authority of Cold War frameworks, ending the absorption of many citizens in the official ideologies of its contenders and detaching some ordinary people from official justifications of power, that made the concept of human rights meaningful. Yet there is no denying that without the further canonization of human rights in the Helsinki process of the Conference for Security and Cooperation in Europe (CSCE), and then Jimmy Carter's explosive affiliation with the language in January 1977, human rights might have remained the preserve of expanding but still minor advocacy groups and their international members and promoters. (Indeed, without Carter, the phrase itself might never have exploded so spectacularly: even after she placed her op-ed pieces that helped Amnesty International publicize suffering prisoners in 1974, Laber recalled, "I did not use the words 'human rights' to describe our cause; it was not part of my everyday vocabulary and would have meant little to most people at that time.")[50]

The CSCE was a fruit of the very Cold War détente between the superpowers that human rights were eventually to unsettle. What began as a Finnish initiative in 1972 for chiefly intra-European imperatives was not intended by negotiators as a stimulus to human rights activism. For the Soviets, the point of the process was to formalize détente by securing international recognition of the three-decade-old takeover of Eastern Europe. Even for human rights advocates, it seemed that for the Soviets the Helsinki accords were "an old dream come true."[51] Not least, the principle of sovereign noninterference was clearly affirmed in the treaty. For West Europeans, and most of all West Germans after Willy Brandt's pioneering *Ostpolitik,* the point was to institutionalize hard-won gains of the relaxation of Cold War tensions. True, this included continuing rhetorical invocations of the human rights that West Europeans had affirmed on paper since World War II. These were sometimes ritually invoked in diplomatic processes, as in the so-called Davignon report of 1970, which outlined a common West European security strategy. And perhaps there were some, like the Dutch, who in the process of negotiating the Helsinki Act for signature in 1975 had the secret intention of overcoming détente rather than producing what one of many skeptical journalists called "a diplomatic gadget that no one will read." Henry Kissinger, who went along with the intra-European process, famously said that the so-called "Third Basket" human rights provisions, which were originally intended to do the minor but important work of allowing family contact and unification across the Iron Curtain, could be written "in Swahili for all I care." But no one—not even the Europeans—had anticipated that the treaty would combine with human rights activism gingerly emerging from below.[52]

Indeed, given the preexisting movements around human rights, the negotiation of the Helsinki accords may have merely added another possible reference for dissidents: appeal to international norms had already begun to occur, and Helsinki provided another set. In their balance of the principles of sovereign impregnability and individual rights, the Helsinki documents reproduced the original contradiction of the UN Charter, rather than shifting in a decisively new direction. The Soviet Union, further, had ratified the international UN covenants around human rights in 1973. The Helsinki accords set up a more meaningful monitoring scheme, but historically sterile UN processes were also being updated in this era, beginning with the creation of the so-called "1235 Procedure," which entertained public debate around gross human rights violations. To more and more contemporaries, however, the Helsinki monitoring process provided an exciting new forum for activism, compared to the creaky UN mechanisms, and institutionalized state-to-state human rights claims for the first time.[53] Beginning with the creation of a Moscow Helsinki Group in May 1976, announced by Yuri Orlov in Sakharov's living room, the Helsinki accords were an essential feature of the crystallization of international human rights consciousness in 1976–77.[54]

In one of those extraordinary convergences in which history is made, human rights also became a potential language of the foreign policy of the Democratic Party in the United States in the early 1970s, before being canonized by its victorious presidential candidate

Jimmy Carter in 1977. In late 1974, one of the most learned observers could still note that "human rights considerations seem likely to play only a relatively limited role in U.S. foreign policy during the next few years."[55] Three years later, the fortunes of human rights could not have looked more different, after a transformation as shocking at the time as it had been accidental in its origins.

In America, human rights started as a way for the contending sides of a Democratic Party at war with itself to restate their pre-existing positions. The strongest impulse clearly came from the left wing of the party, as part of a congressional revolt during the last years of the Vietnam War, in the midst of the Watergate scandal. In the shadow of the War Powers Act and, later, Idaho senator Frank Church's investigations of Cold War malfeasance, some liberal Democrats discovered international human rights. There is little information about why, but beginning in August 1973, Minnesota congressman Donald Fraser used his House Subcommittee on International Organizations and Movements to spotlight human rights norms and mechanisms. As the hearings continued, the Chilean coup intervened, after which Fraser used his Subcommittee on Inter-American Affairs as a forum for discussion of the human rights consequences. One of Fraser's most important conclusions was that the UN processes around human rights seemed unlikely to be reformed, so that governments, in particular the U.S. government, needed to move forcefully to propagate human rights values. It was essentially due to his hearings that Fraser and congressional allies were successful in prompting Henry Kissinger to create a Department of State human rights bureau in 1975, after analysts concluded that "if the Department [of State] did not place itself ahead of the curve on this issue, Congress would take the matter out of the Department's hands." Among other things, the new office began governmental human rights monitoring, though Kissinger made no use of its materials. It was also due to this current that the linkage of foreign assistance to human rights practices began to be introduced.[56] If Fraser pioneered the transformation of human rights into a possible element of U.S.

government policy, there was nevertheless no emergence of human rights as a general slogan and ideological option due to his efforts. They remained too peripheral.

The same could not be said of Jimmy Carter's use of the language in the first months of his presidency. There were, to be sure, other antecedents than Fraser's subcommittee to this departure, most especially on the right wing of the Democratic Party, and in Washington Senator Henry "Scoop" Jackson's agitation for Soviet Jewry in terms of universal human rights. Jackson sponsored his own version of "linkage" in the amendment he cosponsored with Ohio congressman Charles Vanik that denied most favored nation status to the Soviet Union for trade purposes if it refused emigration rights. Starting in late 1972, invoking Solzhenitsyn's ringing claim that there were no longer internal affairs in the world, Jackson doggedly universalized the plight of Soviet Jews, his hatred of détente driving inspiring speeches about universal principles. "I believe in the Universal Declaration of Human Rights," he proclaimed at the Pacem in Terris conference in Washington in October 1973, "and I believe that now, twenty-five years after its adoption by the United Nations, it is not too late or too early to begin to implement it."[57] It was a moment in which Jackson—whose main concern was smashing détente—both discovered the particular cause of Soviet Jews and moved to defend it in universalistic terms.

In doing so, he was one of a number of forces transforming the longstanding cause of Soviet Jewry on the basis of a general principle of freedom of movement and emigration. In this sense, far from driving the large-scale ascendancy of human rights on its own, the cause of "refuseniks" (so-called because of the USSR's denial of exit visas) was caught up in that larger transformation. In the Soviet Union in the early years of the 1970s, Jews pressing for the rights of emigration were only one element in the coalition of dissidents. The combination of the Six Day War and Prague Spring led to a decisive shift in the affiliations of many Jews, and applications for exit visas skyrocketed. The most famous figure, Antatoly Sharansky, became Sakharov's associate and alerted him to a human right he had not made central before in his own move to dissent. Before this era, in both international and American politics, work for Jewish emigration from the Soviet Union had been viewed as an ethnic or even Zionist cause rather a human rights one, even after young activists transformed it into a grassroots movement modeled on civil rights and other advocacy in the era. And though the new AJC Blaustein Institute held a major forum in Uppsala, Sweden in 1972 rediscovering the general human right of freedom of emigration, and Jackson made it central to his legislation invoking the Universal Declaration, the movement still did not immediately incorporate human rights. Rather, the agony of the Soviet Jews slowly became a human rights concern over the course of the 1970s as that larger framework crystallized. The Soviet Jewry movement proved more the beneficiary than the cause of that general transformation.[58]

As late as the end of 1976, in spite of Fraser's dogged efforts and Jackson's passionate rhetoric, there was no sign that human rights were about to achieve any centrality in the Democratic foreign policy lexicon. Even in June of that year, when after Jimmy Carter's unexpected emergence the Democrats' Platform Committee met to iron out the significant differences among the contending factions of the party, human rights had not really been discovered. Antiwar activist Sam Brown, Jr. proposed to embed the principle of linkage to human rights against right-wing autocracies in the platform, to which New York senator (and Jackson ally) Daniel Patrick Moynihan agreed on condition that the principle extend just as much to left-wing totalitarianism. "We'll be against the dictators you don't like the most," Moynihan said to Brown across the table, "if you'll be against the dictators we don't like the most." The next year, Moynihan recalled, the platform result was "the strongest platform commitment of human rights in our history." But it did not affect Carter, and the national media attributed no significance to the moment in real time, even understanding the platform to be in harmony with détente and focused on "amity" with communism, not preparing to move against it.[59]

Jimmy Carter was a coalitional candidate for president in a moment when the party was recovering from its failed post-Watergate feint to the left, which coincided with economic collapse and the decline of popular radicalism. Covering the summer 1976 Democratic convention, prominent *New Yorker* journalist Elizabeth Drew observed that compared to the ideological unity behind George McGovern four years before, there had been "changes in the country as well as within the Democratic Party. . . . The war is over and passions are dead, and many of the delegates to this Convention look, as a friend of mine observed, like 'modified Republicans.'" In 1976, Carter came out of nowhere, and Morris Udall's McGovernite candidacy failed, as had Jackson's (and George Wallace's). Carter emerged as the one whom different factions of the party disliked least.[60]

If there was anything in Carter's campaign that linked him with the contemporary surge of human rights to that point, it was simply his stand for morality in general. Carter's moralism reflected his deep religious convictions after he was "born again" in the mid-1960s. As it continued, the 1976 election became a referendum on détente. His opponent, Gerald Ford, went so far as to prohibit the use of the word in his campaign, but then famously tripped up in the October 6 televised debate in suggesting that the Soviets did not dominate Eastern Europe. Carter made clear moves in the direction of morality and against *Realpolitik* in the summer and fall of 1976, taking maximum advantage of Ford's slip. Carter's personal moralism, and the mood of the American electorate, were a brief match.

In this broad sense, Carter's election, in a campaign suffused with promises of moral transcendence of politics, opened the way for the astonishing explosion of "human rights" across the American political landscape. Even so, through inauguration day Carter mainly invoked ethics and justice as crucial foreign policy principles.[61] It was more a reflection of the primacy of moralism in the last six months of 1976 than the sign of a major departure that even the notoriously cynical Kissinger invoked "human rights" at several public events— even more often than Carter![62] Still by this late date, there were many versions of morality Carter could have invoked as the centerpiece of his foreign policy before he made the fateful choice to turn to human rights in his first months in office. And the conditions that crystallized long enough for Carter to become president were fracturing even as he turned to drive human rights to extraordinary prominence: the country "return[ed] to a normal condition" almost immediately, after which "assailing American wickedness" seemed "out of step."[63] In the right place at the right time, Carter moved "human rights" from grassroots mobilization to the center of global rhetoric.

The year of human rights, 1977, began with Carter's January 20 inauguration, which put "human rights" in front of the viewing public for the first time in American history. This year of breakthrough would culminate in Amnesty International's receipt of the Nobel Peace Prize on December 10. Carter's inaugural address on January 20 made "human rights" a publicly acknowledged buzzword. "Because we are free we can never be indifferent to the fate of freedom elsewhere," Carter announced on the Capitol steps. "Our commitment to human rights must be absolute." The symbolic novelty and resonance of the phrase in Carter's policy is what mattered most of all, since he embedded it for the first time in popular consciousness and ordinary language. Arthur Schlesinger, Jr. once called on the "future historian" to "trace the internal discussions . . . that culminated in the striking words of the inaugural address." No one, however, yet knows exactly how they got there. But soon after, the term was being interpreted as "almost a theological point for Carter. He can't stamp out sin, but he keeps on praying."[64]

Unlike Ford, who had refused Solzhenitsyn's request for a White House meeting in 1975, Carter soon acted to honor dissidents. When New York lawyer and civil libertarian Martin Garbus met with Sakharov in Moscow and hand-delivered a letter from him to Carter, the president took the opportunity to respond (Garbus's wife Ruth smuggled the letter past the KGB in her brassiere). The Soviets responded to the first signs that "human rights" might unsettle hard-won détente, both diplomatically protesting early U.S. State Department affiliations with Sakharov's cause and—as they had in the 1940s —mocking racist America for its hypocrisy. But at this very moment, in an amazing coincidence, tens of millions of Americans were glued to the television set watching Alex Haley's "Roots," the famous African-American family history, which gave full attention to the slave trade and plantation life. ("Can you imagine a week-long series over Soviet TV about life in the Gulag?" *New York Times* columnist William Safire asked playfully.) It was Carter's carefully crafted reply to Sakharov, which the latter released in mid-February, that caused a major uproar and showed that Carter really meant what he said. "Human rights is a central concern of my Administration," reporters transcribed from the copy in Sakharov's apartment. "You may rest assured that the American people and our government will continue our firm commitment to promote respect for human rights not only in our own country but also abroad." The next month, Carter met with dissident Vladimir Bukovsky, in spite of Soviet requests not to do so, and spoke at the United Nations on the importance of human rights. No one—certainly not FDR, among American presidents— had made human rights as central in American, and indeed global, rhetoric.[65] The only senior Western politician to follow suit was David Owen, Britain's dashing new foreign secretary, who tested the theme in 1977–78, after he took office. (In 1978, Owen even published a book laying out his views of the subject.)[66]

"I know there was no specific planning for a particular human-rights campaign or program, such as it is," one foreign policy official told Elizabeth Drew, in a long *New Yorker* article. "I think then fate intervened—happenstance things, letters—that blew the issue up unexpectedly." "The whole thing," another told her, "sort of acquired a dynamic of its own." But by spring, Carter gave a programmatic address at Notre Dame's commencement, laying out a full-scale foreign policy philosophy based on human rights, while Secretary of State Cyrus Vance offered some specifics at the University of Georgia Law School. Even as Carter's subordinates "groped" to define policy, American elites embarked on an extended discussion of human rights, from their historical origins, to their contemporary meaning, to their case-by-case implications. The issue had become relevant and even "chic," Roberta Cohen, executive director of the International League (who would shortly join the Carter human rights bureau), told the *New York Times.* "For years we were preachers, cockeyed idealists, or busybodies and now we are respectable. . . . Everybody wants to get into human rights. That's fine, but what happens if they get bored?" This upsurge in interest could not compare to that of the 1940s, when even the highest officials did not use the language of human rights (except Winston Churchill once out of office), and internationalists were concerned with the UN alone. In the 1970s, by contrast, popular mobilization and then Carter's interest kicked off a much larger and more public discussion that continues in the present.[67]

In the short term, Carter faced accusations of selectivity in the global abuses he singled out for attention. Initially, the Soviet sphere was the overwhelming focus, which led some critics to insist that he broaden his view. Carter protested, "I have never had the inclination to single out the Soviet Union as the only country where human rights are being abridged."[68] Emerging neoconservatives—for whom human rights were understood as anticommunism by another name—warned against pursuing a "false symmetry" in policy, while as early as June 1977 Noam Chomsky from the far left complained that "the human rights campaign is a device to be manipulated by propagandists to gain popular support for counter-revolutionary intervention."[69] Even as he rolled out foreign assistance proposals that cut aid to human rights abusers around the world, Carter faced skeptics from all corners. Some came near to gloating when his diplomacy backfired—first in early March when Ugandan despot Idi Amin responded to Carter's public scolding by threatening Americans in his country. The diplomatic problems with the Soviets that Carter's agenda provoked—Anatoly Dobrynin, the Soviet ambassador, made clear right away he was not pleased, and Leonid Brezhnev gave Vance a very chilly reception in Moscow that spring too—surprised Carter himself. Thereafter, his focus shifted to Latin American dictatorships; emerging news of the "dirty war" in Argentina, where the military had taken control a year before, lent credence to this change.[70]

Even by the end of 1977, the bloom was clearly off the rose for Carter's policy. The difficulty of establishing any consistent line—especially when the policy had emerged without much consideration—led some to claim that Carter had simply "cancelled" his crusade. In response, his own policymakers (notably Patricia Derian, chosen to lead the State Department human rights bureau Kissinger had set up) responded that the campaign had always been meant to be integrated with and qualified by multiple other concerns.[71] Foreign policy experts asked and still ask what a "human rights agenda" really means, but most people are not foreign policy experts. In the long term, American foreign policy discussions were permanently altered, with new relevance for a "moral" option that now referred explicitly to individual human rights. And even more important, Carter introduced the idea in all of its ambiguity to a vast global audience it had never reached—and Americans first among them.

How neatly did human rights fit in American history, and how in the end to make sense of the place of Carter's America in this era of human rights history? There is little doubt that for many Americans, the idea of human rights came to imply a longstanding set of liberal commitments. In spite of immediate attempts to root it in American tradition, however, the shock in response to Carter's invocations of human rights revealed how much novelty there really was. In foreign policy, liberalism had for most of the postwar era taken very different forms than the propagation of rights abroad. In domestic matters, it is tempting to believe that the civil rights movement that had transformed American race relations prompted the new invocations of human rights, but the evidence is thin. Though some participants in the civil rights movement later joined the American human rights movement, the timing of the latter is too late for any truly powerful connection to be made. The civil rights movement experienced its highpoint a decade before the breakthrough of its "successor." And the freefall of civil rights activism beginning the early 1970s meant that the explosion of human rights occurred after earlier trajectories had been interrupted. The gap of years before the spike of human rights suggests it had very different and more immediate sources. Just as important, the early human rights movement omitted the very concerns for more thoroughgoing socioeconomic inequality that had made the later civil rights movement dangerous enough to arouse a conservative backlash.[72]

There were some similarities in the American turn to human rights to those earlier and elsewhere. They were coalitional and strongly featured the promise to replace politics by morality. The Carter administration's checkered history has been summarized as "the agonies of antipolitics."[73] But notwithstanding Carter's own godliness, the coalitions formed by human rights advocates in the American 1970s were not between religious and secular moralists, as in Latin America before, but between factions of the Democratic Party. And the assertion of human rights by the leader of a superpower, and as a set of guiding principles for the exercise of its might, made this assertion of morality obviously different from those that rose from the grassroots. For most liberals, Carter's leadership on human rights afforded not a substitute utopia but a sense of collective national recovery. It was the reestablishment of the country's moral and missionary credentials in the world "after groveling in the moral muck so long" that determined the American meaning of a rights-based internationalism.[74]

At Notre Dame, Carter insisted that a human rights framework allowed for an overall sense of recovery of purpose from the errors of the whole Cold War era. The past to overcome was not simply recent Machiavellianism, since it was the Democratic Party that had begun, and escalated, the Vietnam War a decade before. "For too many years, we've been willing to adopt the flawed and erroneous principles and tactics of our adversaries, sometimes abandoning our own values for theirs," Carter said on the Notre Dame rostrum. "[T]hrough failure we have now found our way back to our own principles and values, and we have regained our lost confidence." This was no cynical ploy: numerous Democratic foreign policy thinkers in Carter's administration had participated in Vietnam to the hilt, and had reflected bitterly since on the tragic consequences. The recovery from long-term mistakes is also what drew in most observers. America, one of Elizabeth Drew's informants told her, "had been back on its heels for so long. We got the impression from two years of travelling around the country of a feeling worse than ennui, of a feeling that time was working against us. That's a very debilitating position for dealing in any sort of relationship. What we're doing has been interpreted by some as Cold Warriorism, but it's not that at all."[75] In a situation when Cold War frameworks had lost their appeal, human rights offered something new, even if it had to be represented in the guise of forgotten national traditions.

Yet even the American turn to human rights only takes on its full meaning against an international background in which old utopias were giving way to a new one. Liberals were moved by the promise of national recovery and responded to Carter's domestic call from above. But from the president to the people, Americans could not have done so without the call from outside and below, since it was far-flung global actors who first made human rights percolate, and were embraced in America as victims. If these two calls were fundamentally different and pointed in different directions—one based on moralizing the state, the other on "the power of the powerless"—it was not obvious at the time. What mattered is that both seemed to converge in the same human rights imperative.

For the power of the powerless, as Václav Havel famously labeled the philosophy of dissent, was only then coming into view. In comparison to the quick rise of human rights in the USSR proper, similar movements after 1968 in the satellite states were delayed, and the investment of hopes in Marxist revisionism survived much longer. Even so, the formation of dissident groups in 1976–77 in Czechoslovakia, Poland, and elsewhere, complete with new appeals to the Helsinki agreements, worked in a similar way. As before, the Committee for the Defense of Workers (KOR) in Poland and Charter 77 in Czechoslovakia, together with the Moscow Helsinki group, made direct appeals to international human rights instruments. But they appeared in a new moment that contrasted sharply with the post-1968 era of ideological confusion, and they brought human rights to its international public acme.

Charter 77 emerged spontaneously, after the Czechoslovak repression of a psychedelic rock band. As in other episodes of dissidence, it brought together a wide range of people—including reform communists who had not learned the same lesson from the collapse of the Prague Spring as their fellows in the movement. And through its range of activities in protest of the regime's persecution of its citizens, it became internationally famous. Along with the Polish workers' committee, Charter 77 did far better than the earliest Soviet dissent in sparking widespread affiliations throughout the Eastern bloc. By late 1978, when he penned his classic meditation on dissidence, Havel could testify, in a reversal of Karl Marx: "A specter is haunting Eastern Europe: the specter of what in the West is called dissent."[76] It was a breakthrough moment.

Havel was a disheveled hero with a countercultural ethos, whose moral intensity gave him iconic status. Though never a revisionist communist, he had welcomed the Prague Spring, and made a prominent call for a pluralization of the parties united by a common goal of building democratic socialism.[77] After Soviet repression, he spent the 1970s away from Prague, in what he described as a state of suspended animation. By the mid-1970s, Havel had signed on to interpret the experience of a generation that "lived through the end of an era; the disintegration of a spiritual and social climate; a profound mental dislocation." As the era of Czechoslovak "normalization" proceeded under Alexander Dubček's replacement Gustav Husák, Havel drew on chiefly existentialist sources to forge a moral critique of the regime, announced in an open letter to Husák in 1975.[78] There is very little that was ideologically new in Havel's most famous statement, "Power of the Powerless," but it perfectly captured the rationale and the conditions for the origins of human rights. As such, it is worth a careful reading.

The first premise of moral dissent was the recognition that ordinary politics were not viable. Havel assumed the lessons of 1968 were now clear. Addressing those who still dreamed the dream of politics, he warned that the worst mistake was to "overestimate the importance of direct political work in the traditional sense." It was for this reason that the first rule was to give up "the intention of presenting an alternative political program." This had been true, he suggested, already in 1968; but there was no excuse now for the failure to grasp that any political initiative "would be liquidated before it had a chance to translate its intentions into action." Revolution and violence were the magic words of a past that had no more meaning in a disenchanted present.[79]

Havel's dearest premises were in an extravagant critique of the modern age: the crisis of the times followed not from totalitarianism, he insisted, but the overdeveloped technology and soulless consumerism of "advanced" society. The obvious failure of totalitarian rule, he thought, had to be seen as a symptom of a much larger, global problem. In such dark reflections, Havel betrayed not just his own reading of specific philosophical texts—most important, those of Czech phenomenologist Jan Patočka, who helped to define the principles of nonrevisionist dissent just as it began. Havel also reflected a temptation common across the world in the 1960s to worry that modernity had gone awry—but he also found a way to translate such malaise into unexpected and portable new form. The roots of Havel's championship of human rights would not accompany their global dissemination. Yet it is crucial to recall that he went so far as to say that dissent mattered not through inspiration from but as warning to the West, where the moral nightmare seemed far worse than in the East, where the totalitarian system made control visible. "Is not the grayness and the emptiness of life in the totalitarian system only an inflated caricature of modern life in general?" Havel asked rhetorically. It was for this reason, he explained, that "traditional parliamentary democracies can offer no fundamental opposition to the automatism of technological civilization. . . . To cling to the notion of traditional parliamentary democracy as one's political ideal and to succumb to the illusion that only this tried and true form is capable of guaranteeing human beings enduring dignity . . . would, in my opinion, be at the very least shortsighted."[80] Havel's deepest aspiration at the time seems to have been for autonomous and small-scale communal existence, which he saw as more authentically connected to life itself.

It was out of the insight into strategic circumstance and on the basis of existentialist morality that Havel made his appeal to human rights. This included a defense of "legalism," the value of law for dissidents. For Havel, it mattered that the communist regime "pretends to respect human rights," and that dissidents could respond through "persistent and never-ending appeal to the laws." Given earlier Soviet dissent, there was nothing strategically original, by this point, in the appeal to international law. But it was very powerful. Charter 77 regularly cited the Helsinki Accords and the international UN covenants on human rights that, through the supreme irony of Czechoslovak ratification in 1975, had become legally binding around the world. True, Havel acknowledged, the appeal to legal forms smacked of bourgeois ideology—a critique that he treated as generally correct.

Yet now the Marxist critique of ideology had to be used to target the Marxist regime, and could incorporate rather than reject legal rights. It was through "words, words, words," as Havel put it, that such a regime established "legitimacy . . . before its own citizens, before schoolchildren, before the international public, and before history." Havel acknowledged forthrightly but strikingly that "law can never create anything better." For now, appeal to legality generally and the law of human rights nevertheless held the most promise.[81]

Pursuing its argument by imagining a humble greengrocer who could be the automaton of an inhuman regime but also possessed inner resources to sap that regime's viability, Havel's essay was a reflection of the quandary in which human rights were really born. Havel was often explicit about the strategic nature of his substitution of legalized morality for politicized struggle. And he insisted that denial of politics could not escape politics and was not meant to do so. Havel sometimes claimed that moral appeals—"living in truth," as Polish dissident Adam Michnik already called it in 1976—were really political immediately and per se. In dissent, Havel wrote, there was "an unambiguous political dimension. If the main pillar of the system is living a lie, then it is not surprising that the fundamental threat to it is living the truth." In this sense, morality had a "very special political significance," establishing what fellow Charter 77 activist Václav Benda dubbed the same year a "parallel polis." Other times, Havel was keen to point out that the moral displacement of politics brought about the conditions for political change even in postponing it. "Whether, when and how [moral dissent] will eventually produce dividends in the form of specific political changes is even less possible to predict. But that, of course, is all part of living within the truth." In this way, Havel promised "unforeseen social unrest and explosions of discontent" as eventual results available only if they were given up as direct ends. The promise of political transformation mattered especially since Havel was speaking to reform communists who still dominated Charter 77 in the earliest years—most notably former government minister Jiri Hájek, who retained his Marxist humanist hopes and insisted that "the contemporary socialist system of our country [is] a self-evident foundation and framework within which these [human rights] treaties are to be realized."[82]

At a deeper level, however, Havel claimed that human rights could not simply mean politics at a later date or by another means. Morality, he maintained, could permanently substitute for politics. In this vein, Havel indulged the belief that politics is a matter of "abstract visions" where morality connects directly with "individual people." The implication was that it was the failure of politics to be concrete enough that also led it to be open to a terrible opportunism. Meanwhile, morality remained "provisional," "negative," "minimal" and "simple." (The resonance of this stance with Amnesty International's philosophy is obvious.) A morality rooted in a "hidden sphere" and not practical concerns provided purity and authenticity, not compromise, violence, and failure. A mentor figure to Havel, Patočka had put this perhaps most clearly in his defense of Charter 77, two months before his death soon after the group formed: "The concept of *human rights*," he wrote, "is nothing but the conviction that states and society as a whole also consider themselves to be subject to the sovereignty of moral sentiment, that they recognize something unqualified above them, something that is bindingly sacred and inviolable even for them, and that they intend to contribute to this end with the power by which they create and ensure *legal* norms."[83]

In this spirit, Havel in the end considered morality—"antipolitics," as Hungarian dissident Gyorgy Konrád dubbed it—something more than strategic, reflecting a genuine and systematic alternative. Aside from somehow leaving a residue in law, Havel insisted, morality rooted in inner life has "nothing to do with politics." Morality would allow for people to transcend politics not as a stopgap necessity but as a permanent achievement, in a bold "reconstitution of the position of people in the world, their relationships to themselves and to each other, and to the universe." Ultimately, there was nothing personal or idiosyncratic about Havel's indecision: was morality the sole and best politics or could it provide a way beyond politics for good? The dilemma defined the origins of widespread appeals to human rights. What Havel called "the purity of this struggle" proposed a brilliant but ambiguous way both to enact and to transcend politics— at least for a time. For its breakthrough was also to be its burden. As one of the premier analysts of East Central European dissidence, Tony Judt, explained in a sympathetic warning, "Precisely because it is functional it also has finitude."[84]

As in the Soviet Union and Latin America before, the explosion of dissent in Eastern Europe depended on coalition, with revisionist standard-bearers as well as with religious forces. In Poland, especially, but Czechoslovakia as well, political Catholicism was of supreme importance, as the role of Karol Wojtyła (John Paul II after his unexpected election as pope in October 1978) in international politics was to show. In Poland, the emergence of human rights claims had depended on an unprecedented alliance of formerly revisionist intellectuals with the Catholic Church, and with constant "insistence on the primacy of ethics [and] the moralization of politics." Human rights figured in this sense in the 1975–76 opposition to new constitutional amendments that proposed to undermine Poland's autonomy in the Soviet sphere. After 1977, the moralization of dissent became ubiquitous.[85]

Without gainsaying the relevance of Christian forces even in the 1970s, what matters in the long view is that they had much less of a propriety claim on human rights than in the 1940s, when Christianity counted so much in both defining and marginalizing the idea. The world had changed since then. Progressive Christianity, both Catholic and Protestant, had exploded around the world without clear connection to human rights. It was not by accident, of course, that Carter gave his classic speech on foreign policy and human rights at Notre Dame University, a Catholic institution, where he was honored along with Brazil's Cardinal Arns.[86] But in America, partisanship for human rights had lost the religious associations of the earlier era, for Catholics and for mainline Protestants.[87] The most revealing case was the Western European one, where transnational Christianity—more particularly, Catholicism—had once done so much to give human rights their meaning. But Christianity entered freefall precisely in these lands in the 1960s.[88] Though some audiences were capable of recognizing the strong religious elements in human rights both under the Eastern bloc and in Latin America, what made the fortune of human rights in the era were the moves of the secular left, including American liberals and the European left, to incorporate the language.

In Europe, there were still other utopian paths available, even ones more prominent in the same era. But they proved to be cul-de-sacs. The easiest to forget remains the new wave of "Eurocommunist" proposals, according to which the still powerful West European communist parties proposed to establish their own "warm" alternative to the refrozen east. For a while in the early 1970s, Eurocommunism looked very promising, to the point that Czech opposition figures pursued connections with it before turning to human rights after 1975. But where Eurocommunism attempted to transcend a Cold War logic, its explicitly political way to do so collapsed. There was also a great deal of attention to so-called Western Marxism, amid a wave of intellectual ferment on the left after 1968 unprecedented in the postwar era. The search for dissident versions of socialism betrayed by history spawned a generation's labor of intellectual recovery, only to face the passing of their moment of inspiration. And some pilgrims, Leszek Kołakowski most notably, were dropping the revisionist schemes that had helped make them icons of the new left. In 1968, the year of his departure from Poland, Kołakowski still insisted that utopianism remained essential, in spite of the now self-evident ease of its perversion, but soon responded to the efflorescence of human rights with the curt argument that no socialism in power would ever respect them.[89] That some found in human rights not a new utopia but rather a response to a god that failed is without doubt, and allowed for deeply conservative interpretations of the idea to find a hearing from the beginning.

As the rise of human rights on the French scene shows, it was nevertheless the transformation of the left that proved the most vital agent of change, since there human rights triumphed due to competition within the left rather than with its rivals, and it transpired through the substitution of utopias. In Paris, as in Latin America in the 1960s, the collapse of the plausibility of Soviet communism did not lead to the demise of revolutionary aspirations: it sparked the search for a better, purer form of communism.[90] After 1968, when a few pioneers began to draw the lessons of Prague, a generation of students was more impressed by the upheaval in Paris, which sparked a huge wave of *gauchisme*. Trotskyism experienced a revival, but it was Maoism that—among a thousand leftist sects—was the most striking beneficiary of the search for revolutionary purity, almost totally unaffected by contemporary exposés of the Cultural Revolution's deadly meaning.

Dissidence first came to the fore within *gauchisme* rather than against it. Mathematician Leonid Plyushch, who mattered most in the early days for the French left because of his Marxist loyalties, came together with revisionist communists suffering under Czech "normalization" who were also made *causes célèbres* in the early 1970s leftist ambiance. Based on a pre-1968 tradition of organizing for dissidents in the name of "socialist legality," and provoked by the Prague Spring and its destruction, intellectuals organized numerous demonstrations and distributed many petitions for dissidents. The October 23, 1975 rally in the Salle de Mutualité for Plyushch's release—he had been a founding member of the Soviet Action Group and was subsequently institutionalized as a psychiatric patient—drew 5,000 participants, apparently the largest such event in these years in any country. When the French Communist Party joined the denunciations and the USSR released the mathematician to travel to Paris, it was a moment of celebration in which it appeared that dissidence could enable leftist activism to cause a seemingly intractable communism to budge.[91]

But soon, such leftist appeals to dissidence to indict the Soviet regime and the archaic French Communist Party took on a life of their own. They reached a kind of self-destructive acme in the form of the "new philosophy," which went so far in the decisive year of 1977 as to indict politics as such, thus bringing French leftists onto a similar terrain as that favoring human rights before and elsewhere. André Glucksmann, the main new philosopher along with Bernard-Henri Lévy, set the tone. Earlier part of the far left, Glucksmann had fastened on Solzhenitsyn in 1974–5 as part of an appeal for an anarchist populism. But Glucksmann's hatred of the Soviet state soon led him to indictments of politics per se, with the move to morality saving the desire for purity from the leftist political entanglements that had once inspired it. In his tome *The Master Thinkers,* Glucksmann indicted all modern philosophical currents for complicity in "power." Lévy's remarkable *Barbarism with a Human Face*—the other master text of the new philosophy—doubtless went furthest in illustrating the conditions for the breakthrough of human rights consciousness. Giving up Glucksmann's vestigial populism, Lévy condemned politics totalistically as a domain of certain failure. A *gauchiste* in the post-1968 moment, Lévy first found in Solzhenitsyn in 1975 the meaning of "the destiny of the Western left." The lesson he soon drew from his reading, however, was a simple one: utopias always come to grief. Lévy's famous book, abetted by his dashing appearance on television, proposed morality instead. He recommended writing "treatises on ethics," and out of allegiance to the moral principles of human rights moved to co-found Action Contre la Faim, a humanitarian group that now exists in many countries. After being too long fooled by the ruses of collective utopia in politics, Lévy explained, the task was now to save individual bodies.[92]

In these transformations, the mobilization of the grassroots and the intellectuals proceeded without any equivalent to Carter's role across the ocean. As Valéry Giscard d'Estaing, then French prime minister, explained, the American president's attitude towards dissidents was a troublesome and disrespectful interference with détente, and his socialist rival François Mitterrand—true to his strategy of coalition-building with communism that eventually brought him to power—agreed.[93] On the ground and in the mind, however, dissidence and dissidents achieved a kind of totemic status; Julia Kristeva—Bulgarian refugee and former Maoist—proclaimed "the dissident" a "new type of intellectual" in 1977, in the teeth of others on the left who denounced the substitution of dissidence for revolution. It was in the atmosphere of the crisis of utopias old and new that human rights broke through. "How not to be astonished at the suddenly restored fortunes of this theme and slogan of human rights that, not long ago, one would have thought amongst the most permanently disqualified for use?" one-time anarchist Marcel Gauchet asked in 1980. "Only yesterday, they were . . . the vulgar instrument of the dominant ideology, dismantled with the smallest effort by the least beginner in the techniques of suspicion," he observed. "Yet somehow the old has become new, and what was most suspect is now beyond suspicion, and now the outmoded, wordy, and hypocritical human rights have regained grace, virginity, and a kind of vivacious audacity in the eyes of the most subtle and exigent members of the avant garde."[94] The impressive transformation was due essentially to the moralistic interpretation of human rights that made such inroads on the ground of the apparent failure of political redemption.

Yet while such moralistic strictures were indeed epochmaking in affording a departure from revolutionary visions, they did not break completely from those visions, either in France, or—with due allowance for national variation—elsewhere. One of the distinctive features of human rights consciousness in the crucial years of the 1970s was that appeal to morality could seem pure even where politics had shown itself to be a soiled and impossible domain. But the French scene makes especially vivid how the break with politics occurred in explicit or implicit fidelity to earlier aspirations. It transferred the aspiration to purity once associated with revolutionary ardor to the less totalistic program of human rights. Human rights were preferable because they were strategically necessary and practically feasible, but also because they were morally pure. The disavowal of earlier utopias took place in part out of the aspiration to achieve through a moral critique of politics the sense of a pure cause that had once been sought in politics itself.

But then, this was Bronislaw Baczko's point, when he diagnosed the move from florid utopianism to one that dared not speak its name in the space of just as few years. In 1968, human rights were in crisis, because their partisans had not found a way to ally themselves with an exploding wave of popular movements. But they hit on a way to do so only amid the exhaustion of utopian energies of the era and through a move from politics to morality. It was the crucial imaginative transformation that mattered. In the long view, what the substitution of moral for political utopianism meant is that human rights came to the world as its partisans abjured the maximalism that had once lent utopias glamor—especially utopias that required profound transformation, or even revolution and violence.

Among the dissidents, explicit debate continued about whether to remain true somehow to socialism, even as Western actors quickly left behind the historical matrix of the origins of human rights consciousness. "Although I have had more than enough opportunity to rage at failed and moribund utopias," Slovak dissident Milan Simecka reflected in the mid-1980s, "now, years later, I have made my peace with them. Not that I believe in their power to save mankind, [but] without them our world would be that much worse. . . . A world without utopias would be a world without social hope, a world of resignation to the status quo and the devalued slogans of everyday political life."[95] Havel, in response, worried that it was crucial to avoid blueprints, "doing without utopias"—although it remained crucial to preserve "a state of openness towards mysteriously changing and always rather elusive and never quite attainable ideals such as truth and morality."[96]

The minimalism of human rights consciousness deeply affected how its "concern" worked in the era. In the near term, to be sure, the campaign for human rights focused overwhelmingly on the Eastern bloc, along with Latin America, rather than on the poorest nations of the developing world. The most famous institutional locus for the crystallization of transnational human rights activities was the Helsinki process, given the follow-up monitoring meetings mandated by the agreement. When it had been signed, no one could have predicted that Eastern bloc dissidents would mobilize in such numbers, or that an American president would throw himself into the cause. Already in 1975, Millicent Fenwick, a New Jersey congresswoman who had traveled to the Soviet Union on an official tour and met Yuri Orlov and other dissidents, proposed the legislation that created a U.S. Helsinki Commission. But in the spring and summer of 1977, in anticipation of the first October meeting in Belgrade, Yugoslavia, the Helsinki process excited much new interest. The Ford Foundation and other philanthropies began to pour money into American initiatives, both organizational and academic. It funded the creation of Helsinki Watch (later Human Rights Watch) and the pioneering Columbia University Center for the Study of Human Rights, to take the most prominent examples of NGO advocacy and academic attention.[97]

But the human rights optic had to become relevant to the entire world stage, and it did so rapidly if selectively. Often, ignorance of some global crimes and single-minded pursuit of others followed from a paucity of information, as in the case of the Cambodian genocide. But ideological factors mattered too. The early enthusiasm of many French leftists for the Khmer Rouge, which was not based on ignorance alone, suggests as much. Concern for Latin American depredations of—sometimes reforming—revolutionaries did not lead Amnesty International to drop its requirement that those who were committed to violence could not become objects of concern. Violence against groups that remained themselves violent did not cross onto the moral radar. Carter's own Cold War selectivity was obvious from the start, in spite of his good intentions. And by 1978 Irving Kristol was already preparing the complaint that Carter's alleged coddling of left-wing dictators compared to his harsh treatment of rightist ones needed to be reversed—which would happen as soon as Ronald Reagan came to power.[98]

The substitution of idealisms affected the selection and framing not least of violent utopias in the "third world," as the case of Indonesia showed. Even as Amnesty International and other Western groups focused on continuing political imprisonment of opponents of the repressive regime in Jakarta, they found nothing outrageous in the much more violent depredations in Indonesia unleashed in East Timor against an indigenous movement for self-determination. While the availability of information mattered here, ideology did too: the East Timorese "resistance" continued to conceive of its cause in terms of postcolonial self-determination, adopting strategies of armed violence, and therefore fell outside the pale of empathy. The triumph of human rights activism thus depended on a decline in elite sympathies for once-romantic anticolonial nationalism. By the late 1970s, self-determination, like other transformative political utopias, had lost its appeal to Western observers, especially because of its frequently violent outcomes. An idealism based on human rights served as an alternative. Not enough is known about the changing terms of resistance to apartheid in South Africa, which had formerly been viewed internationally through an anticolonialist optic, especially when it opted for violence. But its transformation as a cause seems similar. Though it was easy to see the violence on both sides of the Soweto uprising of mid-1976, even when the South African state cracked down on it brutally, the international *movement* against apartheid was evolving into a human rights struggle like others elsewhere.[99]

Whether, with their redefinition in the 1970s and the explosion of their public reputation, human rights made a practical difference is hard to say. Symbolic rhetoric could often be politically powerful, as the risky decision by Brazilian activists to time their denunciation of torture to coincide with Jimmy Carter's visit in March 1978 shows. Even though Carter's administration did not apply human rights policies to Asian affairs, the president's visit to China prompted a self-proclaimed "Human Rights Group" to mount a poster campaign suggesting that Chinese citizens must benefit from human rights too. Meanwhile, the invocations by Carter had unexpected consequences not just abroad but at home. Gay rights activists began to describe their cause (also spiking in public consciousness at this moment) as a human rights campaign. Harvey Milk, the San Francisco activist who became the first openly gay elected official in the nation, incorporated the phrase into speeches, and groups forming nationwide even changed their names to reflect the new relevance of human rights.[100]

For all the complexities of its impact on the way events around the world and at home were singled out for empathy and engagement, the human rights revolution of the 1970s ultimately followed from a transformation of hopes for all peoples everywhere. As Sakharov reflected in late 1978, having witnessed the remarkable upsurge of the language, "the ideology of human rights . . . serve[s] as a foothold for those who do not wish to be aligned with theoretical intricacies and dogmas, and who have tired of the abundance of ideologies, none of which have brought mankind simple human happiness." After their moment of prominence, the hard work began of ushering in an age of institutionalizing simple happiness. Jerome Shestack, member of the International League and the AJC (and later American delegate to the UN Commission on Human Rights) gave a talk in July 1977—a pinnacle moment for human rights—admitting that the "heady times" were also for NGOs "the season of their discontent. Now, at the very height of their popularity, they can slow the tide of human rights abuse only a trifle. . . . They look into a mirror of the times and see not a sleeping Hercules, as they hoped, but Sisyphus."[101] The strenuous, unending labors of Sisyphus that were beginning then have been admirable—and absurdist. Focusing on the exact differences the transnational human rights movement made certainly matters. But it cannot skip over the fundamental prior question: why are this concept and this movement the ones with which many people affiliated at the time and have affiliated since? If human rights have made any historical difference, it was first in their competitive survival as a motivating ideology in the confusing tumult of 1970s social movements, as they became bound up with the widespread desire to drop utopia and have one anyway. And their substitution of plausible morality for failed politics may have come at a price.

5

Today it seems self-evident that among the major purposes—and perhaps the essential point—of international law is to protect individual human rights. "At the start of the new century," one observer writes, "international law, at least for many theorists and practitioners, has been reconceived. No longer the law of nations, it is the law of human rights."[1] If that transformation is one of the most striking there is in modern law and legal thought, it is even more surprising that it really began only yesterday. Not only did the prehistory of international law through World War II provide no grounds for this development; for decades after, there would have been no way to believe or even to guess that human rights might become the touchstones they are today. Neither drawing from the humane spirit of founders centuries ago nor the recoil to World War II's atrocities, human rights for international lawyers too are rooted in a startling and recent departure.

Yet in a short few decades, human rights have occupied the very center of the activities of international lawyers, just as international law itself has taken on a high profile in contemporary moral consciousness. Peripheral before as a widespread framework for improvement, international law is perhaps the prime beneficiary of the recent crisis and recasting of utopian aspirations. After the 1990s, a model of international criminal adjudication, tried and discarded after World War II, was revived as a response to ethnic cleansing and genocide in the former Yugoslavia and Rwanda. Later, it was established as a general international regime, with the International Criminal Court's creation. Though the agenda now called "transitional justice" of responding to past outrages was not envisioned in the 1940s as part of the same enterprise as the formulation of human rights, in their current versions they have been combined. Since 2001, the Geneva Conventions of 1949 governing the conduct of warfare—though they do not mention human rights—have skyrocketed in prominence, especially in campaigns for those detained at the U.S. government's Guantanamo Bay facility for their part in terrorism. Below the level of newspaper headlines, numerous international human rights treaties began to be crafted during the 1970s and have proliferated since, forbidding torture and discrimination against women and proclaiming the rights of children and indigenous peoples.

Debates swirl around whether the injection of human rights law into international affairs genuinely improves them.[2] What has received less attention, however, is how recently international lawyers themselves turned to their now familiar concern with human rights. In organizing themselves in the mid-nineteenth century as a new profession, international lawyers adopted the goal of mastering power through rules. Formalizing actual interstate relations mattered, it was hoped, because formalization itself—the construction of rules supervised by a benevolent and progressive caste of enlightened jurists—would bring more humanity to world affairs. States would not have to sacrifice sovereignty, which indeed had to be regarded as the foundation stone of world order. But international rules achieved through treaty and custom would inevitably lead sovereigns away from fruitless contention and toward harmonious integration. International lawyers would advance civilization through their patient work, as rules themselves—interpreted in an increasingly enlightened way—made belligerency recede. Their mission was, of course, always a difficult one, albeit largely self-imposed. Through World War II, the search for an intellectually plausible, morally sane, and politically acceptable middle point between complacent description of the vagaries of state relations and the grandiose prescription of a

peaceful globe left international lawyers vulnerable to two contending accusations. One was that they had no authority to improve the
world as they found it, the other that they stuck so close to state
power as to foreclose other, and better, moral dreams. Their idolatry
of state sovereignty as the basic unit of international order lent considerable credence to this last charge.[3]

But just for that reason, the inherited program of international
lawyers does very little to explain why international law assumed its
current association with "human rights." Though the connection
now seems natural and necessary, the forms international lawyers—
in the twentieth century, typically university professors, and sometimes functionaries for their states or international organizations—
hoped to embed in world affairs had diverse contents. How long it
took for this moral project to incorporate individual human rights,
let alone move closer and closer toward identifying the very purposes
of international law with their advancement, is so far little known.
This connection did not crystallize before the mid-1970s, prompted
by the widespread reformulation of idealism in terms of "human
rights." The American case sketched in international context here,
cutting across the entire post–World War II era, from the immediate
aftermath of conflict through the decolonization interlude through a
stark 1970s caesura, shows that international lawyers did not so much
guard the flame as join the trend.

The aftermath of World War II, always viewed as a breakthrough
period for human rights, was one in which the concept made next to
no inroads in the discipline of international law. Indeed, a return to
the sources shows that most members of the public international law
bar were convinced years before the Universal Declaration of Human
Rights confirmed their fears that human rights were not to be more
than paper promises in the postwar era. In particular, they were
aware that the Dumbarton Oaks agreements of 1944—which un-
veiled the great power foundations of postwar order for all to see—
meant the end of human rights and not the beginning. The rueful or
enthusiastic acceptance of Cold War division by international law-

yers only reinforced this conclusion. Already by war's end, they knew they could not sally forth under a banner inscribed with dead letters. Just as interesting, international lawyers were so painfully cognizant of the anticolonialist interpretation of human rights in the guise of the right to self-determination of peoples that they rejected human rights as such as dangerous—so dangerous as to be avoided until unexpected developments allowed their appropriation. Only the passing of the anticolonialist moment in human rights history and the surprising reclamation of human rights in their antitotalitarian guise in the 1970s led international lawyers to reevaluate their long-confirmed positions in this regard.

The long-term trajectory of the field looks different when the recent incorporation of human rights is made the focus. Though international law certainly did suffer a relative marginalization in the early Cold War era, developments in the later Cold War and the present era opened the way to a golden age for the discipline beyond the wildest dreams of its Victorian founders. The ultimate—or at least recent—trajectory of international law is not its "fall" but its "rise," as people began to embrace it as a morally attractive mechanism for social change. And it is clear that the circuitous doctrinal path to human rights was an essential part of its reversal of fortune.

The integration of human rights after several decades of bypassing them—especially in the American case—is important for a second reason. It graphically documents the relevance of social movements to legal priorities. Recovering from a long period of cultish admiration for elite judges, especially Earl Warren's Supreme Court, observers of American constitutional politics have learned to praise the indispensable role of social movements in reshaping the national legal agenda.[4] Now, it is far less tempting to celebrate the heroics of the higher judiciary alone without acknowledging that they have depended on the power of social activism surging from below to do their work. Similarly, because human rights achieved no real backing from social movements in the 1940s, international lawyers simply bypassed the concept after flirting with it in wartime. It was only when human rights surged in public consciousness thanks to the energy of later social movements that the concept finally gained its opening as a priority of international lawyers too.

As Allied victory approached in World War II, few of the huge number of proposals for postwar peace arrangements predicted a central role for international law (just as few mentioned the concept of human rights). It was far more common, for instance, to debate how to solve the "German problem" through political means. The basic threat for international lawyers in wartime, in any event, was not the scuttling of human rights but the irrelevance of any idealistic proposal their discipline might make. After the collapse of the League of Nations, and its legalistic reputation, international law during World War II faced a deep challenge. It was in *this* struggle for survival that members of the profession felt they had to intervene: to vindicate any role for their body of rules (and their discipline) after the interwar disaster. Far from favoring human rights, international lawyers confronted a more basic task: to argue that the new order should be based on formalized rules rather than naked arrangements of power, like alliance balancing and security architectures. The case for "peace through law" (in famed émigré Hans Kelsen's phrase) had to be revisited from first principles. And compared to the outcome at the conclusion of World War I, the argument was to be unsuccessful the second time around.[5]

There were both British and American projects, beginning around 1941, to outline the future importance and shape of international law, which would need to be revised in order to play any role once peace came.[6] One American revived an already forgotten interwar proposal for an international declaration of rights; but Americans, from 1942, were most concerned with the preservation of any relevance for their subject.[7] Central British lawyers tended to be less emphatic about the deficiencies of inherited doctrine and less visionary in their reformist hopes, though they yearned for some force to return the field to prominence as a crucial instrument for achieving a stable and progressive international order. "International Law will not exorcise the catastrophe of war; nor will it abolish power politics," leading interwar international lawyer Sir Cecil Hurst allowed in 1947. "Yet we all know that International Law has an essential part to play in the future."[8]

Though state sovereignty had been the central premise of the field during the nineteenth century, the general sentiment during World War II, under the impress of interwar realist and institutionalist critiques of the idea, was that this body of law had to find some additional, alternative footing. A number of Anglo-American figures—Hersch Lauterpacht most famously—were suggesting a turn to the individual not just as the subject of international law, but as a new addressee and partisan. "[A]ll law and all government exist for the benefit of the individual human being," Clyde Eagleton, New York University law professor, declared in 1946. "If he knew that international law could help him, he would give it the support which it needs and without which it can not serve him properly. The international lawyer will not help educate the people in this direction by writing dissertations on the *Clausula rebus sic stantibus* or the *ius postliminii* and doing nothing else." But if there was a rosy era of forward thinking in which the individual surged, it was immediately overtaken by a drive to peace in which international lawyers found themselves in a more elemental struggle for any voice.[9]

The forging of the peace, and especially the founding of the United Nations, signaled to all international lawyers that the reign of state sovereignty had not seen its last days, and by and large they respectfully fell in line. In the Dumbarton agreements, human rights were practically omitted, while in the UN Charter they were reduced to embellishment—a fact that international lawyers were well positioned to understand. It was more worrisome, in any case, that not only human rights but also international law itself seemed to be out of place against the background of the era's grim realism. The campaign that followed, given this more basic challenge, turned around the last-ditch preservation of a role for law of any kind. The General

Assembly, the UN Charter said, reprising what the bar regarded as a critical provision of the League of Nations covenant, must ensure the "encouragement of the progressive development of international law and its codification." But it was clear this was a minor victory. "[I]nternational law has a secondary position in the Charter," one American commented just after its promulgation. "The pendulum of political thinking has swung from the 'idealism' of Woodrow Wilson's day to the other extreme, the 'realism' of . . . San Francisco."[10]

In this crisis of relevance, disarray reigned. It was not even obvious that the promotion of peace that international law was supposed to shoulder in some new way definitely implied a turn to the individual, let alone human rights. Skepticism, not enthusiasm, also applied to what many felt to be rearguard appeals to "natural law." That concept certainly did have some play, following from the temptation to blame twentieth-century disaster on the "positivism" according to which all valid norms originated in the state. But few thought old natural law provided a viable alternative. The same ambivalence surrounded the turn to the individual as a potential subject of international law. In France in particular, interwar criticisms by Léon Duguit and others that saw individualism as the foundation of the modern national sovereignty, not the alternative to it, remained powerful. If so, it would not be easy to enshrine the individual as a new element in international law, when individualism and sovereignty had always been bound up together in theory and practice. Even in England, the lasting memory of the assault on individualist *laissez-faire* on the domestic scene left some proclaiming the need, as sociologist Morris Ginsberg did in late 1944, for "a radical abandonment of individualism in international affairs."[11]

If there was any window in the eyes of international lawyers for the turn to the legalization of individual rights, it was in wartime, not later. Thereafter, it was obvious that grand principles were being marginalized by the UN Charter, not advanced by it. Already in 1946, given the striking paean to sovereignty in the UN Charter's Article 2, leading British international lawyers could dismiss the concept of human rights as little more than "the battle-cry of well-meaning re-formers and a harmless diversionary pastime of less progressive con-temporaries." The realities of the UN's formation, however necessary to embellish for a wider public, had to be stared in the face. "[T]here can be no happy future for the world," one international lawyer re-marked bitterly in 1947, "when citizens, who are free to express them-selves, do not protest and protest again at the chicanery of forty-five important States . . . behaving like vote-catching politicians when power is achieved." But citizens did not protest. Internationalists of the era, indeed, endorsed the settlement as the best available solu-tion. And so international lawyers by and large dismissed human rights as the fig leaf for an international association of states large and small.[12]

If some international lawyers retained a sliver of hope in the or-namental accoutrements of the UN Charter, they were also rebuked for doing so. No less a figure than Manley Hudson, former Harvard law professor and judge at the Permanent Court of Justice, could de-cry in 1948 such readings as not simply wishful but dangerous. "It is difficult to conceive of the possibility of making substantial progress in the development of international law unless a scrupulous respect obtains for the integrity of international instruments," he warned colleagues trying to pretend that UN language bore any serious legal implications. In particular, he insisted, nothing could be inferred from the Charter's Article 56, which merely made the UN's Eco-nomic and Social Council steward of the human rights mentioned in the document's preamble, without giving those rights legal force. Most lawyers agreed with Hudson that charter negotiations had postponed the topic of human rights rather than secured it, as the new international order reposed on the most traditional foundations of state sovereignty. References to peace, justice, and law at San Fran-cisco, not human rights, would have to suffice as potential openings for the profession's role.[13]

Lauterpacht, best known for his championship of human rights ideas in Anglo-American international law circles after the war, tried

valiantly to argue against this realistic conclusion. Starting in wartime with his barebones proposed declaration, he turned in the first
postwar years to agitate within the International Law Association,
and eventually wrote his *International Law and Human Rights* (1950).
But he did so with remarkable candor about the failure of his cause,
both at the level of international organization and within his own
profession. He forthrightly acknowledged that the Atlantic Charter
offered only a "purely verbal" provision for the Four Freedoms. And
while he continued his agitation after Dumbarton Oaks (unlike most
other Anglo-American international lawyers, who read those documents as writing on the wall), he knew the UN Charter made it difficult to believe that traditional principles of sovereignty had been
much undermined.[14]

Famously, Lauterpacht denounced the Universal Declaration as
dangerous because useless, in the name of agitation for a legally
meaningful turn to human rights. But not only were Lauterpacht's
alternatives to sovereignty out of step with developments outside the
discipline; international lawyers themselves were heaping scorn on
those proposals by the late 1940s. In 1949, in a radio talk, Lauterpacht
criticized the declaration for its nonbinding character and emphasized that the charter, for all its concessions to sovereignty, remained
the foundation that alone could authorize any future developments.
But it was thin, and he warned fellow international lawyers not to try
"to kindle sparks of legal vitality" in the Universal Declaration. Instead, he concluded hopefully that the UN Charter's Article 2, which
restated a traditional notion of the impregnability of sovereignty, did
not reduce the UN's potential to enforce human rights in the future
to "a minimum or to render [it] altogether nugatory." A realistic appraisal of the death of human rights in the era had to be the basis for
any hopes for their reanimation in a very indefinite future.[15]

Whatever the textual care of his mild plea to leave room for human rights to return later, however, it can be said that the international law consensus of the time rejected it. The repudiation that met
his doctrinal argument also applied to Lauterpacht's rosy judgment

of the geopolitical situation. Like French opposite number René Brunet, Lauterpacht expressed the hope that the Soviet collectivist suppression of the pioneering rights its "Stalin" Constitution of 1936 had proclaimed would be "transitory"—an assumption which by 1947 was being treated with jeers even by other international lawyers, not simply in the realist circles of the emerging political science discipline of international relations. The world was not about to converge around individual rights simply because the Soviets, too, had listed them so early. Lauterpacht's own reception thus shows that there was no grand annunciation of human rights in international law, whose specialists were indeed aware earlier than most that they were not plausible enough a project to incite allegiance. The doubt, not the confidence, that postwar international lawyers expressed about the prospects of human rights is what matters in judging the trajectory of the discipline later.[16]

At this moment of crisis and uncertainty, it was tempting to look back to foundations for guidance. But even as Lauterpacht claimed that Hugo Grotius, the early modern Dutch natural law thinker, would have welcomed human rights, others concluded that their founder had lost his authority. The idea of a "Grotian tradition" had never been much more than a revealing act of retroactive canonization, and could not afford any authority for the international protection of human rights. In his famous paper on Grotius, Lauterpacht acknowledged that his predecessor's texts offered the idea of "fundamental rights and freedoms of the individual" no support. But what, Lauterpacht asked, if Grotius' failure to do so were regarded as an "exception" to "the otherwise uniformly progressive trend" of his thought—a kind of inadvertent mistake? But just as he was almost alone in his championship of human rights in the field, Lauterpacht was also alone in pretending that Grotius would have championed them if he had simply thought about it harder. Others, like University of London international law professor H. A. Smith, saw that not only the distant history of Grotius and company but even the recent past of interwar authorities were now in abeyance—inapplicable to the emerging situation of superpower standoff, which had never obtained before. "The world in which we now live is more remote from that of our fathers than that of our fathers from the age of Grotius."[17]

For such reasons, there is very little evidence that the international law bar welcomed the Universal Declaration of Human Rights when it came, as they were well aware that its achievement had come at the price of legal enforceability.[18] Apart from the Frenchman René Cassin and the Canadian John Humphrey, lawyers were not prominent in its formulation in 1946–48. The Institut de Droit international—the discipline's central historic institution—began meeting again in August 1947, and the first item on the agenda was a draft declaration of rights with a view to a prospective binding convention. Introducing the discussion in Lausanne, Charles de Visscher, a highly admired jurist through the postwar era, decried the fact that the UN Charter had forsaken the moral principles on which the postwar order was supposed to be based. Yet for the institute after 1947, human rights became a nontopic. And while as late as 1949 the American Society of International Law could still give some attention to the prospect of international rights covenants, the obvious stall of the move to legality made human rights uninteresting.[19]

As a result, no major textbooks or treatises of the 1950s or even 1960s give international human rights much attention, and they did not crystallize as the prominent subfield within the discipline they are today. "I want to tell you how deeply I feel about human rights," émigré international lawyer Josef Kunz, who taught at the University of Toledo, assured his audience in 1951. "On the other hand, we must approach the task as scholars, i.e., objectively and critically. Beautiful words alone cannot solve difficult problems." For this reason, the grandiose agenda proclaimed scant years before had been a flash in the pan. "The proposal of some," Kunz wrote in reference to Lauterpacht, "to make individuals direct subjects of international law and to grant them a right of action in a special international court against their own state, has no chance to be realized, for theoretical as well as for practical reasons. Theoretically, it must be understood that our international law and the United Nations Charter are based on the principle of the sovereignty of states. . . . The practical reason is the simple fact that the states are not willing and ready to accept such proposals." Strikingly, it was not even worth guarding the flame.[20]

Far from smashing naïve hopes, the Cold War confirmed lawyerly insight into the persisting realities of power and the imperative against excessive utopianism. Even as they incorporated a heavy dose of realism, of course, international lawyers also committed themselves to finding some progressive uses for rules. They remained committed to the long-term project of mastering power through law, but not human rights law, except indirectly or by other means. Columbia law professor Philip Jessup provides an excellent example of the general path of strategic retreat. In the 1940s, he had shared in the brief hopes for a more thoroughgoing erosion of the principle of sovereignty in favor of individual human rights, but his 1950 *A Modern Law of Nations* registered clearly that these hopes were not viable. The right of nationality as the best way to protect individual rights in the international system, with UN development of human rights systems unlikely to occur, now was the best strategy. Alluding to Theodore Roosevelt's quip that some form of utopia stood as the only alternative to hell, Jessup commented glumly in 1953 that "the choice is not easy when one finds intimations in the learned journals that the 'Utopians' are those who disregard the national interests of their country. Whether it is realistic to believe in Hell, or hellish to believe in realism, I am not prepared to say." In such a climate, he worried that even the name of his august community of international lawyers might have to be changed to "American Society of International Realism."[21]

The marginalization of international law by the Machiavellianism of "international relations," in any case, was not restricted to

America, since it reflected a general paradigm change in a Cold War of global dimensions. It was Hans Morgenthau, a renegade international lawyer and the inventor of international relations, who argued for that shift most strenuously. But there were many others within international law who supplemented an account of the virtues of rules with a picture of the realities of power—with particularly disastrous consequences for any potential emphasis on human rights. Georg Schwarzenberger, an international lawyer born and trained in Germany who taught at University College in London for forty years after the war, had argued already during it that if international law was to become relevant to politics it would have to give up its scientific pretenses and neutralist pose and wade into the fray against totalitarianism left and right. From within international law, much as Morgenthau was doing in America, he pioneered a realist conception that identified interstate power as the true motor of history, with international law its "disguise" after the fact. There was no doubt that these perceptions were general. Even Lauterpacht could acknowledge, for example in a Hebrew University lecture in 1950, that "the lawless conduct of the Second World War" on the Axis side, but even more so "the very part which power played in conquering lawlessness," had "tended to enthrone power as an end in itself."[22]

Not surprisingly, in the postwar period Schwarzenberger argued even more strenuously for the incorporation of insights about power politics into international legal discourse, for a world in which finishing the struggle against totalitarianism mattered most. The prospect of human rights law, he warned, could lead international lawyers to place an ill-advised campaign above the realistic assessment of the politics that drove the World War II alliance apart. "[T]he post-war world woke up to the reality of an unparalleled disregard of human rights," he wrote, not long after the Cold War crystallized. "The last minute attempt at the Conference of San Francisco to make the United Nations responsible for the promotion of human rights and fundamental freedoms was a merely nominal success for the protagonists of this course," Schwarzenberger recorded, almost gleefully. "To assume that a common denominator of human rights could be found between West and East was to ignore the true structure of the people's 'democracies.'"[23]

A year later, Schwarzenberger revised his *Power Politics* (originally published during the war) to include a chapter devastating to the recent flirtation with human rights. It was unsurprising, he insisted, that the achievement of "the draftsmen of our contemporary human rights in the international sphere" had been for nought. "[T]he task of protecting the individual against the sovereign State, and the world powers in particular, has been trustingly left with the representatives of the very powers whose discretionary power is to be curtailed." The verdict of meaninglessness or even counterproductivity applied both at the level of ideology in general and that of UN bureaucracy in particular. After the 1947 *non possumus* decision that the UN Commission on Human Rights must simply throw away any petitions that came its way, Schwarzenberger entered a caustic response. "[T]he activities of the Commission on Human Rights, need hardly be mentioned."[24]

The concept of human rights remained yet more peripheral in legal affairs outside the small college of international lawyers, not simply because of American Cold War imperatives, but also because of the effect of legal realism on many law professors. Pretending to play the skunk at the garden party at the meeting of the American Society of International Law in 1959, international relations specialist Stanley Hoffmann put things bluntly: "in a world in which total politicization has eliminated those areas of domestic and international affairs from which governments used to stay away, it seems to me perfectly vain to hope for an escape from politics . . . To press forward in the field of *universal* definitions of human rights is an invitation to hypocrisy and to heightening political tensions." But the fact of the matter was that he was preaching mostly to the long since converted. If the formalistic project of international law was to hibernate in these circumstances, it meant dropping, not sheltering, human rights. The intellectual and especially the new political forces were simply too powerful to do otherwise.[25]

As the Cold War crystallized, Jessup's highly chastened plea for relevance for his discipline effectively captured the concessions of an international law bar whose pretension to speak for the universal conscience of civilization had no purchase in a bipolar world in which both sides proceeded politically rather than legally. "What has happened within the last thirty years," noted H. A. Smith already in 1947, "is that the loss of common cultural unity upon which the law was originally founded has been destroyed by its own original home, that is to say, in Europe. The process began, but unfortunately did not end, with the Bolshevik revolution in Russia in 1917." For Lord Cyril Radcliffe in 1950—a lawyer then famous for his role in the South Asian partition—human rights were "clothes made too fine for human wear," because the cultural unity required for international law to be meaningful had evaporated. "We smile now to read how a century ago James Lorimer could argue that an Islamic state ought not be admitted into the family of nations because of the essentially intolerant character of Islam," Clive Parry of Cambridge University remarked in a 1953 survey of the state of European international law. "But if we substituted Communism for Mohammedanism, we may perhaps confess that the problem is as large as it ever was, if not larger." Similarly, in 1953 Princeton international lawyer Percy Corbett concluded that anyone interested in the values of human rights would want to pursue them through legalistic enactment least of all. There was no doubt that time had brought "a frosty wind of political reality into the garden planted with such labor and skill by the intellectuals. The climate, it seems, remains obdurately unsuitable; but the pictures in the seed-catalogues are lovely, and who knows when the climate may change?"[26]

As of 1945, therefore, human rights were already on the way out for the few international lawyers who had made them central in wartime, with the Cold War extending rather than upsetting their fate. One important reason was the persistence of state sovereignty in postwar doctrine. True, European international lawyers seem to have preferred far earlier than their American colleagues a slight relaxation of the state's centrality in international law. Cassin could argue that with human rights a breakthrough had occurred with a great future ahead of it. Other Europeans agreed, albeit less exultantly. Max Huber, a Swiss international lawyer famed for his interwar sociological work, treated the human rights developments of the 1940s optimistically, citing Lauterpacht's work approvingly, without mentioning the supervening Cold War; in one of his last articles, Boris Mirkine-Guetzévitch, interwar founder of comparative constitutionalism, wrote similarly. In West Germany and Austria, the move from positivism to naturalism in law waned as time passed, but some— notably Alfred Verdross, once Kelsen's student—argued for human rights as the necessary inference from human dignity for decades.[27]

If, however, Europeans preserved human rights, it was in the frequently Christian, "personalist" key that allowed the concept to take on a conservative meaning as the postwar era began. Personalism provided a powerful idiom for West European incorporation of human rights, as leading figure Charles de Visscher testified in championing the topic when the famed Institut de Droit international coalesced again. Human rights, he wrote, could rely on "a powerful current of ideas that has arisen against the nameless abuses that we have witnessed: it is the personalist conception of society and power." As time passed, such personalism more and more simply rephrased anticommunism and Western unity rather than offering a philosophy of global amity. Even as a scholastic literature grew up around the European Convention on Human Rights (1950) in the early years, there was no serious promotion by European international lawyers of human rights as a wider project, as the European Convention signaled values without bringing a serious legal regime into being. Geographical localization of human rights proved an alternative to their global universalization, not a step toward it. Its result did matter for scholarship, turning European international lawyers interested in human rights toward the doctrinal and institutional particulars of their region. But the same did not happen in the case of Americans and their own regional "inter-American" system. Even compared to its still-backwater European cousin, it had little real significance.[28]

For this reason, human rights as an organizing concept were largely absent through the 1950s and 1960s from the American discipline. And the unfolding of postwar history showed that the last-ditch utopia of rules and its strategic combination with realist insights into power could often marginalize the concept of human rights yet further, rather than husbanding doctrine to await more propitious circumstances. The work of Louis Sohn at Harvard Law School, at the far idealist end of the spectrum in the United States, provides a very illuminating example. Sohn worked throughout the postwar era with the American Association for the United Nations, and occasionally contributed reflections on the state of human rights proposals to its deliberations. Yet when he published, together with Grenville Clark, his idealistic revision proposal for the UN Charter in 1958, he gave priority to democratizing membership and representation, with the premium on peace in a nuclear world, and next modernizing economic development, with the plan explicitly not "extend[ing] to any attempted protection of the individual against the action of his own government." Indeed, the "Bill of Rights" Clark and Sohn appended to their proposal was meant, evidently on the model of American constitutionalism, to provide negative rights *against the United Nations itself* (presumably due to the relative strengthening of the federal center, just as had eventually become necessary when the U.S. Constitution was framed). In other words, through much of the era Sohn was very far from moving toward direct protection of the individual as the path he later claimed international law followed all along.[29]

The case of the dominant Columbia (or larger "Manhattan") school in the United States in this period forces similar conclusions. It inherited the now much chastened idealism of the prior generation, keeping faith in the hope that an "invisible college" of international lawyers—the label Columbia professor Oscar Schachter applied to his brethren—could exercise beneficent influence on mankind. Early in his career, when he still worked for the United Nations, Schachter boldly argued, not simply for Lauterpacht's view of the charter, but even for its powerful implications for American domestic law. But the time was not right for such a view, and Schachter did not pursue it as the 1950s continued.[30]

His colleague Louis Henkin, eventually to become perhaps the most iconic law school activist for the centrality of human rights in the field, focused even less on the topic in his early work. Continuing his teacher Jessup's cautious internationalism, Henkin pursued a two-track academic agenda of investigating the conditions under which the world might avoid nuclear disaster through arms agreements and the constraints American constitutional law might place on incorporation of international legal norms. One of his early publications on the latter track mentioned human rights norms, including the norm against genocide, as examples of a subject that, even without ratifying international legislation, Congress might have the latitude to address for domestic purposes under an expanded view of its foreign affairs power.[31]

Yet Henkin's first actual publication on the topic of human rights, which appeared only in 1965 (thus, when he was about fifty years old), conceded that there was little reason to treat what had once been announced so hopefully as more than moral norms to protect through the general strategy of securing peace and offsetting inequality. "Few appear prepared to build a kingdom of rights built with beams taken from their own eye," he acknowledged—and he was not one of those few. "The principal hope for human rights," he insisted, "lies in continuing international peace, in reduced international tensions, in internal stability, in developing political institutions, and in rising standards of living. For the most part, human rights can only be promoted indirectly." In other words, human rights could not be taken as doctrinal ends in themselves; and the international legal community could best stick to its continuing mission of establishing a secure world and promoting well-being. Not surprisingly, in the first versions of Henkin's classic work on observance of international law, *How Nations Behave,* attention to human rights as a specific feature of the norms that—as he famously argued—most nations followed most of the time was nil. He, too, was very far from the program, in his eventual phrase, of promoting "human rights as rights."[32]

As for that interesting and urbane thinker, Wolfgang Friedmann, who had taught a number of places in the Anglophone world before settling in at Columbia from 1955, he gave even less evidence of devotion to human rights as a central prospective element of international law. His Continental formation made him very different from his "Columbia school" colleagues Henkin and Schachter in this regard. It led him to a sociological contextualization of law generally, not just international law, and prompted him to call for a permanent end to wordy idealism in the discipline. But while he searched in the postwar period for evolutionary and progressive tendencies in the social foundations of law, and claimed international law was moving from coexistence to cooperation, he rejected any move to the individualization of international law, and did not cherish the concept of human rights. As late as 1969, he drily deemed Lauterpacht's doctrinal proposals "somewhat over enthusiastic," with any move to direct individual protection by international law likely "only to a very limited extent." Noting that same year how few countries had ratified the UN covenants on human rights in their first three years of existence, he predicted that "[t]he enormous divergencies between the ideology, political and social systems of the member States of the United Nations make anything like a universal covenant on human rights a rather distant aspiration." Reprising this argument in 1972, Friedmann recommended that it be "to fields less affected by basic political and social beliefs that we . . . turn for some hope that the sheer urgencies of civilized survival will promote the development of international legal institutions and standards." His slaying in a mugging outside Columbia Law School the same year meant he did not live to see the human rights explosion that immediately followed.[33]

In some respects it was the rival "New Haven school" of Myres McDougal and his various associates that at first made far more doctrinal room than any American competitors for human rights. Early in the postwar period, this "policy-oriented" school embedded human rights as one element of the minimum world order it treated as a practical baseline toward which international organization could aim for now. And it named human dignity as the central value in the fuller-bodied maximal order it held out on the horizon for later. Given the blatant Cold War commitments of the school, which were its defining feature, it is surely not wrong to conclude that its members "failed to protect their postulated goal values from a critique of being either an old-fashioned naturalism in disguise or a smoke screen for a defense of American foreign policy." All the same, in comparison, the formalist remnant in the "Manhattan school" and at Louis Sohn's Harvard Law School was less specifically tethered to human rights as a central doctrinal plank.[34]

It was the process of decolonization that made the fortune of human rights at the United Nations—albeit with a stark reconceptualization of their meaning, grounded in the collective right of self-determination. Paradoxically, this transformation made rights still less central for international lawyers. The very priority accorded self-determination in the course of the long move toward the United Nations covenants, far from providing a step toward the vindication of a long-sought project, led to the further marginalization of human rights for the very international lawyers now identified with them.

One might go so far as to claim that it was not World War II and genocide, but anticolonialism and decolonization, that really broke international lawyers' long-term apologia for the state and its projects. Even before decolonization, the state continued its doctrinal rule. Already in the immediate postwar moment, before widespread decolonization, Latin American states championed a clarification of the *droits des États* to correspond with any human rights that the United Nations might try to promote. And lawyers were well aware that, in its first decades, the United Nations was much more the forum for the promotion of sovereign nations than it was for individual human rights. They drew the obvious conclusion that no radical renovation of their discipline away from the state was in the offing. The experts on the UN International Law Commission, charged with formulating a "Declaration of the Rights and Duties of States" right away, could not win the General Assembly's approval for it. But doctrinally, and not just politically, international lawyers continued to think of their subject as a reflection of the affairs of sovereign states.[35]

Then the new states exploded onto the stage of history. The "decolonization of international law" prompted immediate reflections, and slower transformations. The speed of decolonization—and the recomposition of the UN General Assembly—were too rapid and shocking to ignore. After a century-long dalliance with imperialism, however, the difficult process of decolonization of the discipline's assumptions and the pluralization of its membership only made fundamental inroads in the 1970s and 1980s. Even then, not everyone agreed that the old international law could incorporate such novelty. In 1973, Jessup—recently retired from a decade stint on the International Court of Justice—noted that the destabilizing role of the new nations in the international forum had led him to "despair the universals which are accepted in theory if not in practice by the international community." Until the old states and the new states could see eye to eye, he concluded, international law might better simply give up any hope of generalist pretensions.[36]

The forced reflection on the rise of the human rights revolving at the UN around self-determination was only one small facet of the general mood of anxious misgiving that beset international law in its traditional capitals of Europe and its somewhat newer ones on American shores. More than any other development, however, understanding the critique of self-determination by Western international lawyers shows how replete with irony the rise of human rights really was in the 1970s—especially in the doctrinal interests of this discipline. For it was not only the politics of the peace and the origins of the Cold War that extinguished the minor earlier interest in human rights; decolonization made them seem not simply hypocritical slogans, but downright treacherous ones. Some international lawyers had a creditable reason for rejection of self-determination: it was hard to forget the interwar politics of self-determination in Europe, with the disastrous consequences for individuals and groups victimized as contiguous ethnonational groups sought collective redemption. But another clear reason for disciplinary resistance was a more problematic opposition to any fundamental decolonization of international law as new sorts of peoples claimed sovereignty.

Most leading figures were well aware of—and scandalized by— the anticolonialist "capture" of the UN's human rights project, with its installation of self-determination as the first of all human rights. "It would seem difficult more completely to confuse values and to wander farther from the spirit in which the defense of human rights was contemplated," de Visscher, the Belgian, commented acidly on the rise of self-determination, in a classic text of postwar international law. Perhaps characteristically, British jurists criticized the development less with angry vitriol than cutting irony. The British jurist Samuel Hoare (later an early authority in European human rights machinery) made his point most sardonically in the General Assembly:

> In 1948 when the General Assembly had adopted the Universal Declaration of Human Rights, it had not apparently regarded self-determination as a fundamental human right, for the document which was intended to be comprehensive contained no mention to it. The first reference to a "right" of peoples and nations to self-determination occurred in a General Assembly Resolution of 1950; yet by 1952 it was spoken of as "a prerequisite to the full enjoyment of all fundamental human rights." Consequently either the General Assembly had inadvertently omitted the very corner-stone of human rights

from the Declaration or the various delegations at the subsequent session had been so carried away by their enthusiasm and their desire to affirm an important principle that they had failed to give due consideration to the legal and political effects of converting a principle into a universal right.

To this theoretical observation, as time passed, others added practical condemnation of self-determination. Oxford law professor J. E. S. Fawcett worried in the 1960s that "the U.N. has appeared to understand and apply the principle of self-determination for the protection of human rights in ways . . . which have had political effects that are not in the long term in the interest of human rights." There was no way to even contemplate returning human rights to the doctrinal agenda after the Cold War stymied them, without reckoning with the priority of self-determination that Western international lawyers were most apt to treat with considerable misgivings.[37]

It was thus not just Americans for whom the formation of the postcolonial nation-state as the first item on the agenda of human rights was an appalling affront. If they paid attention to human rights in the era, leading American international lawyers who did so wholeheartedly agreed about the perversity of their new framework. As for Hoare, the conversion of self-determination from a principle into a "right" drew especially intense fire. Writing in *Foreign Affairs,* Clyde Eagleton fumed that "the arguments advanced and the action taken would seem to give each individual human being a right to be an independent country. . . . It is sad that anti-colonial resentment should have distorted so noble a principle." Quincy Wright—University of Chicago expert who had advocated human rights strenuously in wartime—posed his objection in logical and doctrinal terms.

> Self-determination is not an individual but a collective right, if indeed it is a right at all, and so has no place in the covenants. If, however, this position is accepted, then the question arises, What is the collectivity that has the right? Is it the imperial state recognized as

a person in international law or is it the colony, minority, or people demanding self-determination and aspiring to such recognition? Clearly, simultaneous "self-determination" by these different collectivities would be likely to precipitate conflict. If, on the other hand, self-determination is an individual right, then all political authority would cease. Every individual could himself determine to change allegiance and to assert his own sovereignty.

Whether in anger or by argument, American lawyers refused to follow human rights where the UN's new states took them.[38]

There was only one interpreter—the forgotten but crucial figure Egon Schwelb—who seriously explored a way to put a progressive face not just on the Cold War delay of the covenant process but also on the anticolonialist rethinking of human rights. A Prague lawyer and city official in the interwar period, Schwelb did long service in the UN Human Rights Division before retiring to Yale Law School, where he taught the first human rights course in the country. Precisely because of the long failure of the covenants, he suggested in 1963, the Universal Declaration "assumed a far greater measure of importance than many of its authors intended." In this era, Schwelb argued, international lawyers could now reclaim Lauterpacht's lost argument of the 1940s by suggesting that there might be a legal obligation to protect human rights inherent in the charter after all—or even in the declaration itself. "The Declaration," Schwelb explained, "took over the function originally contemplated for the International Bill of Rights." Schwelb acknowledged that Lauterpacht had originally decried the toothlessness of the Universal Declaration in 1950. But, Schwelb reported, shortly before his death in 1960 Lauterpacht had "qualified in the light of events the negative attitude which he had taken." Though it confirmed the transformation in meaning of human rights in the spirit of self-determination, Schwelb even appealed to the Declaration for the Granting of Independence to Colonial Countries of 1960 for undermining the assumption that the Universal Declaration could be of no legal validity without the covenants. After all, Schwelb wrote, while the earlier declaration had been labeled a mere "standard of achievement," the newer one proclaimed its agenda "a present necessity," and in effect updated its predecessor from hortatory to obligatory force.[39]

Of course, few if any international lawyers sympathized with this creative argumentation, which dwelled on United Nations texts without regard to its practices. But its almost solitary incubation of a progressive fiction of the unfolding of human rights across the postwar era mattered in the long run. Shortly after, more and more international lawyers began to agree about the increasing legality of the Universal Declaration, though they did so typically not through Schwelb's route but through suggesting that the declaration could advance through custom and opinion. Among Americans, Sohn argued soon after Schwelb for that conclusion, and by March 1968, at Montreal, an evanescent Assembly for Human Rights (a collection of international lawyers and officials called together by Sohn and Seán MacBride of the International Committee of Jurists) could proclaim that the "Universal Declaration of Human Rights constitutes an authoritative interpretation of the Charter of the highest order, and has over the years become a part of customary international law."[40]

These moves were, all the same, experiments by a tiny minority in the face of the more widespread anxiety that the rise of self-determination as the first human right inspired—even among international lawyers. The ingenious arguments made the best of a bad situation—a UN rights regime dead on arrival and saved from its Cold War neutering only by the unexpected rise of the new states. But in these shadowy years, they were not much more than proposals to activate later. At the turn of the 1970s, there was little reason to be enthusiastic about human rights, as Wisconsin law professor Richard Bilder, who prided himself on objective assessment, noted. The notion retained "a rather hollow ring. . . . [T]he condition of man over the last quarter-century seems largely unchanged; indeed, things often seem to be getting worse [and] even some of the concept's staunchest supporters are skeptical whether international efforts offer substantial promise in achieving human rights goals." Of course, things might change, he acknowledged. "One generation's hypocrisy may be the next generation's fighting creed."[41]

It was far more the essential, and external, context of global ideological change in the 1970s that accounts for how human rights became central to American international law for the first time. As a proxy for that development in the largest sense, it is useful to examine the evolution of the career of Louis Henkin, who became the single leading figure on the American scene. Precisely because he was such a disciplinary hero, it is valuable to see that even in his case the development of enthusiasm for human rights came almost out of nowhere and at a surprisingly late date—and due to external circumstances. Other figures did matter, like Frank C. Newman, a Berkeley law professor who turned enthusiastically to human rights between the mid-1960s and the mid-1970s (when he became a California Supreme Court justice). While Schwelb had taught the subject shortly before, Newman's interest in joining advocacy and activism led him to found what was the first law school clinic for human rights in the country. For a number of years, he led his "Berkeley crew" of students to meetings of the UN Commission on Human Rights to assist with claims, and made connections with international academic networks, especially that of Cassin and his colleagues.[42]

It would be hard to overstate Henkin's eventual centrality as "grandfather" of human rights in American international law, idol for younger generations, and model of a career in the field. In his earliest serious engagement with the topic of human rights, however, Henkin shared the general skepticism of what human rights had come to mean at the high tide of anticolonialist sentiment. His arguments were not at all unusual when he registered the common complaint, in his first essay on human rights of 1965, that human rights had now been made unusable, whatever their potential original promise. "[T]he struggle to end colonialism," he wrote, "swallowed up the original purpose of co-operation for promotion of human rights. . . . Anticolonialism . . . colored the human rights covenants[:] Self-determination was added to the roster of human rights as an additional weapon against colonialism though there was no suggestion that this was a right of the individual." He had not addressed the topic before, except in an atmosphere of Cold War skepticism, and now decolonization had made things worse.[43]

Henkin's initial impulse to engage anew with human rights came, it would seem, through his connection with the world of American Jewish advocacy. The American Jewish Committee had made human rights lobbying at the United Nations one facet of its international political agenda. At an AJC-sponsored 1963 conference, Henkin was invited to play the realist rather than the idealist, casting cold water on the more optimistic notion that binding legal covenants—assuming they were feasible at all—were likely to improve enforcement of human rights standards. As he had argued before, the only hope for the values embodied in human rights remained indirection: arms control in bilateral relations, and keeping a watchful eye on UN theatricality. But in the decade after 1968, things changed rapidly, in a series of nonlinear steps.[44]

Tasked by the AJC to evaluate likely political trends in the 1970s, Henkin signed on to the organization's long-affirmed position that "Jewish rights are human rights." No doubt in reference to the recriminations of the recent Tehran conference where self-determination (and criticism of Israeli occupation) ruled, he advised caution: he remarked on behalf of his committee that the United Nations had proved a highly unreliable forum for rights claims, "although Arabs succeeded in airing their charges that Israel had violated human rights in the occupied territories." Even as human rights were gaining in moral authority, if not real legality, they were now proving to be a double-edged sword for Jews. True, Jews had "been in the forefront of organized efforts to improve international recognition, promotion, and protection of human rights." But in view of anticolonialist rhetoric, in the form of abuse of Israel in the international forum, they were right to show "signs of discouragement and doubt about their effort."[45]

In spite of this worry, around the same time Henkin took the lead in setting up the American sister to the International Institute for Human Rights in Strasbourg, which Cassin had founded with his Nobel monies. Like Cassin's outfit, this American institute saw its primary mission as educational, at the university level. Its initial activities included sponsorship of the first-ever compilation of a human rights casebook. Henkin taught his and Columbia Law School's first course on international human rights in 1971–2; Sohn—who strikingly taught the first Harvard Law School course on the topic the same year—published the pioneering casebook in 1973, together with Thomas Buergenthal, his influential student. Late the same year, Henkin testified at Donald Fraser's congressional hearings on American foreign policy and human rights. There, he ruefully reported no real consensus around even what human rights meant, given the developments since the immediate postwar moment when "the U.N. was much smaller and dominated by Western states and Western ideas." Now, except for more general agreement on egalitarianism, the rise of the third world, along with the continuing influence of communism, meant conflict over the very definition of the idea. The only imaginable remedy for the "sense of crisis about international protection of human rights" was UN reform. Given that the rise of grassroots NGOs (which Henkin rarely mentioned) and even Fraser's own hearings mattered because they portended bypassing the UN as an exclusive forum for the human rights idea, it is a revealing affirmation.[46]

For even at this late date, the die was not yet cast. Participating in a 1974 McGill University colloquium on Judaism and human rights, Henkin continued to suggest that the main story of human rights protection was idealistic disappointment. Henkin explicitly warned that idealists would only repeat their past mistakes by pining for radical transformation in the fortunes of their cause. The unavoidable conclusion is that even by that moment in the mid-1970s, with the percolation of dissidence skyrocketing and other forces gathering, no tipping point for the championship of human rights as a doctrinal matter had occurred, for Henkin at least. This was not a personal failing unless he is forced to play the role of prophet: his inability to imagine an impending novelty is simply testimony to how unpredictable it really was.[47]

The discontinuity of 1975–1977 in human rights history in general is there to see in Henkin's career in particular. It is not anticipated in anything he wrote, even as his publications of the immediate moment register its transformative power. From that exciting time, Henkin threw himself completely into the cause, without ever explicitly reflecting on the nonlegal conditions that had made his drastic self-reinvention possible. In 1977, he began a series of colloquia at Columbia University and the next year founded the first human rights center at an American university. (Around the same time, Henkin's wife Alice joined the Aspen Institute and began a series of influential human rights conferences.) Continuing his ties with the AJC projects that had originally drawn him into human rights discussions, Henkin argued now much more emphatically for the centrality of human rights to Jewish politics, after the period in which so many Jews had felt betrayed by the uses of the language against Israel: "The answer to politicization in international forums is to fight it," Henkin argued, "not to abandon those who do and to leave the field to the enemies of human rights." In apparent recognition of the previously unsuspected power of forces outside the United Nations—notably nongovernmental organizations—to define and advance human rights, Henkin joined the board of the Lawyers Committee for Human Rights in 1978 and played a guiding role in its early years. (This NGO is now known as Human Rights First.) And he was not alone among international lawyers, whether they were old hands or recent converts, in registering that the human rights idea had experienced a sudden revolution. Whatever the minor antecedents,

American international lawyers entered their current phase of pursuing human rights in larger numbers and from diverse angles at this moment.[48]

Yet in many ways, in spite of this bumpy trajectory, Henkin's own new enthusiasm for human rights suppressed the exact historical conditions for its occurrence, whether in his own career or in the larger context of forces like NGOs and events like Carter's presidency that made it possible. His pivotal 1978 book *The Rights of Man Today* lays out a potted history of the origins of Euro-American rights, a model pioneered by Lauterpacht before; turns to what is essentially an exercise in the comparison of national constitutions as the chief forum in which the globalization of rights could be achieved; and concludes with a survey of the more newfangled but complementary project of defending rights above and beyond nations. Interestingly, major departures in this progression—most notably that of the caesura between the history of domestic constitutionalism and the history of international law or, within international law, between an age of disappointed expectations and new hope—are given essentially no analysis, even though they were so critical for Henkin's ability to proclaim a new era of rights.[49]

Equally remarkable in the context of the postwar history of international human rights was Henkin's Americanization of the concept, beginning with his historical narrative. It was mainly here that Henkin diverged from Lauterpacht's 1950 work, on which *The Rights of Man Today* otherwise leaned heavily. One obvious explanation for Henkin's warmly patriotic universalism is that it was a strategic move. America's commitment to the idea of international human rights since 1945 had been wayward at best, particularly when it came to the country's acceptance of formal treaties like the human rights covenants. (The United States had ratified none so far.) In 1977, in a letter to the *New York Times*, however, Henkin—besides reassuring worrywarts that such agreements lacked force in any event—insisted that the International Covenant on Civil and Political Rights was not simply "an amazing tribute to Western values" but, even more specifically, to bedrock American assumptions: "It has made our ideology the international norm."[50]

But together with strategy, there was heartfelt belief. As Henkin's *Rights of Man Today* makes abundantly clear, Henkin felt a genuine investment in the superiority of the American political and social model as synonymous with a commitment to human rights. The United States, Henkin argued, pioneered commitment to the values to which even its opponents were now forced to pay lip service. Henkin fits best into the general story of American liberalism of the era, which proceeded through human rights in a moment of ideological recovery in the 1970s after a disastrous earlier form of globalism. Unlike Carter, however, Henkin did not explicitly reflect on what American liberalism had to recover from or present human rights as an American ideology ever interrupted or betrayed. And he did not register the significance of short-term international sources of ideological change—notably shifting brands of utopianism—that had allowed for the human rights breakthrough of which Henkin was, far more than has been recognized, the beneficiary rather than the cause.

In this sense, Henkin's case remains powerfully illustrative. To this day, there has been very little self-reflexive understanding among American international lawyers about what the exact historical conditions were in which they made human rights central. From this moment, Henkin and others threw themselves into the mission of popularizing international law's renovated purposes. Beyond a breathtaking shift of interpretive protocols, devotion to teaching the new international law, another hallmark of disciplinary reinvention, took pride of place.[51] Of course, one cannot take the story of conversion, either by Henkin or by the larger discipline, too far. Henkin famously rejected the concept of sovereignty, even as in his revised theory of international law states retained their centrality, perhaps even as a normative commitment, and not simply as a matter of the facts of the world. And Henkin's overwhelming enthusiasm was for political and civil rights, not others—which once again made him a man of his time. But in the postwar discipline of American international law, it was a grand departure. In Henkin's career, and for the future of the discipline through the present, the age of rights—certainly for international lawyers—had been born.[52]

What possible explanations are there for the rise of human rights among international lawyers, especially American figures for whom they had seemed peripheral for so long? The most common explanation the discipline itself offers—in part because it gives the discipline itself a causal role—places weight on the progressive evolution of juristic sensibility as a powerful force of change. "Human rights are undergoing a stage of continuing evolution," Theodor Meron, Sohn's student and New York University professor, explained, advocating this evolution not simply through idealizing interpretation of formal treaty law but also through asserting advance in informal custom. "Through a process of accretion," Meron explained, "elements of state practice and *opinio juris* form new customary norms of human rights. This continuing process, in which *opinio juris* appears to have greater weight than state practice, is more interesting than [a] static picture of human rights . . . More rights will be added in the course of time."[53] In this scheme, the history of human rights in international law is primarily one of constant evolutionary pressure on the part of jurists themselves.

By itself, however, such a theory of the customary growth of norms does very little to explain the startling move of human rights from the periphery to the center of the discipline—since it took place almost overnight. If "evolution" there was, it occurred on a kind of catastrophe model, in which change happens in nonlinear moments of unforeseeable mutation: a model that does not fit well with usual theories of customary progress in the law. It is far more plausible to believe that *opinio juris*, not least in reigning opinion about the status of the Universal Declaration itself, changed in response to external factors rather than driving disciplinary assumptions from the inside as enlightenment exercised its gentle force of improvement. International lawyers never abjured their commitment to humanity and improvement through legal formalities, however chastened that commitment became in the Cold War tempest. But it took a revolution outside their ranks for human rights to become the content of their forms.

A crucial—though negative—external factor is certainly the waning of the age of decolonization. Once, skepticism about human rights in the guise of anticolonialist self-determination had reigned. Soon, enthusiasm for human rights as potential interference in sovereign jurisdiction took its place. The prominent Italian jurist Antonio Cassese explained this drastic shift as the transition from the era of *external* self-determination to *internal* self-determination. The human rights explosion of the 1970s could be cast as continuous with the rest of postwar history if human rights were understood as requiring the aggressive championship of indigenous freedom from colonial powers in a first moment, which once over could then give way to the pursuit of freedom within groups in a second moment.[54] But besides suppressing the widespread anxiety of Western international lawyers about "external" self-determination in that first moment, Cassese's retrospective contrast of external versus internal self-determination disguises more than it explains about the radical transformation. After all, the abrogation of the once sacrosanct sovereignty implied by external self-determination through the international concern with the rights of individuals of "internal self-determination" is not the unfolding of a single idea in different phases: it is a shift from one idea to another.

That the waning of anticolonialism allowed for international lawyers to make human rights central does not explain why they actually did so, of course. Given no explanation in the intellectual lineage of international law—whether a mythical Grotian tradition in the long term or a commitment to the New Deal or the post–World War II human rights moment in the shorter term—one might wonder whether there is help to be found in the changing composition of the discipline. One obvious feature of the development of postwar international law, and eventually human rights, is the startling prominence of Jews within it—especially in America, where the postwar era saw the succession to centrality in the field of émigrés and the children of immigrants. (There were many Jews among pre-World War II French international lawyers, and Lassa Oppenheim and Hersch Lauterpacht were prominent in Britain long before Jews succeeded to central positions in American international law.) In the United States, the succession from Manley Hudson to Louis Sohn at Harvard Law School is the most graphic symbol of this change. And all of the key members of the "Columbia school" were Jews, and this mattered to Henkin not least. But while undoubtedly an important feature of the professional sociology of international law, as of so many other academic fields, the succession of Jews to positions of academic centrality does not, on reflection, explain much of substance. Of the founders of human rights in American international law, only Buergenthal survived the Holocaust; and given the chronological delay of Holocaust consciousness even for Jews, it is important not to assume that this specific event drove their thinking. More important, the principal realist dissidents from and within international law, like Morgenthau and Schwarzenberger, were also Jews, along with their more formalist colleagues. But the chief reason that neither Jewish identity nor early memory of the Holocaust can be seen as much more than background factors in the disciplinary move to human rights is that they do not explain the timing, and they do not explain the specifics of the work. Instead, it seems from a look at a career like Henkin's that it was the radical shift in public climate that best accounts for the mutation that occurred. Human rights were reclaimed from anticolonialism, and made a central part for the first time of the foreign policy of American liberalism.

The best positive explanation of the rapid identification of international legal projects in the United States with individual human rights is precisely the larger extra-disciplinary context of postwar transformation. Like many original founders of human rights, many

European lawyers who were involved from the beginning often represented spiritualistic, conservative personalism, focused as it was on a new politics of "human dignity." American lawyers, however, followed a very different path to human rights. It was a late and external change in the definition of idealism—the substitution of one utopia for another—that best explains the switch in the meaning of their discipline. This was so even when, as for the American liberals of the Carter mold, they mainly inherited a new consensus around human rights due to a concatenation of other forces, without having adopted more full-blown utopias before. In particular, international lawyers were witnesses to the creation of a whole new set of possibilities for human rights beyond the United Nations, where they had shown their limitations.

Yet it would be misleading to suggest that international law provided simply one domain among others where the power of this human rights explosion registered. The turn by dissidents like Aleksandr Esenin-Volpin and Václav Havel to human rights was also, and explicitly, a revival of the plausibility of abstract norms as a vehicle of moral progress; and though they owed the general intellectual renewal of formalism to arguments by Eastern European dissidents, it was fateful that international lawyers were the existing custodians of international legal forms to which those very figures appealed. The lawyers had husbanded formalism without rights during an era of realist dominance. But they were the natural inheritors of a reactivated formalism revolving around the rights they had earlier marginalized. Hence the paradox: the rise of human rights in international law occurred not for reasons internal to international law as a profession, but due to the ideological changes that set the stage for a moral triumph of human rights—one that in turn gave a whole new relevance to the field's mission.

It is impossible to isolate the path of the law from its intersections with social action. Human rights, like other similar norms, depended on a rising social movement to be canonized by lawyers, certainly as a professional idea and priority. But the human rights movement was simply one social movement among others. A prior and far more global social movement, anticolonialism, received a considerably more guarded reception in the theory and practice of Western, including American, international lawyers. The version in which international human rights spiked in the West in general—with overwhelming focus on political and civil rights—meant that the earliest affiliations of most international lawyers gave those commitments exclusive priority too. Henkin's career provides an excellent illustration of both facts. This starting point had a profound effect on doctrine and practice, and explains why the huge panoply of rights theorized and pursued by international lawyers since the 1970s have had to be added over time rather than pursued from the outset. Even as human rights provided the grounds for a reconstitution of their discipline, international lawyers, like members of other sectors of the human rights movement, faced the forbidding task of determining how this late-come concept could address a growing range of global political concerns.

Today, the law plays an altogether unprecedented and unusual role in how the international forum is imagined and how aspirations for change in its arrangements are pursued. Thanks to the new plausibility it gave abstract norms, the human rights movement made international law a privileged instrument of moral improvement and, indeed, provided it enormous appeal as a framework for idealistic pursuits. But it was to be fateful for the future that international law could come to occupy a role in the moral imagination that, given the discipline's own circuitous path to human rights, it had not won for itself. And the debt of international lawyers to a very specific social movement meant that they would not simply inherit a fund of powerful energy but also face serious constraints in advancing an idealistic agenda in later years.

When the history of human rights is told beyond myths of deep origins, it illustrates the persistence of the nation-state as the aspirational forum for humanity until recently. The state was the incubator for rights claims, both in the rise of the absolutist state, with its well-disciplined interior order and colonialist exterior expansion, then in the creation of the modern nation, in which citizenship and rights, identification and contestation, were always bound up with each other. The relevance of the nation-state was amplified, rather than qualified, in the World War II alliance politics that led to the marginalization in the United Nations of the human rights that some wartime rhetoric had featured. It was geographically dispersed in the anticolonialist imagination, in which the new human rights were understood as a subversive instrument against imperial rule in the name of liberation and the construction of new states around the world. The perceived crisis of the postcolonial world, however, made the globalization of the nation-state unattractive as the sole formula for the achievement of modern freedom. Accordingly, rights finally lost their long connection with revolution.

When the history of human rights acknowledges how recently they came to the world, it focuses not simply on the crisis of the nation-state, but on the collapse of alternative internationalisms—global visions that were powerful for so long in spite of not featuring individual rights. The crisis of popular consent for the machinations of Cold War geopolitics left people looking for new causes to believe in, even as the decade after 1968 put unforgiving pressure on newer alternatives, especially if those alternatives were internationalist in scope. The answer to why human rights emerged is thus not "globalization." Whether the subaltern versions of internationalism that coexisted so uneasily with anticolonialist nationalism (most obviously, pan-Arabism and pan-Africanism), or communism and attempts to save it through "Marxist humanism," it was not only the loss of faith in the nation-state but also the desertion of the stage by alternative promises to transcend the nation-state that accounts for the relevance of human rights in the last three decades.

The international human rights movement became so significant, then, neither because it offered a rights-based doctrine alone nor because it forged a truly global vision for the first time. Rather, it was the crisis of other utopias that allowed the very neutrality that had made "human rights" wholly peripheral to the aftermath of World War II—when taking sides in a contest of programmatic visions seemed so pressing—to become the condition of their success. As a number of its partisans in the 1970s were well aware, human rights could break through in that era because the ideological climate was ripe for claims to make a difference not through political vision but by transcending politics. Morality, global in its potential scope, could become the aspiration of humankind.

But the very neutrality that allowed for human rights to survive in the 1970s, and prosper as other utopias died, also left them with a heavy burden later. For even if their breakthrough depended on their antipolitics, human rights were soon affected by two transformative changes. First, the moment that favored pure moral visions passed, not least in American party and electoral politics, as Jimmy Carter's brief presidential career illustrates so vividly. Second, and more important, partisans of the human rights idea were forced to confront the need for political agenda and programmatic vision—the very things whose absence allowed for their utopia to emerge so spectacularly and discontinuously in the first place. If human rights were born in antipolitics, they could not remain wholly noncommittal toward programmatic endeavors, especially as time passed.

For these reasons, the dynamics of the birth of the era of human rights in the later 1970s gave way to different ones in the youthful and adolescent struggles for the concept through the present day. But correctly identifying the historical origins of contemporary human rights aspirations is the only way to reckon with the profound dilemmas human rights continue to face as a utopian ideal and movement. If they had really been the fruit of democratic revolution, they would not have faced the demand for programmatic vision. If they had been forged in a moment of post-Holocaust wisdom, they would have had a completely different historical bearing, both focused on genocide prevention from the beginning and restricted to that incontestable cause without having to shoulder the burden of addressing all global ills and diverse political agendas. But they were neither of these things. Because they were born at a moment when they survived as a moral utopia when political utopias died, human rights were compelled to define the good life and offer a plan for bringing it about precisely when they were ill-equipped by the fact of their suprapolitical birth to do so.

Signs of trouble came when the contingency of their emergence—acknowledged by many in the moment of their startling breakthrough—was quickly forgotten. It was convenient almost immediately to represent human rights as a matter of longstanding tradition. In this regard, one of the most fascinating testaments to the breakthrough of "human rights" in the late 1970s is the response of philosophers, who after a moment of confusion about their novelty assimilated them to natural rights principles that were themselves being revived.

When John Rawls famously reclaimed individual rights, in his epoch-making *A Theory of Justice* (1971), it had no apparent consequences for either the general or the philosophical ascent of human rights (an expression Rawls did not use). This fact is perhaps unsurprising: the renaissance of rights in Anglophone thought of the era at first remained as restricted to the nation-state as rights claims had always been. Whatever else disappears in Rawls's "original position," the plurality of nations and the arbitrariness of borders among them remains. There had been next to no serious philosophical support for natural rights (let alone human rights) in the twentieth century to that point—except to the extent Christianity still helped define the discipline after World War II, as Jacques Maritain's career makes clear. Yet even after Rawls's démarche, rights prospered independently of human rights. Strikingly, in a tiny bibliography on rights composed by political theorists in 1978, next to no authors treated "human rights" as such.[1] (The main exception was the British liberal philosopher Maurice Cranston, whose contributions had little echo until after the mid-1970s.)[2]

When the human rights revolution occurred, a long half-decade after Rawls's groundbreaking treatise, philosophers at first registered their confusion at whether it involved what Rawls taught them to talk about. "Although the concept of 'natural rights' has not been completely displaced," one remarked, "the expression human rights certainly has a greater popularity today than has been true of 'natural rights' since the days of Tom Paine. . . . [P]eople differ about the significance of the shift in terminology from 'natural' to 'human' rights. Is this shift merely terminological? Or may it be that to speak of 'human' rather than 'natural' rights implies and fosters alteration of the original understanding of 'fundamental' rights?"[3] Philosophers, however, did not stick with that question, deciding instead to assimilate the surge of human rights to the Rawlsian revival, as if the former followed from the latter. The immediate homogenization of the two separate developments obscured the essential novelty of human rights, which still goes almost unmentioned in histories of rights penned by philosophers today.

It was at this moment that long historical trajectories in the history of early modern and Enlightenment natural law were widely invoked as the precedents for human rights.[4] It was more understandable that in other languages—where no new phrase was popularized—it was assumed that *droits de l'homme* and *Menschenrechte* were the same concepts across time. In the English language, the phrase "human rights" still seemed strange in the 1970s, and so the assimilation of rights and human rights had to be quite intentional. Though he had developed his own demand for "taking rights seriously" in the later 1960s and never before mentioned human rights in their international relevance, Ronald Dworkin's response to the events of 1977 was simply to introduce the phrase to his vocabulary as if he had always been talking about them. When invited by the Columbia University General Education Seminar to address the topic late that year, Dworkin gave a lecture called "Human Rights" but simply rehearsed his analysis of rights as so-called moral trumps.[5] Thomas Scanlon, another proponent of the revival of liberal rights, did turn to the independent novelty of human rights after the explosion, but in the long run he and others were understandably intent on allowing the rights revival and international human rights to combine.[6] It would be tempting to argue that the rediscovery of rights by Rawls and the birth of human rights were successors, except that there is no evidence for it. The historical fact of the matter is that the rights revival did not give rise to a specific concern with international human rights; without external stimulation, philosophers could easily have remained stuck in a discussion of rights in their state-based foundations and consequences. In fact, they did: even as philosophers learned the new phrase, the new era of philosophical rights by and large postponed current interest in global justice until a generation later. The rediscovery of rights and the invention of "human rights" did interact—but first of all to disguise immediately the novelty of the new phrase, and the political implications of that novelty.

Others who were interested in human rights in their role as a prominent new language of international legitimacy, however, were aware that their political implications had to be worked out, whatever the deep authority timelessness or tradition might provide. Already Carter's elevation of human rights to a policy of the state meant that the "politics of human rights" was introduced as the much-debated problem that it remains. The injection of morality into foreign policy, for example, compelled the leading realist thinkers of the postwar era to turn to it immediately—no mean accomplishment for moralists, to gain the attention of theorists who reduced international affairs to power alone.[7] In the short term, in the United States, Ronald Reagan's election in 1980 meant a crossroads for the relationship of the human rights movement to state power.[8] During the Carter administration, to which it clearly owed its newfound public role, the human rights movement generally treated government as an ally. Reagan's victory—not least when he nominated declared enemy of rights Ernest Lefever as lead State Department official—complicated this relationship profoundly. The era of Reagan foreign policy brought about a disturbing assimilation of human rights to the independently developed program of "democracy promotion," with early neoconservatives arguing that human rights were best served by placing them in a larger framework. Unrelenting opposition to communist regimes that would never reform, they claimed, had to be balanced with a friendly attitude towards rightist dictators supposedly on a path to liberalism. The argument was to have many tragic consequences at the time and since.[9] In light of such events, it is perhaps more understandable that the Marxist critique of rights has never truly disappeared, even reshaping itself in light of the new concept of "human rights" of recent decades.[10]

There is no doubt that, after decolonization and the civil rights movement ended formal empire and racism, the language of human rights provided a potent antitotalitarian weapon for the first time. The claim that the proliferation of human rights activism brought the Soviet Union down, however, should not obscure the fact that human rights actually emerged out of exasperation with the Cold War and the hope for a way beyond its divisions. In any case, Reaganites were far from alone in making human rights into a language of partisan politics, to which private individuals could sign on and against which governments were willing to measure their foreign policy, at least on paper. The emergence of "democracy promotion" revealed that human rights would have to incorporate concrete policy commitments and fuller-bodied social thinking to be meaningful, and to address the wide range of problems that required more than a set of abstract moral norms. The pure struggle of morality would have to enter the realm where political visions clash, with its hard choices, compromising bargains, and dirty hands.

Neoconservative democracy promotion, in spite of its almost immediate redefinition of human rights, nevertheless proved only one path among others. In America, the human rights community has sprouted many organizations and magnified its activities over the years. It opposed the rhetoric of democracy promotion as an excuse for repressive governments, but not without taking on a huge range of new concerns and activities of its own. Yet the slow but sure move toward a politics of human rights was most visible in Western Europe starting in the 1980s, where human rights NGOs proliferated and the newly prominent European Court in Strasbourg symbolized the great strides a rhetoric of human dignity and rights made at every level of the continent's affairs. Some observers, indeed, were led to believe that at domestic, regional, and international levels European nations had gone so far in embracing human rights as to have substituted principle entirely for power—a charge that, though untrue, suggested the path of human rights from antipolitics to program that Europeans had indeed taken.[11]

Could human rights have remained a minimalist utopia of antipolitics, as it was in its era of breakthrough? It seems unlikely, for the obvious reason that the more it seemed like the last utopia standing in world affairs, the more substantive a role international rights norms would have to take in how individuals lived out their aspirations and how nation-states and supranational organizations sought public legitimacy. If there ever really was a "global human rights revolution," it has occurred only since the 1980s, when a variety of groups around the world, and all governments, learned to speak the language. Close to the ground, one of the most hotly debated issues is whether this process of "vernacularization" of human rights was one in which ordinary people in different places winnowed their demands in the direction of acceptability to Western audiences, or whether they were able to use them from below in creative and transformative ways.[12] Not surprisingly, having lately incorporated human rights ideas themselves, international lawyers assumed an altogether new prominence, along with the staffers of expanding and bureaucratizing NGOs, as the professionalized stewards of what human rights might mean beyond their use as a tool of moral resistance.[13] In this atmosphere, the grassroots character that had made Amnesty International so pioneering and exemplary entered relative decline, as new forms of expertise pushed the human rights movement away from the original conditions of its breakthrough. Human rights were forced to move not simply from morality to politics, but also from charisma to bureaucracy.

One of the most globally significant shifts in the concerns of the human rights agenda—and indeed in the immediate implications of the phrase human rights—was the unexpected rise in the imperative of genocide prevention. It is remarkable how little this humanitarian norm figured in public consciousness either in the 1940s or even in the 1970s. Popular concern about the Holocaust, though it was getting off the ground in the later era, seems like an originally separate development without profound connection to the contemporaneous surge in human rights. Strikingly, perhaps the major early examples of rising interest in preventing genocide, over the crises in Biafra and Bangladesh in the late 1960s, did not spark the creation of the international human rights movement. In that era, genocide consciousness continuing to make its way in the world gave rise to calls for aid, and a revival of the nineteenth-century tradition of humanitarian intervention (especially after India's invasion of Pakistan in 1971).[14] But neither was yet conceptualized as part of a global human rights revolution. That had not yet become imaginable.

By the 1990s, a monumental change had occurred. Although it is still unclear whether, when, and how the popularization of Holocaust memory helped construct norms of universalist responsibility, it is quite striking that, with the possible exception of American Jewish guilt over prior inaction driving concern for co-religionists under Soviet rule, Holocaust memory was peripheral to the explosion of human rights in the crucial era of the 1970s.[15] The contest of utopias was far more relevant. Human rights and genocide prevention, separate in their 1940s invention, were independent as late the creation of movements around both after the 1960s. Yet somehow—since revelations of the Cambodian genocide, and certainly by the mid-1990s resurgence of "ethnic cleansing" on the European continent—genocide prevention is now among the first items on the human rights agenda.[16]

But the amazingly belated integration of genocide consciousness as a human rights concern is only one dimension of a far larger shift: the slow amalgamation of humanitarian concern for suffering with human rights as both a utopian idea and a practical movement.[17] Humanitarianism, with its origins in Christian pity and Enlightenment sympathy through its high era of imperialist entanglement in the nineteenth century, had developed in historical independence of rights talk. It entered into international organizations in the interwar League of Nations, with its concern over the "white slavery" of traffic in women and children, and in the cause of refugees, which also assumed a central place in United Nations affairs. Christian and secular NGOs like the Red Cross, Oxfam, and others, inheriting the philanthropic impulse of the nineteenth century, provided succor for the horrors of war and campaigned against famine and hunger all along. But it is simply mistaken to conceive of these as human rights organizations, as they were almost never understood in that way by their participants. Conversely, as late as the 1970s, the breakthrough for human rights—far more an antitotalitarian reflex—occurred in striking autonomy from humanitarian concern, particularly for global suffering. In their explosive moment, human rights were pursued for dissidents under Eastern European totalitarianism and victims of Latin American authoritarianism, not those in miserable circumstances in general. Highly restrictive in the sorts of depredations singled out for agitation in its earliest period, Amnesty International added only torture and disappearances to the list in its glory years. Yet today, human rights and humanitarianism are fused enterprises, with the former incorporating the latter and the latter justified in terms of the former.

In other words, the concern for genocide abroad is simply one dimension of the conversion of human rights into the worldview that sought to provide an answer to any area of global concern. Only in view of this shift from minimalism to maximalism can one understand the eruption in the varieties of rights claims, both by Western elites and local actors. And only as a struggle to overcome its enabling restrictions can one understand the logic of this expansion. From having triumphed because it lacked a political blueprint, the human rights movement was forced to draw up plans to remedy a crisis-ridden world. If human rights "occupied the space" left open by the departure of other utopian schemes, it was not wholly a matter of filling a vacuum.[18] The move to pervasive relevance required intellectual creativity and hard work, but also typically unacknowledged entry into a very contested political terrain—one that human rights had broken through by promising a way to avoid.

In this way, human rights were brought to new geographic areas around the globe and unsuspected concerns of substance, and into both the difficulty and drama of fundamental transformation from antipolitics to program. One obvious example of that creative mutation was the forging of "transitional justice," which in the 1980s was invented as an optic based on the Latin American experience to allow human rights to be not just an external moral criticism of terrible regimes but an internal political resource in the erection of their successors.[19] But the history of what have been known as "social rights" is perhaps even more revealing than the move to transitional justice of how human rights, born in moral transcendence of politics, had to become a political agenda.

Among the most striking paradoxes of the trajectory of social and economic rights is their decline precisely when "human rights" came into their own. Why were those rights so prominent at the time of the discreet coinage of the concept in the 1940s (not to mention in the earlier history of citizenship struggles during the French Revolution and since) but so absent in the 1970s when human rights were canonized? The fact that the idea of "human rights" was forged in the 1940s, a time of some commitment to social equality and the common good, meant that social rights were comparatively uncontroversial. Yet at that time it was not the commitment to social rights by itself, but whether reformed capitalism or revolutionary communism would best protect them, that made human rights peripheral rather than central. In contrast, the conditions of totalitarian and authoritarian rule that were the context for the breakthrough of human rights in the 1970s meant that social rights simply did not figure on the agenda, as the world moved on from the high tide of social democratic commitments. Social rights were absent from Eastern bloc dissidence, and Latin American leftists seeking alliance abroad muted their critiques of capitalism to do so, while their Western audiences in an era of economic shock stripped down their appeals to focus on political and civil basics.

In the end, however, the conditions of breakthrough were not to continue. For some, like Aryeh Neier, a founder of Human Rights Watch, social rights—let alone other entitlements—were never crucial. When confronted with them, he argued for sticking with concern for so-called negative liberties instead of incorporating more positive entitlements that he treated as dubious. If he lost that argument, in his organization and in general, it was not simply the better arguments of other human rights activists in favor of expanding their concerns that explain why.[20] The main reason is that it was not clear, after the collapse of alternative utopias, what other ideology could address global wrongs, especially as events led the gaze to shift from totalitarian and authoritarian rule to global immiseration—notably on the African continent, which is now the privileged site of human rights concern. Put differently, it was precisely the increasing role of human rights in Western social discourse, together with the collapse of alternative frameworks, which meant that practically all political concerns had to be reformulated in their terms and addressed by them. As totalitarianism and authoritarianism waned, social and economic rights consciousness could not help but surge.

The history of social rights suggests clearly, therefore, that the great irony of the larger history of human rights is the forced movement toward the very sort of maximalist utopia whose collapse in other forms in the 1970s allowed the concept to triumph on account of its minimalism. Human rights were compelled to assume exactly the sort of burden that had brought other ideologies low. Social and economic rights were not alone in these processes of inclusion or outright invention, even if they are the most vivid example. From women's rights—which were not a significant part of human rights consciousness in developed countries during its 1970s inception in spite of an exploding domestic and international women's movement—to various other rights of culture, indigeneity, and environment, the story of human rights since the 1970s has inevitably pushed the idea away from the particular conditions in which it emerged.[21] If human rights consciousness needs to be met "from below" by third-world constituencies lacking before, or to be "transformed" in view of truly outrageous global distress, it is because it arose when it did and in the specific form it did.[22]

Even as human rights continued to draw on the claim that their source of authority transcended politics, their transformation into the dominant framework of the government and improvement of human life in far-flung global locales changed them profoundly. The turn of the human rights movement to concerns with "governance" in postcolonial states around the world is perhaps the most vivid illustration of the embrace of politics.[23] It seemed obvious that episodic kinds of concern, in reaction to episodic crises, would never solve the problems that gave rise to those wrongs in the first place. And the notion of "governance" as a move from spectacular to structural wrongs, besides illustrating the transition from antipolitics to program, is now frequently combined in the human rights movement with a revived and rethought version of a Cold War theory of social development once notorious for its disinterest in rights but now based on them. On reflection, this evolution is unsurprising. Much as in the original history of rights in the nineteenth century and domestic civil rights in a later age, the early assertion of abstract entitlements prompted their advocates to scrutinize conditions for the enjoyment of entitlements, which are unfailingly structural, institutional, economic, and cultural.

In this process, the star-crossed trajectory of the notion of a "right to development" to which suffering humanity might be entitled is especially thought provoking. Contrary to what is sometimes suggested, the content of such a right was not a fundamental departure, given that anticolonialism had long since redefined human rights in the direction of nationalistic self-determination and collective development. But it was a specific act of creative appropriation when Senegalese jurist Kéba M'Baye—disciple of Léopold Senghor and associate of René Cassin's Institut des droits de l'homme— coined the phrase "right to development" in 1972, almost a decade before it figured in the 1981 African Charter on Human and Peoples' Rights (the UN General Assembly passed its Declaration on the Right to Development in 1986).[24] To that point, not least during the heyday of Western and especially American Cold War doctrines of modernization and development, rights had not figured as central concepts. And while it was precisely in the 1970s that the high tide of anticolonialism found expression in the attempt to craft a subaltern politics of development, international agencies as well as state and private actors in the decades since have devised schemes of development in which honoring human rights is conceived as both the means and the end.[25] Intellectually, the theoretical and doctrinal energy harnessed to the project of finding a vision of human rights adequate to global immiseration graphically illustrates the sheer distance from the landmark of their antitotalitarian invention that human rights have had to travel.[26] The jury is clearly still out on whether a rights framework for global poverty is the right framework.[27] But the verdict is debated only because human rights were forced to face—and it seemed believable that they might be able to face—problems that had been addressed by other schemes, and contending utopias, before.

Were human rights disabled by the circumstances of their birth from making precisely the moves they have made—and that so many demanded they make—from antipolitics to program? Was the movement too hobbled by its formulation of claims as individual entitlements, or its inattention to the relevance of economic and larger structural relationships for the realization of those entitlements, or was its challenge rather its far more general refusal of ideology? Is the process of its troubled expansion merely the story of the difficulty of combining cooperation with existing governmental and intergovernmental programs with criticism of them, or is its originally critical attitude toward power to blame? These are questions that are only beginning to be asked, based on perceived limitations of human rights as the best vessel of aspirations for a better world—dissatisfactions that are at the very least the burden of its success, but whose weighty consequences over the long term it is too soon to assess.

Instead of turning to history to monumentalize human rights by rooting them deep in the past, it is much better to acknowledge how recent and contingent they really are. Above all, it is crucial to link the emergence of human rights to the history of utopianism—the heartfelt desire to make the world a better place. That it is only one form of utopianism, indeed one that exists today because it weathered the recent storm in which others were shipwrecked, ought to be clear by now. But not every age need be as unsympathetic to political utopia as the recent one in which human rights came to the fore. And so the program of human rights faces a fateful choice: whether to expand its horizons so as to take on the burden of politics more honestly, or to give way to new and other political visions that have yet to be fully outlined.

In some ways, the choice has already been made: to the extent the human rights agenda has extended its purview or been forced to do so, it inevitably became something new. Yet this transformation is neither an easy nor an obvious process, and should happen consciously rather than inadvertently. Henry Steiner, a law professor who eventually became an expert in the field and led Harvard Law School's human rights program until recently, lucidly cautioned the human rights movement that it needed to carefully distinguish two missions that it was apt to confuse: between human rights as catastrophe prevention and human rights as utopian politics. "The human rights corpus is very spacious in the rights, freedoms and liberties that it embraces," Steiner noted. "[Some] norms express what one could call the 'anti-catastrophe' goal or dimension of the human rights movement: stopping the massive disasters that have plagued humanity. That goal is complemented by another, related but distinct utopian dimension to human rights: giving people the freedom and capacity to develop their lives and the world. . . . When you get past the core, the absolute 'no's,' there is inevitable ambiguity and outright conflict."[28] Historically, Steiner's contrast is false. In fact, it was due to minimalism and utopianism, indissociably and together, that human rights made their way in the world. But the conditions for this combination were fleeting. And they are long since gone.

Today, these goals—preventing catastrophe through minimalist ethical norms and building utopia through maximalist political vision—are absolutely different. One remains more compatible with the moralized breakthrough of human rights in the first place; the other follows from aspirations human rights have incorporated since that time, aspirations that are emphatically visionary but also necessarily divisive. The first version can honestly confront its lack of answers and acknowledge that it must make room for the contest of genuinely political visions for the future: seeking ways to constrain the contest so it does not lead to disaster, perhaps, but playing no other role. Yet then human rights cannot be a general slogan or worldview or ideal. If it draws authority from its appeal to morality, the other, utopian version of human rights easily becomes a recipe for the displacement of politics, forcing aspirations for change to present themselves as less controversial than they really are, as if humanity were not still confused and divided about how to bring about individual and collective freedom in a deeply unjust world.

Born of the yearning to transcend politics, human rights have become the core language of a new politics of humanity that has sapped the energy from old ideological contests of left and right. With the advancement of human rights as their standard, a huge number of schemes of transformation, regulation, and "governance" contend with one another across the world. But if in the thirty years since their explosion in the 1970s human rights have followed a path from morality to politics, their advocates have not always forthrightly acknowledged that fact. Born in the assertion of the "power of the powerless," human rights inevitably became bound up with the power of the powerful. If "human rights" stand for an exploding variety of rival political schemes, however, they still trade on the moral transcendence of politics that their original breakthrough involved. And so it may not be too late to wonder whether the concept of human rights, and the movement around it, should restrict themselves to offering minimal constraints on responsible politics, not a new form of maximal politics of their own. If human rights call to mind a few core values that demand protection, they cannot be all things to all people. Put another way, the last utopia cannot be a moral one. And so whether human rights deserve to define the utopianism of the future is still very far from being decided.

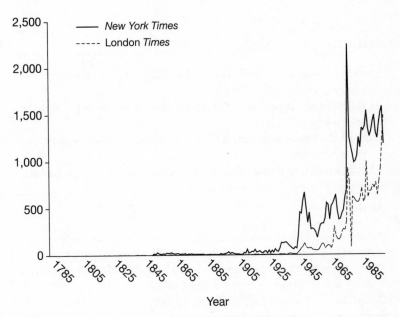

"Human rights" in Anglo-American news, with 1977 breakthrough

1941

Franklin Delano Roosevelt's State of the Union address announces "four freedoms" (January)

Atlantic Charter signed by FDR and Winston Churchill in Placentia Bay, Newfoundland (August)

Inter-allied Meeting at St. James's Palace, London endorses the Atlantic Charter (September)

Churchill travels to Washington, D.C. for Arcadia conference (December)

1942

White House, with Churchill in residence, issues Declaration of the United Nations, mentioning human rights for the first time (January)

Commission to Study the Bases of a Just and Durable Peace (American Protestants) releases guiding principles (March)

American Law Institute begins draft list of rights

Jacques Maritain writes in *Fortune* magazine on "the rights of the human person" (April)

International League of the Rights of Man is founded in New York

Beveridge Report, proposing welfarist protection, published in Great Britain (December)

1943

Wendell Willkie's bestseller *One World* is published

Commission to Study the Bases of a Just and Durable Peace publishes *Six Pillars of Peace*

Témoignage chrétien publishes booklet, "Human and Christian Rights"
Allied leaders meet in Tehran (November–December)

1944

FDR proposes "Second Bill of Rights" in State of the Union address (January)
Dumbarton Oaks meetings on postwar international organization begin, Washington, D.C. (August)
American Law Institute publishes draft bill of rights

1945

Hersch Lauterpacht publishes *An International Bill of Rights*
Allied leaders meet in Yalta (February)
Chapultepec Act affirms sovereignty as first principle of American sphere (March)
FDR dies (April 12)
San Francisco Conference, forming United Nations, begins (April)
Victory in Europe Day (May 8)
UN Charter signed (June 26)
Allied leaders attend Potsdam conference (July–August)
Hiroshima bombed with nuclear device (August 6)
Allies sign International Military Tribunal Charter, announcing concept of "crime against humanity" (August 8)
Nagasaki bombed with nuclear device (August 9)
Victory over Japan Day (August 14–15)
Fifth Pan-African Conference held in Manchester, England (October)
UN Charter enters into force (October 24)

1946

UN Commission on Human Rights begins to meet
India petitions United Nations regarding plight of South Asians in South Africa

1947

Communist takeover in Czechoslovakia (February)

Truman doctrine announced (March)

UN Economic and Social Council decides Commission on Human Rights may not consider petitions (summer)

Institut de Droit international, international law's central historic association, reconvenes after ten-year hiatus (August)

South Asian partition and formal independence of India and Pakistan (August)

W. E. B. Du Bois submits petitions to UN on African-American subordination (October)

Hungary, Bulgaria, and Romania are excluded from the UN (1947–1948)

1948

Mohandas Gandhi assassinated (January)

American Declaration of the Rights and Duties of Man passes in Bogotá (spring)

State of Israel declares independence (May)

Congress of Europe meets (May)

World Council of Churches coalesces in Amsterdam meeting (August)

Gerhard Ritter, German conservative, writes first history of human rights (November)

UN General Assembly passes Genocide Convention (December 9)

UN General Assembly passes Universal Declaration of Human Rights (December 10)

Cardinal József Mindszenty, Primate of Hungary, is interned, leading to the premier international human rights cause of the era (December)

1949

Cardinal Josef Beran of Czechoslovakia is put under house arrest (June)

International community drafts new Geneva Conventions governing warfare, including novel civilian protection

Council of Europe meets, debates rights principles (August–September)

1950

European Convention on Human Rights opened for signature (November)
UN Third Committee meets to consider whether human rights apply within
   empires
Lauterpacht publishes *International Law and Human Rights*

1968

International Year for Human Rights
UN Conference on Human Rights held in Tehran (April–May)
Andrei Sakharov's "Thoughts on Progress. . ." appears in *New York Times* (July 20)
Leszek Kołakowski, *Towards a Marxist Humanism,* appears
Warsaw Pact troops invade Czechoslovakia (August 20)
Conference of NGOs in Consultative Status (September)
Chronicle of Current Events begins in Moscow (September)
René Cassin accepts Nobel Prize for Peace (December)

1969

Action Group for Human Rights (Moscow) emerges (May)
Organization of American States opens American Convention on Human Rights for ratification
Cassin founds Institute for Human Rights in Strasbourg

1970

Human Rights Committee (Moscow) appears
Davignon report, outlining European security strategy, appears
Louis Henkin founds branch of Cassin Institute in the United States
Alexandr Solzhenitsyn accepts Nobel Prize for Literature (December)

1971

Henkin teaches a class on human rights, a first for him and a first for Columbia Law School; Louis Sohn teaches first Harvard Law School class on human rights
Jacob Blaustein Institute for Human Rights founded by the American Jewish Committee

1972

Index of Censorship, by Writers and Scholars International, appears
Amnesty International opens Campaign against Torture, publishes on torture, and opens petition drive
Cassin and Blaustein institutes hold forum on emigration rights in Uppsala, Sweden

1973

Soviet Union ratifies international covenants on human rights
Military seizes power in Uruguay (summer)
Conference for Security and Cooperation in Europe founded (July)
Congressman Donald Fraser's hearings on international human rights begin in Washington, D.C. (August)
President Salvador Allende of Chile overthrown in coup and killed (September 11)
Hedrick Smith's profile of Sakharov appears in *New York Times Magazine* (November)
International League of the Rights of Man awards Sakharov the Human Rights Prize (December)
Rose Styron publishes article on torture in *The New Republic* (December)

1974

Jeri Laber places op-eds for Amnesty International in the *New York Times*
Now ex-Marxist Kołakowski explains his "correct views about everything" to E. P. Thompson in *Socialist Register*

Seán MacBride, who helped start Amnesty Campaign against Torture, accepts Nobel Prize for Peace (December)

1975

Helsinki Final Act signed (August 1)
Operación Condor, rightist international alliance, begins in Latin America
Brazil's human rights movement crystallizes
Henry Kissinger creates Department of State human rights bureau
Gerald Ford turns down Solzhenitsyn's request for White House meeting
Millicent Fenwick, New Jersey congresswoman, proposes legislation creating U.S. Helsinki Commission
Rally held in Paris for dissident Leonid Plyushch's release, 5,000 attend (October)
Czechoslovakia ratifies international human rights covenants, bringing them into force (December)
Sakharov awarded Nobel Prize for Peace, wife Elena Bonner accepts (December)

1976

Cardinal Silva Henriquez of Chile founds Vicariate of Solidarity (January)
Argentine armed forces overthrow President Isabel Martínez de Perón (March)
Moscow Helsinki Group founded (May)
Kissinger praises human rights at Organization of American States meeting (June)
Democrats' Platform Committee meets, before human rights discovered (June)
Soweto uprising in South Africa (June)
Jimmy Carter's two minor campaign speeches on human rights (September–October)
Committee for the Defense of Workers (KOR) founded in Poland
Amnesty International opens office in Washington, D.C.

1977

Charter 77 in Czechoslovakia founded (January)
Carter declares absolute commitment to human rights at his inauguration (January)
Carter letter to Sakharov revealed to press (February)
Carter meets Vladimir Bukovsky at White House (March)
Idi Amin threatens Americans in Uganda in response to Carter's public scolding (March)
Julia Kristeva proclaims "the dissident" a "new type of intellectual"
Carter delivers major speech on human rights in foreign policy (May)
Noam Chomsky warns of human rights being "manipulated by propagandists" (June)
Belgrade follow-up meeting in Helsinki process begins (October)
Year-long seminar on human rights begins at Columbia University (fall)
Amnesty International wins Nobel Peace Prize (fall)

1978

Helsinki (later Human Rights) Watch founded
Cardinal Henriquez of Chile declares "year of human rights"
Václav Havel writes "The Power of the Powerless"
Henkin publishes *The Rights of Man Today,* helps found Lawyers Committee for Human Rights (later Human Rights First)
UNESCO International Congress on the Teaching of Human Rights, held in Vienna (September)
Karol Wojtyła elected pope (October)
Columbia University Center for the Study of Human Rights founded

Prologue

1. See U.N. Doc. A/Conf.32/SR.1–13 (1968) for the conference proceedings. Compare Roland Burke, "From Individual Rights to National Development: The First UN International Conference on Human Rights, Tehran, 1968," *Journal of World History* 19, 3 (2008): 275–96.
2. Moses Moskowitz, "The Meaning of International Concern with Human Rights," in *René Cassin: Amicorum Discipulorumque Liber,* 4 vols. (Paris, 1969), 1: 194.
3. Philip Roth, *American Pastoral* (New York, 1997), 87.

1 Humanity before Human Rights

1. Jorge Luis Borges, "Kafka and His Precursors," in *Selected Non-Fictions,* ed. Eliot Weinberger (New York, 1999), 364–65, emphases added.
2. Hannah Arendt, *The Origins of Totalitarianism,* 3rd ed. (New York, 1968), chap. 9.
3. Cf. Lynn Hunt, *Inventing Human Rights: A History* (New York, 2007).
4. Jeanne Hersch, ed., *Birthright of Man* (Paris, 1969), a sprawling UNESCO publication to mark the twentieth anniversary of the Universal Declaration suggesting the universality across time and space of human rights.
5. See, for example, Pierre Lévêque, *Bêtes, dieux, et hommes: l'imaginaire des premières religions* (Paris, 1985), and Richard Bulliet, *Hunters, Herders, and Hamburgers: The Past and Future of Human-Animal Relationships* (New York, 2005), chaps. 2–3.

6. See Elaine Pagels, "Human Rights: Legitimizing a Recent Concept," *Annals of the American Academy of Political and Social Sciences* 442 (March 1979): 57–62, also available as "The Roots and Origins of Human Rights," in Alice H. Henkin, ed., *Human Dignity: The Internationalization of Human Rights* (New York, 1978).

7. "There has been," Sheldon Pollock concludes in his comparative study of the rival universalisms of the premodern Latin and Sanskrit language zones, "not just one cosmopolitanism in history but several." Sheldon Pollock, *The Languages of the Gods in the World of Men: Sanskrit, Culture, and Power in Premodern India* (Berkeley, 2006), 280. See also Carol A. Breckinridge et al., eds., *Cosmopolitanism* (Raleigh, 2002), notably Pollock's chapter.

8. The classic version of this argument is provided by Ernst Troeltsch, "Das stoisch-christliche Naturrecht und das moderne profane Naturrecht," *Verhandlungen des ersten deutschen Soziologentages vom 19.-22. Oktober 1910 in Frankfurt a.-M.* (Tübingen, 1911), in English as "Stoic-Christian Natural Law and Modern Profane Natural Law," in Christopher Adair-Toteff, ed., *Sociological Beginnings: The First Conference of the German Society for Sociology* (Liverpool, 2006).

9. Cf. Richard Reitzenstein, *Werden und Wesen der Humanität im Altertum: Rede zur Feier des Geburtstages Sr. Majestät des Kaisers am 26. Januar 1907* (Strasbourg, 1907).

10. Hannah Arendt, *On Revolution,* rev. ed. (New York, 1965), 107. Cf. James Q. Whitman, "Western Legal Imperialism: Thinking about the Deep Historical Roots," *Theoretical Inquiries in Law* 10, 2 (July 2009): 313. Whitman's own critique of putative Roman theoretical and legal sources applies exactly and equally well to his own thesis of Christian origins, as legal imperialism is only one facet of contemporary human rights.

11. Cf. J. H. Elliot, "The Discovery of America and the Discovery of Man," *Proceedings of the British Academy* 48 (1972): 101–25, and John M. Headley, *The Europeanization of the World: On the Origins of Human Rights and Democracy* (Princeton, 2008).

12. There is a deep history here; see, for instance, Robert von Keller, *Freiheitsgarantien für Person und Eigentum im Mittelalter: eine Studie zur Vorgeschichte moderner Verfassungsgrundrechte* (Heidelberg, 1933), and

Kenneth Pennington, *The Prince and the Law, 1200–1600: Sovereignty and Rights in the Western Legal Tradition* (Berkeley, 1993).

13. See Gilles Couvreur, *Les pauvres ont-ils des droits? Recherches sur le vol en cas d'extrême nécessité depuis la Concordia de Gratien (1140) jusqu'à Guillaume d'Auxerre (1231)* (Rome, 1961).

14. See Richard Tuck, "Scepticism and Toleration in the Seventeenth Century," in Susan Mendus, ed., *Toleration: Conceptual and Historical Perspectives* (Cambridge, 1987), and Jeffrey R. Collins, "Redeeming the Enlightenment: New Histories of Religious Toleration," *Journal of Modern History* 81, 3 (September 2009): 607–36. See also Patrick Collinson, "Religion and Human Rights: The Case of and for Protestantism," in Olwen Hufton, ed., *Historical Change and Human Rights* (New York, 1995), and John Witte, Jr., *The Reformation of Rights: Law, Religion, and Human Rights in Early Modern Calvinism* (Cambridge, 2007).

15. Cf. Gerald Stourzh, "Liberal Democracy as a Culture of Rights: England, the United States, and Continental Europe," in *From Vienna to Chicago and Back: Essays on Intellectual History and Political Thought in Europe and America* (Chicago, 2007), esp. 308, which glosses over the distinction between English and natural rights.

16. Edmund Burke, *Reflections on the Revolution in France,* ed. J. G. A. Pocock (Indianapolis, 1987), 51, emphasis added.

17. See, e.g., David Brion Davis, *The Problem of Slavery in Western Culture* (Ithaca, 1966). One historian, Lynn Hunt, has recently argued that the fellow-feeling of secular humanitarianism was the primary force in the origins of both the universalism and the "rights of man" of early modern revolution. But on inspection, this proposal is surprisingly weak. For one thing, humanitarianism—whose sources were primarily religious, not secular in the beginning—hardly pointed unilaterally in the direction of individual rights. As Lynn Festa has shown in her *Sentimental Figures of Empire in Eighteenth-Century Britain and France* (Baltimore, 2006), it likewise informed imperialism abroad in the eighteenth century, and probably far more than it did the expansion of concern even at home. But the notion that sympathy with others' pain prompted the large-scale extension of the list of rights is a yet more dubious proposition. At least until very recently, the history of humanitarianism is best understood as a separate topic from the history of

rights. For some sources, see my "Empathy in History, Empathizing with Humanity," *History & Theory* 45, 3 (October 2006): 397–415.

18. J. W. von Goethe, *Hermann and Dorothea,* trans. Thomas Conrad Porter (New York, 1854), 97.

19. Philip Mitsis, "Natural Law and Natural Right in Post-Aristotelian Philosophy: The Stoics and Their Critics," and Paul Vander Waerdt, "Philosophical Influence on Roman Jurisprudence? The Case of Stoicism and Natural Law," both in *Aufstieg und Niedergang der römischen Welt* II.36.7 (1994): 4812–900. But the meaning of *ius* in Roman law and its difference from the notion of a "subjective" claim in later legal systems is even disputed, notably by Michel Villey. See Villey, "L'idée du droit subjectif et les systèmes juridiques romains," *Revue historique de droit français et étranger* 4, 23 (1946): 201–27.

20. Jane Burbank and Frederick Cooper, "Empire, droits, et citoyenneté, de 212 à 1946," *Annales E.S.C.* 63, 3 (May 2008): 495–531.

21. See esp. Tuck, *The Rights of War and Peace: Political Thought and the International Order from Grotius to Kant* (Oxford, 1999).

22. Thomas Hobbes, *Leviathan,* rev. ed., ed. Tuck (Cambridge, 1996), 91.

23. "It cannot be a coincidence," Tuck writes, "that the modern idea of natural rights arose in the period in which the European nations were engaged in their dramatic competition for domination of the world." Tuck, *Rights,* 14. See also Anthony Pagden, "Human Rights, Natural Rights and Europe's Imperial Legacy," *Political Theory* 31, 2 (2003): 171–99, and Duncan Ivison, "The Nature of Rights and the History of Empire," in David Armitage, ed., *British Political Thought in History, Literature, and Theory* (Cambridge, 2006).

24. Cf. Knud Haakonssen, "Protestant Natural Law Theory, A General Interpretation," in Natalie Brender and Larry Krasnoff, eds., *New Essays on the History of Autonomy: A Collection Honoring J. B. Schneewind* (Cambridge, 2004), 95.

25. See Morton White, *The Philosophy of the American Revolution* (New York, 1978), chaps. 4–5.

26. Georg Jellinek, *Die Erklärung der Menschen- und Bürgerrechte: ein Beitrag zur modernen Verfassungsgeschichte* (Leipzig, 1895); Émile Boutmy, "La Déclaration des droits de l'homme et du citoyen et M. Jellinek," *Annales des sciences politiques* 17 (1902): 415–43; Jellinek, "La

Déclaration des droits de l'homme et du citoyen et M. Boutmy," rpt. in *Ausgewählte Schriften und Reden,* 2 vols., ed. Walter Jellinek (Berlin, 1911). For comment, see Otto Vossler, "Studien zur Erklärung der Menschen- und Bürgerrechte," *Historische Zeitschrift* 142, 3 (1930): 516–45; Wolfgang Schmale, "Georg Jellinek et la Déclaration des Droits de l'Homme de 1789," in *Mélanges offerts à Claude Petitfrère: Regards sur les sociétés modernes (XVIe–XVIIe siècle),* ed. Denise Turrel (Tours, 1997) and Duncan Kelly, "Revisiting the Rights of Man: Georg Jellinek on Rights and the State," *Law and History Review* 22, 3 (Fall 2004): 493–530.

27. Along with Jellinek, see Gilbert Chinard, *La déclaration des droits de l'homme et du citoyen et ses antécédents américains* (Washington, 1945).

28. *The Federalist Papers,* ed. Clinton Rossiter (New York, 2003), 512 (No. 84).

29. Self-evidence is an *intellectual category* in Enlightenment thought; if so, the proclamation of rights as self-evident does not at all mean historians can assume they actually were. Cf. David A. Bell, "Un dret égal," *London Review of Books,* November 15, 2007.

30. Cf. Dan Edelstein, *The Terror of Natural Right: Republicanism, the Cult of Nature, and the French Revolution* (Chicago, 2009).

31. On America, see, for example, Larry D. Kramer, *The People Themselves: Popular Constitutionalism and Judicial Review* (New York, 2005). On France, see, for example, Philippe Raynaud, "Des droits de l'homme à l'État de Droit," *Droits* 2 (1985) and Alec Stone Sweet, *The Birth of Judicial Politics in France: The Constitutional Council in Comparative Perspective* (New York, 1992).

32. David Armitage, *The Declaration of Independence: A Global History* (Cambridge, Mass., 2006), esp. 17–18.

33. Cf. Istvan Hont, "The Permanent Crisis of a Divided Mankind: 'Contemporary Crisis of the Nation-State' in Historical Perspective," *Political Studies* 42 (1994): 166–231, esp. 191–98, and J. K. Wright, "National Sovereignty and the General Will: The Political Program of the Declaration of Rights," in van Kley, ed., *The French Idea of Freedom.*

34. Alexander Bevilacqua, "Cloots, Rousseau and Peaceful World Order in the Age of the French Revolution" (M.Phil. thesis, University of Cambridge, 2008) and Albert Mathiez, *La Révolution et les Étrangers:*

Cosmopolitisme et défense nationale (Paris, 1918); on German theorizing, see Pauline Kleingeld, "Six Varieties of Cosmopolitanism in Late Eighteenth-Century Germany," *Journal of the History of Ideas* 60 (1999): 505–524, and Kleingeld, "Defending the Plurality of States: Cloots, Kant, and Rawls," *Social Theory and Practice* 32 (2006): 559–578.

35. See Marc Bélissa, *Fraternité universelle et intérêt national (1713–1795): les cosmopolitiques du droit des gens* (Paris, 1996), and *Repenser l'ordre européen, 1795–1802: de la société des rois aux droits des nations* (Paris, 2006).

36. Cf. Martha Nussbaum, "Kant and Stoic Cosmopolitanism," *Journal of Political Philosophy* 5, 1 (March 1997): 1–25, rpt. as "Kant and Cosmopolitanism," in James Bohman and Mathias Lutz-Bachmann, eds., *Perpetual Peace: Essays on Kant's Cosmopolitan Idea* (Cambridge, Mass., 1997).

37. Cited in Lloyd Kramer, *Lafayette in Two Worlds: Public Cultures and Personal Identities in an Age of Revolutions* (Chapel Hill, 1996), 255–56.

38. Citations from Lewis B. Namier, "Nationality and Liberty," rpt. in Eugene C. Black, *European Political History, 1815–1870: Aspects of Liberalism* (New York, 1967), 139–41, except for the last, from Yael Tamir, *Liberal Nationalism* (Princeton, 1995), 124. Cf. Michael Walzer, "Nation and Universe," in *Thinking Politically: Essays in Political Theory* (New Haven, 2007) and C. A. Bayly and Eugene Biagini, eds., *Giuseppe Mazzini and the Globalisation of Democratic Nationalism, 1830–1920* (Oxford, 2008).

39. Tony Judt, "Rights in France: Reflections on the Etiolation of a Political Language," *Tocqueville Review* 14, 1 (1993): 67–108. See also Norberto Bobbio, "Diritti dell'uomo e del cittadino nel secolo XIX in Europa," and other essays in Gerhard Dilcher, et al., eds., *Grundrechte im 19. Jahrhundert* (Frankfurt, 1982).

40. See Steven B. Smith, *Hegel's Critique of Liberalism: Rights in Context* (Chicago, 1991).

41. See Herbert A. Strauss, *Staat, Bürger, Mensch: die Debatten der deutschen Nationalversammlung 1848/1849 über Grundrechte* (Aarau, 1947); cf. Brian E. Vick, *Debating Germany: The 1848 Frankfurt Parliamentarians and National Identity* (Cambridge, Mass., 2002); for

some texts, Heinrich Scholler, ed., *Die Grundrechtsdiskussion in der Paulskirsche: eine Dokumentation* (Darmstadt, 1973).

42. Arendt, *Origins*, 293.

43. A fine Anglo-American overview is Jeremy Waldron, "The Decline of Natural Right," in Allen Wood and Songsuk Susan Hahn, eds., *Cambridge History of Nineteenth Century Philosophy* (New York, forthcoming).

44. Elie Halévy, *The Growth of Philosophic Radicalism,* trans. Mary Morris (Boston, 1955), 155.

45. This claim is due to Marcel Gauchet, "Les droits de l'homme ne sont pas une politique," *Le Débat* 3 (July–August 1980), rpt. in *La condition politique* (Paris, 2007).

46. See, e.g., Adam Hochschild, *Bury the Chains: Prophets and Rebels in the Fight to Free an Empire's Slaves* (New York, 2005), Jenny S. Martinez, "Antislavery Courts and the Dawn of International Human Rights Law," *Yale Law Journal* 117, 4 (January 2008): 550–641, or Gary J. Bass, *Freedom's Battle: The Origins of Humanitarian Intervention* (New York, 2008).

47. Abigail Green, "The British Empire and the Jews: An Imperialism of Human Rights?" *Past and Present* 199 (May 2008): 175–205; Lisa Moses Leff, *The Sacred Bonds of Solidarity: The Rise of Jewish Internationalism in Nineteenth-Century France* (Stanford, 2006).

48. Cf. Carole Fink, *Defending the Rights of Others: The Great Powers, the Jews, and International Minority Protection, 1878–1938* (Cambridge, 2004), and Mark Mazower, "Minorities and the League of Nations in Interwar Europe," *Daedalus* 26, 2 (1997): 47–64.

49. Cited in David Donald, *Charles Sumner and the Rights of Man* (New York, 1970), 423.

50. Remarkably, in her discussion of the "invention of human rights," Lynn Hunt omits even to mention either the right of private property or the 1793 articulation of social rights. See Jean-Pierre Gross, *Fair Shares for All: Jacobin Egalitarianism in Practice* (Cambridge, 1997), 41–46, 64–72, and chap. 6. On the right to work, see Pierre Rosanvallon, *The New Social Question: Rethinking the Welfare State,* trans. Barbara Harshav (Princeton, 2008), chap. 5.

51. Gareth Stedman Jones, *An End to Poverty? A Historical Debate* (New York, 2003), 13.

52. "The Right to Work Denied," in *The Utopian Vision of Charles Fourier,* ed. and. trans. Jonathan Beecher and Richard Bienvenu (Boston 1971), 137. On Thelwall, see Gregory Claeys, *The French Revolution Debate in Britain: The Origins of Modern Politics* (New York, 2007).

53. Cited in Beecher, *Victor Considerant and the Rise and Fall of French Romantic Socialism* (Berkeley, 2001), 143. See also Rosanvallon, *The New Social Question,* for other French invocations.

54. T. H. Marshall, "Citizenship and Social Class," in *Citizenship and Social Class, and Other Essays* (Cambridge, 1950).

55. See, e.g., Edward S. Corwin, "The 'Higher Law' Background of American Constitutionalism," *Harvard Law Review* 42, 2 (December 1928): 149–85, and 42, 3 (January 1929): 365–409.

56. See Robert Green McCloskey, *American Conservatism in the Age of Enterprise, 1865–1910* (Cambridge, Mass., 1951), chap. 5, "Judicial Conservatism and the Rights of Man." See also Richard A. Primus, *The American Language of Rights* (Cambridge, 1999), which leaves this seemingly important era out.

57. See, most accessibly, Léon Duguit, "Law and the State," *Harvard Law Review* 31, 1 (November 1917): 1–185 and "Objective Law," *Columbia Law Review* 20, 8 (December 1920): 817–31. Compare, for the tip of the iceberg on illiberal twentieth century regimes and social rights, Pedro Ramos Pino, "Housing and Citizenship: Building Social Rights in Twentieth Century Portugal," *Contemporary European History* 18, 2 (May 2009): 199–215.

58. See Joan Wallach Scott, *Only Paradoxes to Offer: French Feminists and the Rights of Man* (Cambridge, Mass., 1996), chap. 4.

59. See, e.g., William D. Irvine, *Between Justice and Politics: The Ligue des Droits de l'Homme, 1898–1945* (Stanford, 2007); Paul L. Murphy, *World War I and the Origins of Civil Liberties in the United States* (New York, 1978); and K. D. Ewing and C. A. Gearty, *The Struggle for Civil Liberties: Political Freedom and the Rule of Law in Britain, 1914–1945* (Oxford, 2001).

60. Hidemi Suganami, "A Note on the Origin of the Word 'International,'"

British Journal of International Studies 4 (1978): 226–32. Cf. Arendt, "The Seeds of a Fascist International," in *Essays in Understanding, 1930–1954*, ed. Jerome Kohn (New York, 1994).

61. See *Annuaire des organisations internationales* (Geneva, 1949), as well as Martin H. Geyer and Johannes Paulmann, eds., *The Mechanics of Internationalism: Culture, Society and Politics from the 1840s to World War I* (Oxford, 2001).

62. The recent collapse of the border between human rights and humanitarianism has led the usual case for continuity to revolve around events in the law of war—which, however, "humanized" warfare for the soldiers involved only, without appeal to "the rights of man" as a basis.

63. Cf. Monique Canto-Sperber and Nadia Urbinati, eds., *Le socialisme libéral: Une anthologie* (Paris, 2003).

64. See Madeleine Rébérioux, "Jaurès et les droits de l'homme," *Bulletin de la Société d'Etudes Jaurésiennes* 102–103 (July 1986).

65. As Leszek Kołakowski points out, the German translation of the (originally French) lyrics used the phrase "die 'Internationale' erkämpft die Menschenrecht" for rhyming reasons, and against ideological proclivity. Leszek Kołakowski, "Marxism and Human Rights," *Daedalus* 112, 4 (Fall 1983): 81.

66. The total omission of this basic fact remains perhaps the most startling feature of backstories of contemporary internationalism composed in recent years. See esp. Akira Iriye, *Global Community: The Role of International Organizations in the Making of the Modern World* (Berkeley, 2002).

67. Martti Koskenniemi, *The Gentle Civilizer of Nations: The Rise and Fall of International Law* (Cambridge, 2001), 67–76.

68. See, e.g., Lloyd Kramer, who says anachronistically that "[m]ost liberal nationalists in the early nineteenth century . . . stressed the link between universal rights and national independence without fully recognizing how national claims could overwhelm other claims for universal human rights." Kramer, *Lafayette*, 255–56. That this insight was unavailable is not a failure on their part but a clue to the conditions under which "universal human rights" could later become salient. With similar anachronism, Louis Henkin concluded *The Rights of Man Today*

(Boulder, 1978), discussed further in Chapter 5 of this book, by saying: "Paine proclaimed the rights of man in national society [but] would have welcomed international human rights" (137).

69. See Marc Bloch, *The Historian's Craft*, trans. Peter Putnam (New York, 1953), chap. 1.

70. Arendt, *Origins*, 299; cf. Giorgio Agamben, *Homo Sacer: Sovereign Power and Bare Life*, trans. Daniel Heller-Roazen (Stanford, 1997), 132–33.

2 Death from Birth

1. One agenda item for this chapter is to heal the separation between the history of human rights and the history of international organization generally, the latter as in John W. Wheeler-Bennett and Anthony Nicholls, *The Semblance of Peace: The Political Settlement after the Second World War* (New York, 1972) and G. John Ikenberry, *After Victory: Institutions, Strategic Restraint, and the Rebuilding of Order after Major Wars* (Princeton, 2001), chap. 6.

2. Moses Moskowitz, "Whither the United Nations Human Rights Program?" *Israel Year Book on Human Rights* 6 (1976): 82.

3. See, brilliantly, Jill Lepore, *The Name of War: King Philip's War and the Making of American Identity* (New York, 1998) and for mostly British statements, Phyllis Bottome's Penguin special collection of speeches, *Our New Order or Hitler's?* (London, 1943).

4. Theodore A. Wilson, *The First Summit: Roosevelt and Churchill at Placentia Bay 1941* (Boston, 1969).

5. See *Foreign Relations of the United States: The Conferences at Washington, 1941–1942, and Casablanca, 1943* (Washington, D.C., 1968), 370–71. Based on the British archives, Brian Simpson complains: "Quite how human rights found their way into the text is not as clear as one would like," and scholars examining American sources have not done better. A. W. B. Simpson, *Human Rights and the End of Empire: Britain and the Genesis of the European Convention* (Oxford, 2001), 184.

6. "Human Rights League," *New York Times*, March 15, 1933, organized by the president of City College with participation by John Dewey and others; "New Group Appears to 'X-Ray' New Deal," *New York*

Times, September 10, 1934, which mentions a "Roosevelt Human Rights League" whose "subversive" activities need to be opposed. "Hoover Denounces New Deal as Foe of Human Liberty," *New York Times,* September 4, 1934; "Text of the Socialist Party Platform," *New York Times,* May 27, 1936. Interestingly, a few years later, after the New Deal revolution, the U.S. Supreme Court could be credited for championing "Human Rights . . . over Property Rights." Frederic Nelson, "Human Rights with Cream," *The New Republic,* February 1, 1939.

7. Pius XI, Mit brennender Sorge (March 14, 1937), as translated in Georges Passelecq and Bernard Suchecky, *The Hidden Encyclical of Pius XI,* trans. Steven Rendall (New York, 1997), 105; Ingravescentibus Malis (September 29, 1937), as summarized in "Pagans and Reds Are Held by Pope to Menace the World," *New York Times,* September 30, 1937; "Pope Bids Church to Guard Man's Rights," *New York Times,* October 13, 1938.

8. Robert E. Lucey, "A Worldwide Attack on Man," *Voice for Human Rights* 1, 2 (September 1940): 7; in the same issue, see "Change of Name Shows Broader Application of Principles," *Voice for Human Rights* 1, 2 (September 1940): 10, which explains the move to human rights language.

9. McCormick had frequently reported about papal rhetoric; and in early 1942 she joined a secret State Department committee to work on postwar affairs. Anne O'Hare McCormick, "The Reawakening that Hitler Failed to Mention," *New York Times,* October 4, 1941. Compare her *New York Times* pieces, "For State or—Church," March 1, 1936; "The New Pope," March 3, 1939 ("Pius XI felt obliged to raise his voice on every possible occasion in the defense of liberty of conscience and the inalienable rights of the individual soul"); and later "Papal Message a Momentous Pronouncement," December 25, 1944, all reprinted in McCormick, *Vatican Journal 1921–1954,* ed. Marion Turner Sheehan, intro. by Clare Booth Luce (New York, 1957), at 98.

10. Compare State Department work in 1942 on the idea of a bill of rights within the framework of economic and social reconstruction: Ruth B. Russell, ed., *A History of the United Nations Charter: The Role of the United States, 1940–1945* (Washington, 1958), chap. 12.

11. I draw on existing surveys in light of this point. See Elizabeth Borgwardt, *A New Deal for the World: America's Vision for Human Rights* (Cambridge, Mass., 2006); Paul Gordon Lauren, *The Evolution of Hu-*

man Rights: Visions Seen, 2nd ed. (Philadelphia, 2003), chap. 5; and esp. Simpson, *Human Rights*, chap. 4.

12. For the origins, see William Draper Lewis, "An International Bill of Rights," *Proceedings of the American Philosophical Society* 85, 5 (September 1942): 445–47.

13. Hersch Lauterpacht, "The Law of Nature, the Law of Nations, and the Rights of Man," *Transactions of the Grotius Society* 29 (1943): 1–33; Lauterpacht, *An International Bill of Rights* (New York, 1945); for more on Lauterpacht, see below, chap. 5; Robert P. Hillman, "Quincy Wright and the Commission to Study the Organization of Peace," *Global Governance* 4, 4 (October 1998): 485–499; Glenn Tatsuya Mitoma, "Civil Society and International Human Rights: The Commission to Study the Organization of Peace and the Origins of the UN Human Rights Regime," *Human Rights Quarterly* 30, 3 (August 2008): 607–630.

14. See Robert A. Divine, *Second Chance: The Rise of Internationalism in America during World War II* (New York, 1967), 22–23.

15. Commission to Study the Bases of a Just and Durable Peace, *A Righteous Faith* (New York, 1942), 101, 103; and *Six Pillars of Peace: A Study Guide* (New York, 1943), 72–81. Cf. Heather A. Warren, *Theologians of a New World Order: Reinhold Niebuhr and the Christian Realists, 1920–1948* (New York, 1997), esp. chap. 6.

16. The earliest publications are "The Natural Law and Human Rights" (Windsor, Ontario, 1942), an award acceptance speech dated January 18, 1942 and published as a pamphlet; and "Natural Law and Human Rights," *Dublin Review* 210 (April 1942): 116–24. He then wrote *Les droits de l'homme et la loi naturelle* (New York, 1942), translated into many languages. Maritain, "Christian Humanism," *Fortune*, April 1942. Similar views ricocheted throughout Catholic thought thereafter; see, e.g., Joseph T. Delos, "The Rights of the Human Person Vis-à-Vis the State and the Race," in Delos et al., *Race-Nation-Person: Social Aspects of the Race Problem* (New York, 1944), or Tibor Payzs, "Human Rights in a World Society," *Thought* 22, 85 (June 1947): 245–68.

17. The American Jewish Committee made clear the shift of Jewish strategy from prewar mechanisms like intervention, bilateral treaty, or a minorities regime to "international machinery." But while it treated human rights after the war as the successor to minority rights, this was

surely not the general public meaning of the phrase. American Jewish Committee, *To the Counsellors of Peace* (New York, [March] 1945), esp. 13–24; and "A Post-War Program for Jews," *The New Republic*, April 30, 1945. Cf. Jacob Robinson, *Human Rights and Fundamental Freedoms in the Charter of the United Nations* (New York, 1946); and "From Protection of Minorities to Promotion of Human Rights," *Jewish Year Book of International Law* 1 (1949): 115–51; as well as Mark Mazower, "The Strange Triumph of Human Rights, 1930–1950," *Historical Journal* 47, 2 (2004): 379–98.

18. Wm. Roger Louis, *Imperialism at Bay: The United States and the Decolonization of the British Empire* (Oxford, 1977); Warren F. Kimball, *The Juggler: Franklin Roosevelt as Wartime Statesman* (Princeton, 1991), chap. 7; see also Chapter 3.

19. Goebbels cited in Karl Dietrich Bracher, *The Nazi Dictatorship: The Origins, Structure, and Effects of National Socialism,* trans. Jean Steinberg (New York, 1970), 10. On British silence, see Simpson, *Human Rights,* 204–5, ascribing this to traditional British allergies to formal declarations. For the Pope and Continental Catholicism, see esp. the encyclical Summi Pontificatus (October 20, 1939), which reads that "man and the family are by nature anterior to the State, and that the Creator has given to both of them powers and rights and has assigned them a mission and a charge that correspond to undeniable natural requirements"; François and Renée Bédarida, eds., *La Résistance spirituelle 1941–1944: Les cahiers clandestins du "Témoignage chrétien"* (Paris, 2001), 159–86; and Paul A. Hanebrink, *In Defense of Christian Hungary: Religion, Nationalism, and Antisemitism, 1890–1944* (Ithaca, 2006), 170–80.

20. See Dallek, *Franklin Roosevelt,* 419–20, 482; Kimball, *The Juggler,* chap. 6, Kimball, "The Sheriffs: FDR's Postwar World," in David B. Woolner et al., eds., *FDR's World: War, Peace, and Legacies* (New York, 2008); Robert C. Hilderbrand, *Dumbarton Oaks: The Origins of the United Nations and the Search for Postwar Security* (Raleigh, 1990); and esp. Christopher D. O'Sullivan, *Sumner Welles, Postwar Planning, and the Quest for a New World Order, 1937–1943* (New York, 2008). See also, for general discussion of the relation between globalism and regionalism for Americans (which involved sometimes expanding and some-

times protecting the Monroe Doctrine's hemispheric security zone), Neil Smith, *American Empire: Roosevelt's Geographer and the Prelude to Globalization* (Berkeley, 2003), chap. 14.

21. Hilderbrand, *Dumbarton Oaks*, 16.

22. *Foreign Relations of the United States: Diplomatic Papers 1944 (General)* (New York, 1966), 791; Jebb cited in Hilderbrand, *Dumbarton Oaks*, 92.

23. Charles Webster, "The Making of the Charter of the United Nations" (based on a 1946 lecture), in *The Art and Practice of Diplomacy* (New York, 1962), 79. For the idea of the events that followed as a "people's peace," see Lauren, *Evolution*, chaps. 5–6. Cf. Farrokh Jhabvala, "The Drafting of the Human Rights Provisions of the UN Charter," *Netherlands International Law Review* 44 (1997): 3–31.

24. Dorothy B. Robins, *Experiment in Democracy: The Story of U.S. Citizen Organizations in Forging the Charter of the United Nations* (New York, 1971), 157; Vera Micheles Dean, *The Four Cornerstones of Peace* (New York, 1946), 9. The book consists of pamphlets originally prepared for the Foreign Policy Association and published in 1944–45.

25. Ralph Barton Perry, "Working Basis Seen," *New York Times*, January 7, 1945. Cf. Robins, *Experiment*, 74–75, citing a Christian newsletter to the effect that "the real choice . . . is not between an imperfect peace agency and an adequate agency, but between an imperfect organization which can keep the peace for a generation and gradually evolve into something better, and an open struggle for power which cannot keep the peace at all." Reinhold Niebuhr, "Is This 'Peace in Our Time'?" *The Nation*, April 7, 1945. Brian Simpson is clearly wrong to say that "[i]n the USA itself the failure to emphasize the importance of human rights became the main criticism." Simpson, *Human Rights*, 251.

26. Robins, *Experiment*, 151; "This Is It," *Time*, June 18, 1945.

27. José Cabranes, "Human Rights and Non-Intervention in the Inter-American System," *Michigan Law Review* 65, 6 (April 1967): 1147–82, which stresses the reasons for commitment to sovereign impregnability, esp. 1161–62 on the Bogotá declaration. Cf. Lauren, *Evolution*, and Mary Ann Glendon, *A World Made New: Eleanor Roosevelt and the Universal Declaration of Human Rights* (New York, 2001).

28. Herbert V. Evatt, "Risks of a Big Power Peace," *Foreign Affairs* 24, 2 (January 1946): 195–209; and *The United Nations* (Oliver Wendell Holmes lectures, 1947) (Cambridge, Mass., 1948).

29. Webster, "The Making," 86; Vandenberg cited in Clark M. Eichelberger, *Organizing for Peace: A Personal History of the United Nations* (New York, 1977); Virginia Gildersleeve, *Many a Good Crusade* (New York, 1954), 330–31. On Smuts, see Mark Mazower, *No Enchanted Palace: The End of Empire and the Ideological Origins of the United Nations* (Princeton, 2009), chap. 1; see also Saul Dubow, "Smuts, the United Nations, and the Rhetoric of Race and Rights," *Journal of Contemporary History* 41, 1 (2008): 45–74. For the addition of the Commission on Human Rights to the charter, due to Christian and Jewish representatives, as well as the American Association for the United Nations, see Eichelberger, *Organizing for Peace*, 269–72; Robins, *Experiment*, 129–32; Benjamin V. Cohen, "Human Rights under the United Nations Charter," *Law and Contemporary Problems* 14, 3 (Summer 1949): 430–37 at 430–31; cf. William Korey, *NGOs and the Universal Declaration of Human Rights* (New York, 1998), chap. 1. See also Frederick Nolde's memories in *Free and Equal: Human Rights in Ecumenical Perspective* (Geneva, 1968).

30. "Les droits fondamentaux de l'homme, base d'une restauration du droit international," *Annuaire de l'Institut de Droit International* 41 (1947): 153–54.

31. Cf. Albert Verdoodt, *Naissance et signification de la Déclaration universelle des droits de l'homme* (Louvain, 1964); and, most exhaustively, Johannes Morsink, *The Universal Declaration of Human Rights: Origins, Drafting, and Intent* (Philadelphia, 1999).

32. See Jason Berger, *A New Deal for the World: Eleanor Roosevelt and American Foreign Policy* (New York, 1981).

33. The Ligue des Droits de l'Homme, at its Dijon Conference in 1936, announced the need for a new set of social rights, to add to the political and civil ones it had defended since the Dreyfus Affair; see Ligue des Droits de l'Homme, *Le Congrès national de 1936: Compte-rendu sténographique* (Paris, 1936), 219–305 and 415–23, "Projet de complément à la Déclaration des Droits de l'Homme." For postwar social rights, see also Georges Gurvitch, *The Bill of Social Rights* (New York, 1946).

34. See the narrative in Cass Sunstein, *The Second Bill of Rights: FDR's Unfinished Revolution and Why We Need It More than Ever* (New York, 2004). The changing nature of the New Deal after 1937 in the direc-

tion of individual rights is the main thesis of Alan Brinkley, *The End of Reform: New Deal Liberalism in Recession and War* (New York, 1995), though Brinkley makes no attempt to connect this rights-based deradicalization to wartime internationalism.

35. For a general picture, see my "Personalism, Community, and the Origins of Human Rights," in Stefan-Ludwig Hoffmann, ed., *A History of Human Rights in the Twentieth Century* (Cambridge, 2010). On Roosevelt, see Glendon, *A World Made New;* on Humphrey, see Clinton Timothy Curle, *Humanité: John Humphrey's Alternative Account of Human Rights* (Toronto, 2007).

36. See esp. A. J. Hobbins, "René Cassin and the Daughter of Time: The First Draft of the Universal Declaration of Human Rights," *Fontanus* 2 (1989): 7–26, one document in a subsidiary and frequently nationalistic literature intent on awarding credit to a single founder.

37. René Cassin, "L'État-Léviathan contre l'homme et la communauté humaine," *Nouveaux cahiers,* April 1940, rpt. in Cassin, *La pensée et l'action* (Paris, 1972), citing Pius XII's encyclical Summi Pontificatus. It may be, in his case alone, that the rhetoric of the human person retained some link to older, generally overthrown neo-Kantian ideas of the turn of the century. On Cassin, see Marc Agi, *René Cassin, fantassin des droits de l'homme* (Paris, 1979); Eric Pateyron, *La contribution française à la rédaction de la Déclaration universelle des droits de l'homme: René Cassin et la Commission consultative des droits de l'homme* (Paris, 1998); and J. M. Winter, *Dreams of Peace and Freedom: Utopian Moments in the Twentieth Century* (New Haven, 2006), chap. 2. For a flavor of Cassin's views in this era, see Cassin, "The United Nations and Human Rights," *Free World* 12, 2 (September 1946): 16–19; "The UN Fights for Human Rights," *United World* 1, 4 (May 1947): 46–48; or "La Déclaration Universelle des Droits de l'Homme," *Évidences* 1 (1949). For memories, see various texts in Cassin, *La pensée et l'action.* For bibliography and reminiscences, see the special issue of *Revue des droits de l'homme* (December 1985).

38. Edward Said, *Out of Place* (New York, 1999), esp. 265. A serious study of Malik is a desideratum, but see Raja Choueri's revealing *Charles Malek: Discours, droits de l'homme, et ONU* (Beirut, 1998), which stresses his religiosity and loyalty to the American missionary tradition

that led to the founding of the American University of Beirut where he studied and later taught. Malik's most full-blown endorsement of Christian personalism in public at the time occurs in E/CN.4/SR.14 (1947), esp. 3–4.

39. John Humphrey, *Human Rights and the United Nations: A Great Adventure* (Dobbs Ferry, 1983), 65–66. The Bogotá declaration, often said to be the first international declaration of rights in world history, had been preceded by the Geneva Declaration of the Rights of the Child (1924).

40. For a much more laudatory view of the role of "small states" at this point, see Glendon, "The Forgotten Crucible: The Latin American Influence on the Universal Human Rights Idea," *Harvard Human Rights Journal* 16 (2003): 27–40; and esp. Susan Waltz, "Reclaiming and Rebuilding the History of the Universal Declaration of Human Rights," *Third World Quarterly* 23, 3 (2002): 437–48; and Waltz, "Universalizing Human Rights: The Role of Small States in the Construction of the Universal Declaration of Human Rights," *Human Rights Quarterly* 23 (2001): 44–72. On Latin America, cf. Paolo G. Wright-Carrozza, "From Conquest to Constitutions: Retrieving a Latin American Tradition of the Idea of Human Rights," *Human Rights Quarterly* 25, 2 (May 2003): 281–313.

41. See UNESCO, *Human Rights: Comments and Interpretations*, intro. Maritain (New York, 1948), 9; [Melville Herskovits et al.], "Statement on Human Rights," *American Anthropologist*, n.s., 49 (1947): 539–43, and 50 (1948): 351–55 at 543, which includes Julian Steward's criticism of the residual universalism of the anthropological plea for difference; cf. Karen Engle, "From Skepticism to Embrace: Human Rights and the American Anthropological Association from 1947–1999," *Human Rights Quarterly* 3 (2001): 536–59.

42. UN ESC Res. 75 (V), August 5, 1947; Humphrey, *Human Rights and the United Nations*, 28; Mehta cited in Manu Bhagavan, "A New Hope: India, the United Nations and the Making of the Universal Declaration of Human Rights," *Modern Asian Studies* 44, 2 (March 2010): 311–47.

43. Charles Malik, "How the Commission on Human Rights Forged Its Draft of the *First* Covenant," *United Nations Weekly Bulletin*, June 1, 1950.

44. See Andrew Martin, "Human Rights and World Affairs," *Year Book of World Affairs* 5 (1951): 44–80 at 48.

45. George L. Kline, "Changing Attitudes toward the Individual," in Cyril Black, ed., *The Transformation of Russian Society* (Cambridge, 1960); John N. Hazard, "The Soviet Union and a World Bill of Rights," *Columbia Law Review* 47, 7 (November 1947): 1095–1117; Rupert Emerson and Inis L. Claude, Jr., "The Soviet Union and the United Nations: An Essay in Interpretation," *International Organization* 6, 1 (February 1952): 20–21. For the best narrative of the Soviets and the Universal Declaration, see Kamleshwar Das, "Some Observations Relating to the International Bill of Human Rights," *Indian Yearbook of International Affairs* 19 (1986): 12–15, citing UN Doc. E/CN.4/SR.89, 12.

46. Jennifer Amos, "Embracing and Contesting: The Soviet Union and the Universal Declaration of Human Rights, 1948–1958," in Hoffmann, ed., *A History of Human Rights*, and Waltz, "Universal Rights: The Contribution of Muslim States," *Human Rights Quarterly* 26 (2004): 813–19.

47. "The declaration was, in certain respects, not based on reality, because it described man as an isolated individual and overlooked the fact that he was also a member of a community." U.N. Doc. A/PV.183 (1948), 916. As late as 1965, Harvard Law School's Harold Berman, among other things expert in Soviet jurisprudence, could write that the USSR's approach to human rights, for all its flaws, remained "a genuine response to the crisis of the 20th century, which has witnessed the breakdown of individualism—in law as well as in other areas of spiritual life." Berman, "Human Rights in the Soviet Union," *Howard Law Journal* 11 (Spring 1965): 341.

48. See, e.g., Ivo Lapenna, *Conceptions soviétiques de droit international public* (Paris, 1954), 222–23, 293–99. Further, it would appear that post-1948 attempts to formulate a "socialist international law" did not prioritize human rights in any way. Ibid., 149–53. On the Soviets at the UN more generally, see Alexander Dallin, *The Soviet Union at the United Nations: An Inquiry into Objectives and Motives* (New York, 1962).

49. For the resolutions, all from early 1949, see UN G. A. Res. 265 (III) (South Asians), 272 (III) (Hungary and Bulgaria), and 285 (III) (Soviet wives, brought by Chile, whose ambassador's son found himself af-

fected). See also, later, UN G. A. Res. 294 (IV) (1949) and 385 (V) (Hungary and Bulgaria again).

50. See, e.g., their role in Louis Sohn and Thomas Buergenthal, *International Protection of Human Rights* (Indianapolis, 1973). On early activity around South Africa, see R. B. Ballinger, "UN Action on Human Rights in South Africa," in Evan Luard, ed., *The International Protection of Human Rights* (London, 1967).

51. See Martin, "Human Rights in the Paris Peace Treaties," *British Yearbook of International Law* 24 (1947) and Stephen D. Kertesz, "Human Rights in the Peace Treaties," *Law and Contemporary Problems* 14, 4 (Autumn 1949): 627–46; and, for canny analysis of the international (including UN) uproar around Mindszenty, see Gaetano Salvemini, "The Vatican and Mindszenty," *The Nation*, August 6, 1949.

52. This era remains to be studied in much detail, but for now see Barbara Metzger, "Towards an International Human Rights Regime during the Inter-war Years: The League of Nations' Combat of Traffic in Women and Children," in Kevin Grant et al., eds., *Beyond Sovereignty: Britain, Empire, and Transnationalism* (New York, 2007); Keith David Watenpaugh, "'A Pious Wish Devoid of All Practicability': The League of Nations' Eastern Mediterranean Rescue Movement and the Paradox of Interwar Humanitarianism," *American Historical Review* (forthcoming); and Claudena M. Skran, *Refugees in Inter-War Europe: The Emergence of a Regime* (Oxford, 1995). It is anachronistic, however, to conflate humanitarianism and human rights, which reflects contemporary assumptions.

53. Cf. Daniel Maul, *Menschenrechte, Sozialpolitik und Dekolonisation: Die Internationale Arbeitsorganisation (IAO) 1940–1970* (Essen, 2007); in English, see Maul, "The International Labour Organization and the Struggle against Forced Labour," *Labor History* 48, 4 (2007): 477–500 and "The International Labour Organization and Human Rights," in Hoffmann, ed., *A History of Human Rights*.

54. Aron cited in Marco Duranti, "Conservatism, Christian Democracy, and the European Human Rights Project, 1945–1950" (Ph.D. diss. Yale University, 2009), 88; E. H. Carr, "The Rights of Man," in UNESCO, ed., *Human Rights*, 20. Compare Carr's argument against the isolation of

formal guarantees to the importance of social protection by various mechanisms. "Nor are political rights and political principles the dominant preoccupation of the contemporary world. The statement often, and justly, made that the future of democracy depends on its ability to solve the problem of full employment illustrates the subordination of political to social and economic ends in the modern world. Internationalism, like nationalism, must become social." Carr, *Nationalism and After* (London, 1945), 63.

55. Cf. Mark Philip Bradley, "The Ambiguities of Sovereignty: The United States and the Global Human Rights Cases of the 1940s and 1950s," in Douglas Howland and Luise White, eds., *The Art of the State: Sovereignty Past and Present* (Bloomington, 2008).

56. G. K. A. Bell, *Christianity and World Order* (Harmondsworth, 1940), 104; Bell, "The Church in Relation to International Affairs" (address at Chatham House), *International Affairs* 25, no. 4 (October 1949): 407, 409; Emil Brunner, "Das Menschenbild und die Menschenrechte," *Universitas* 2, 3 (March 1947): 269–74 and 2, 4 (April 1947): 385–91 at 269; cf. R. M. MacIver, ed., *Great Expressions of Human Rights* (New York, 1950), with chiefly religious authors and contents, including famed American Catholic theologian John Courtney Murray's personalist and communitarian interpretation. Cf. Richard McKeon's "The Philosophic Bases and Material Circumstances of the Rights of Man," in UNESCO, ed., *Human Rights*, and the autobiographical and other reflections in McKeon, *Freedom and Reason and Other Essays*, ed. Zahava McKeon (Chicago, 1990), and the epilogue to this book on the philosophical revival of rights in the 1970s.

57. Gerhard Ritter, "Ursprung und Wesen der Menschenrechte," *Historische Zeitschrift* 169, 2 (August 1949): 234. These paragraphs follow my "The First Historian of Human Rights," *American Historical Review*, forthcoming.

58. Ritter, "Die englisch-amerikanischen Kirchen und die Friedensfrage," *Zeitwende* 18 (1949): 459–70, citation at 469. For Dulles and Nolde at Amsterdam, see Dulles, "The Christian Citizen in a Changing World," and Nolde, "Freedom of Religion and Related Human Rights," in World Council of Churches, *Man's Disorder and God's Design*, vol. 4:

The Church and the International Disorder (London, 1948), 73–189, esp. 107–8 on the international bill of rights. For a different view of the centrality of human rights to the WCC, see John Nurser, *For All Peoples and All Nations: The Ecumenical Church and Human Rights* (Washington, 2005). Malik himself testified, prefacing Nolde's later memoirs, that "I felt that if we should lose th[e] Article on freedom of conscience and religion, namely, if man's absolute freedom were to be derogated from in any way, even by the subtlest indirection, my interest in the remainder of the Declaration would considerably flag." Malik, "The Universal Declaration of Human Rights," in Nolde, *Free and Equal*, 10. In a similar vein, see the essays by Malik and Nolde in Marion V. Royce and Wesley F. Rennie, eds., *We, the People, and Human Rights: A Guide to Study and Action* (New York, 1949).

59. Cited in Simpson, *Human Rights*, 227.

60. William D. Irvine, *Between Justice and Politics: The Ligue des Droits de l'Homme, 1898–1945* (Stanford, 2007).

61. See, however, Willy Strzelewicz, *Der Kampf um Menschenrechte: Von der amerikanischen Unabhängigkeitserklärung bis zur Gegenwart* ([Stockholm, 1943,] Hamburg 1947) for a social democratic narrative. Lora Wildenthal's work shows that after the war, civil liberties activism could incorporate some allusions to the new international language, without profoundly changing the terms of its activities. Wildenthal, "Human Rights Activism in Occupied and Early West Germany: The Case of the German League for Human Rights," *Journal of Modern History* 80, 3 (September 2008): 515–56. The cases of the postwar Ligue and ACLU suggest similar conclusions.

62. Wolfram Kaiser, *Christian Democracy and the Origins of the European Union* (Cambridge, 2007). Cf. Michael Newman, *Socialism and European Unity: The Dilemma of the Left in Britain and France* (London, 1983).

63. Duranti, "Conservatism," which I follow here.

64. Aimé Césaire, *Discourse on Colonialism*, trans. Joan Pinkham (New York, 1972), 17. The story of French opposition to the European Convention is told in Duranti, "Conservatism," conclusion. On Belgian and Dutch affairs, there is much more to be done, but see, e.g., Peter Mal-

content, "Myth or Reality? The Dutch Crusade against the Human Rights Violations in the Third World, 1973–1981," in Antoine Fleury, et al., eds., *Les droits de l'homme en Europe depuis 1945* (Bern, 2003).

65. On Cyprus, see Simpson, *Human Rights,* chaps. 17–19. On Lawless, see Ian Brownlie, "The Individual before Tribunals Exercising International Jurisdiction," *International and Comparative Law Quarterly* 11, 3 (1962): 701–20; and Jack Greenberg and Anthony R. Shalit, "New Horizons for Human Rights: The European Convention, Court, and Commission of Human Rights," *Columbia Law Review* 63 (1963): 1384–1412. For caseload, see, e.g., Steven Greer, *The European Convention on Human Rights: Achievements, Problems, and Prospects* (Cambridge, 2006), chap. 1, esp. the charts on 34–35.

66. This assertion is based on a full analysis of the stenographic record. On Nuremberg and the Genocide Convention, see Donald Bloxham, *Genocide on Trial: War Crimes Trials and the Formation of Holocaust History and Memory* (Oxford, 2001); and Mira Siegelberg, "The Origins of the Genocide Convention," *Columbia Undergraduate Journal of History* 1, 1 (2005): 34–57.

3 Why Anticolonialism Wasn't a Human Rights Movement

1. Cited in Dixee R. Bartholomew-Feis, *The OSS and Ho Chi Minh: Unexpected Allies in the War against Japan* (Lawrence, 2006), 243.

2. Ho Chi Minh, "Declaration of Independence of the Democratic Republic of Viet-Nam," in *On Revolution: Selected Writings 1920–66,* ed. Bernard B. Fall (New York, 1967), 143.

3. Ibid., emphasis added. According to Jack Rakove, already "in writing the preamble to the Declaration, Jefferson was seeking neither to strike a blow for the equality of individuals, nor to erase the countless social differences that the law sometimes created and often sustained. The primary form of equality that the preamble asserts is an equality among peoples, defined as self-governing communities." Rakove, "Jefferson, Rights, and the Priority of Freedom of Conscience," in Robert Fatton, Jr. and R. K. Ramazani, eds., *The Future of Liberal Democracy: Thomas Jefferson and the Contemporary World* (New York, 2004), 51.

4. Laurent Dubois makes such a claim about the Haitian Revolution, and

Lynn Hunt, writing on the same era, has followed him. Laurent Dubois, *A Colony of Citizens: Revolution and Slave Emancipation in the French Caribbean, 1787–1804* (Chapel Hill, 2004). Lynn Hunt, *Inventing Human Rights: A History* (New York, 2007), chap. 4.

5. Cf. Florence Bernault, "What Absence Is Made Of: Human Rights in Africa," in Jeffrey N. Wasserstrom et al., eds., *Human Rights and Revolutions* (Lanham, 2000), esp. 128.

6. Cited in Raoul Girardet, *L'idée coloniale en France* (Paris, 1972), 183.

7. In this sense, the title of Bonny Ibhawoh, *Imperialism and Human Rights: Colonial Discourses of Rights and Liberties in African History* (Albany, 2007), is seriously misleading. For claims that an interesting indigenous rights movement in Ghana in the late nineteenth century anticipated later developments, cf. S. K. B. Asante, "The Neglected Aspects of the Gold Coast Aborigines Rights Protection Society," *Phylon* 36, 1 (1975): 32–45.

8. Erez Manela, *The Wilsonian Moment: Self-Determination and the International Origins of Anticolonial Nationalism* (Oxford, 2007).

9. On the interpretation of the Atlantic Charter by the Allies themselves as the war continued, see Wm. Roger Louis, *Imperialism at Bay: The United States and the Decolonization of the British Empire, 1941–1945* (New York, 1978). See also Neil Smith, *American Empire: Roosevelt's Geographer and the Prelude to Globalization* (Berkeley, 2003), chap. 13. FDR is cited in Robert Dallek, *Franklin Roosevelt and American Foreign Policy 1932–1945* (Oxford, 1979), 324.

10. Efforts to add self-determination to the Universal Declaration were, as noted in the previous chapter, chiefly a concern of the Soviet and Eastern bloc delegates, and were rejected. For Ho, see William J. Duiker, *Ho Chi Minh: A Life* (New York, 2000), 341.

11. Elizabeth Borgwardt, *A New Deal for the World: America's Vision for Human Rights* (Cambridge, Mass., 2005); Borgwardt, "'When You State a Moral Principle, You Are Stuck With It': The 1941 Atlantic Charter as a Human Rights Instrument," *Virginia Journal of International Law* 46, 3 (Spring 2006): 501–62.

12. Paul Kennedy, *The Parliament of Man: The Past, Present, and Future of the United Nations* (New York, 2006), 179. Among the Nigerians examined by Ibhawoh, "the introduction of the [Universal Declaration] did

not stimulate the kind of impassioned debates about the right to self-determination that followed the Atlantic Charter" (160). This is not surprising, since the declaration did not mention self-determination.

13. Mohandas Gandhi, "A Letter Addressed to the Secretary-General of UNESCO," in Jacques Maritain, ed., *Human Rights: Comments and Interpretations* (New York, 1948); Jawaharlal Nehru, "To the United Nations" (November 1948), in *Independence and After* (Delhi, 1949). Cf. G. S. Pathak, "India's Contribution to the Human Rights Declaration and Covenants," in L. M. Singhvi, ed., *Horizons of Freedom* (Delhi, 1969).

14. On the League, formed in Brussels in 1927 with communist funding and organization, see Vijay Prashad, *The Darker Nations: A People's History of the Third World* (New York, 2007), 31–50.

15. For a panoramic view, see Christopher Bayly and Tim Harper, *Forgotten Wars: Freedom and Revolution in Southeast Asia* (Cambridge, Mass., 2007), esp. 127, 141 for the impact of the Atlantic and UN charters.

16. For the best study to date, see Kweku Ampiah, *The Political and Moral Imperatives of the Bandung Conference: The Reactions of the US, UK, and Japan* (Kent, 2007).

17. "Declaration to the Colonial Peoples of the World," in Kwame Nkrumah, *Revolutionary Path* (New York, 1973).

18. For the text, see Rachel Murray, *Human Rights in Africa: From the OAU to the African Union* (Cambridge, 2004), Appendix 1, at 271.

19. C. L. R. James, *The Black Jacobins: Toussaint L'Ouverture and the San Domingo Revolution*, new ed. (New York, 1963), 24, 116, 139.

20. Aimé Césaire, *Discourse on Colonialism*, trans. Joan Pinkham (New York, 1972), 15. Cf. Léopold Sédar Senghor, "L'UNESCO," in *Négritude et humanisme* (Paris, 1964); or "La Négritude est un humanisme du XXe siècle," in *Négritude et civilisation de l'universel* (Paris, 1977). For background, Gary Wilder, *The French Imperial Nation-State: Negritude and Colonial Humanism between the World Wars* (Chicago, 2005).

21. Senghor's Senegal hosted, for instance, a January 1976 conference in Dakar on Namibia, with its moving spirit, Kéba M'baye, invoking his "civilization of the universal" as grounds for indicting South Africa's illegal trusteeship on grounds of anticolonialism and human rights. See

the proceedings and Declaration of Dakar in *Revue des droits de l'homme* 9, 2–3 (1976).

22. Frantz Fanon, *The Wretched of the Earth,* pref. Jean-Paul Sartre, trans. Constance Farrington (New York, 1963), 317.

23. W. E. B. Du Bois, "750,000,000 Clamoring for Human Rights," *New York Post,* May 9, 1945, rpt. in *Writings by W. E. B. Du Bois in Periodicals Edited by Others,* ed. Herbert Aptheker, 4 vols. (Millwood, 1982), 4: 2–3. See also Du Bois, "The Colonies at San Francisco," *Trek* (Johannesburg), April 5, 1946, rpt. in ibid., 4: 6–8.

24. See Louis, *Imperialism at Bay,* Parts III–IV and Gordon W. Morrell, "A Higher Stage of Imperialism? The Big Three, the UN Trusteeship Council, and the Early Cold War," in R. M. Douglas et al., eds., *Imperialism on Trial: International Oversight of Colonial Rule in Historical Perspective* (Lanham, 2006).

25. Still, unlike Chapter XI, the "Declaration Regarding Non-Self-Governing Territories," the trusteeship track did at least open that prospect with its language in Art. 76 of "their progressive development towards self-government or independence as may be appropriate to the particular circumstances of each territory and its peoples." For the figure, Harold Karan Jacobson, "The United Nations and Colonialism: A Tentative Appraisal," *International Organization* 16, 1 (Winter 1962): 45. The literature on trusteeship is surprisingly thin, but see William Bain, *Between Anarchy and Society: Trusteeship and the Obligations of Power* (Oxford, 2003), chap. 5, esp. 108–14 on the Atlantic Charter. On procedural developments around nonself-governing territories, see Yassin El-Ayouty, *The United Nations and Decolonization: The Role of Afro-Asia* (The Hague, 1971).

26. Cited in Martin Duberman, *Paul Robeson: A Biography* (New York, 1989), 297.

27. These are the subtitles of Evan Luard, *A History of the United Nations,* 2 vols. (New York, 1982, 1989), covering 1945–1955 and 1955–1965, respectively. Cf. Jacobson, "The United Nations," and David W. Wainhouse, *Remnants of Empire: The United Nations and the End of Colonialism* (New York, 1964).

28. These events are well explored in a pair of articles by Lorna Lloyd, "'A Family Quarrel': The Development of the Dispute over Indians in

South Africa," *Historical Journal* 34, 3 (1991): 703–25; and "'A Most Auspicious Beginning': The 1946 United Nations General Assembly and the Question of the Treatment of Indians in South Africa," *Review of International Studies* 16, 2 (April 1990): 131–53. See also Mark Mazower, *No Enchanted Palace: The End of Empire and the Ideological Origins of the United Nations* (Princeton, 2009), chap. 4.

29. Compare the first debate in a joint session of the First and Sixth Committees to the plenary debate: U.N. Doc. A/C.1&6/SR.1–6 (1946) and A/PV.50–52 (1946). Carlos Romulo, for instance, spoke in both debates in favor of the Indian concerns: A/C.1&6/SR.3 (1946), 29–30, and A/PV.51 (1946), 1028–30.

30. In an otherwise excellent study, compare the misleading concluding chapter in Marilyn Lake and Henry Reynolds, *Drawing the Global Colour Line: White Men's Countries and the International Challenge of Racial Equality* (Cambridge, 2008).

31. U.N. Gen. Ass. Res. 44 (I), December 8, 1946. The issue of South-West Africa was also of major significance. See, e.g., R. B. Ballinger, "UN Action on Human Rights in South Africa," in Evan Luard, ed., *The International Protection of Human Rights* (London, 1967).

32. Cited in Ampiah, *The Political and Moral Imperatives*, 147. For some specific analyses of the percolation of self-determination in UN politics on which I have drawn, see Benjamin Rivlin, "Self-Determination and Colonial Areas," *International Conciliation* 501 (January 1955): 193–271; Muhammad Aziz Shukri, *The Concept of Self-Determination at the United Nations* (Damascus, 1965); and Rupert Emerson, "Self-Determination," *American Journal of International Law* 65, 3 (July 1971): 459–75. For larger effects on the organization, see D. N. Sharma, *The Afro-Asian Group in the United Nations* (Allahabad, 1969); David A. Kay, "The Politics of Decolonization: The New Nations and the United Nations Political Process," *International Organization* 21, 4 (Autumn 1967): 786–811; and Kay, *The New Nations in the United Nations, 1960–1967* (New York, 1970).

33. U.N. Doc. A/C.3/SR.292 (1950), 133.

34. U.N. Gen. Ass. Res. 421(V), December 4, 1950.

35. U.N. Doc. A/C.3/SR.361 (1951), 84.

36. U.N. Doc. A/C.3/SR.362 (1951), 90.

37. U.N. Doc. A/C.3/SR.366 (1951), 115.

38. U.N. Doc. A/PV.375 (1952), 517–18.

39. U.N. Gen. Ass. Res. 545(VI), February 5, 1952. The resolution also called for the covenant to "stipulate that all States, including those having responsibility for the administration of Non-Self-Governing Territories, should promote the realization of that right," which in effect, if unofficially, revised the charter's Chapter XI. Down into the 1970s, leading international lawyers could attack this retroactive change as an illegitimate revision of the charter outside its own amendment procedures. See Leo Gross, "The Right of Self-Determination in International Law," in Martin Kilson, ed., *New States in the Modern World* (Cambridge, Mass., 1975). For the continuing debate on self-determination and rights at the UN, see Roger Normand and Sarah Zaidi, *Human Rights at the UN: The Political History of Universal Justice* (New York, 2008), 212–24.

40. Louis Henkin, "The United Nations and Human Rights," *International Organization* 19, 3 (Summer 1965): 513.

41. Vernon Van Dyke, *Human Rights, the United States, and the World Community* (Oxford, 1970), 77.

42. Kay, *New Nations*, 87; cf. Kay, "The Politics of Decolonization," 802. See also many of the analyses in Hedley Bull and Adam Watson, eds., *The Expansion of International Society* (Oxford, 1984), esp. Bull's "The Revolt against the West" and R. J. Vincent's "Racial Equality."

43. U.N. Gen. Ass. Res. 1514 (XV), December 14, 1960; Amilcar Cabral, "Anonymous Soldiers for the United Nations" (December 1962), in *Revolution in Guinea: Selected Texts*, trans. Richard Handyside (New York, 1969), 50–51. After Sharpeville, see U.N. Gen. Ass. Res. 1598 (XV), April 15, 1961, passed with only Portugal voting no; and later 1663 (XVI), November 28, 1961; 1881 (XVIII), October 11, 1963; and 1978 (XVIII), December 17, 1963. And, for comment, Ballinger, "UN Action," Moses E. Akpan, *African Goals and Diplomatic Strategies in the United Nations* (North Quincy, 1976); and Audie Klotz, *Norms in International Relations: The Struggle against Apartheid* (Ithaca, 1995), esp. 44–55. In the same years, there were also resolutions on the long-simmering

South-West Africa dispute, and the shocking decision by the International Court of Justice that other African countries had no standing in the forum to bring an action.

44. U.N. Gen. Ass. Res. 1775 (XVII), December 7, 1962; 1904 (XVIII), November 20, 1963; 2106A (XX), December 21, 1965; and 2131 (XX), December 21, 1965.

45. They were seriously undercut at the last moment by revision of implementation provisions, though a coalition of African and Asian countries also introduced the Optional Protocol to the covenant on civil and political rights intended to allow for individual complaint. See, e.g., Egon Schwelb, "Notes on the Early Legislative History of the Measures of Implementation of the Human Rights Covenants," in *Mélanges offerts à Polys Modinos: Problèmes des droits de l'homme et de l'unification européenne* (Paris, 1968); and Samuel Hoare, "The United Nations and Human Rights: A Brief History of the Commission on Human Rights," *Israel Year Book of Human Rights* 1 (1971): 29–30.

46. On gross violations and, a few years later, a formal procedure for petitioning for their investgiation, see ESC Res. 1235 (XLII) (1967) and Res. 1503 (XLVII) (1970); cf. Schwelb, "Complaints by Individuals to the Commission on Human Rights: Twenty-Five Years of an Uphill Struggle (1947–1971)," *International Problems* 13, 1–3 (January 1974): 119–39; and for one survey of the results of the so-called 1503 procedure, Ton J. M. Zuijdwijk, *Petitioning the United Nations: A Study in Human Rights* (New York, 1982). For the larger picture, and esp. the Commission on Human Rights's Sub-commission on Prevention of Discrimination, see Jean-Bernard Marie, *La Commission des droits de l'homme de l'ONU* (Paris, 1975), Moses Moskowitz, *The Roots and Reaches of United Nations Actions and Decisions* (Alphen aan den Rijn, 1980); and Howard Tolley, *The United Nations Commission of Human Rights* (Boulder, 1987).

47. This is the title of the article rpt. in Bill V. Mullen and Cathryn Watson, eds., *W. E. B. Du Bois on Asia: Crossing the World Color Line* (Jackson, 2005).

48. See the careful survey of responses to the Atlantic Charter in Penny M. von Eschen, *Race against Empire: African-Americans and Anticolonialism, 1937–1957* (Ithaca, 1997), 25–28.

49. Du Bois, *Color and Democracy: Colonies and Peace* (New York, 1945), as well as "The Negro and Imperialism" (1944) and "The Pan-African Movement" (his Manchester address reviewing prior conferences), both in Du Bois, *W. E. B. Du Bois Speaks: Essays and Addresses 1920–1963*, ed. Philip S. Foner (New York, 1970). See on all this the early chapters of Gerald Horne, *Black and Red: W. E. B. Du Bois and the Afro-American Response to the Cold War, 1944–1963* (Albany, 1986).

50. Du Bois, "750,000,000 Clamoring," 3; Du Bois, *Color and Democracy,* 10–11, 43, 54, 73, 140–41.

51. I infer this from the material presented in Carol Anderson, *Eyes Off the Prize: The United Nations and the African American Struggle for Human Rights* (Cambridge, 2003), chap. 1. Besides von Eschen, *Race,* 74–85, see also Daniel W. Aldridge III, "Black Powerlessness in a Liberal Era: The NAACP, Anti-Colonialism, and the United Nations Organization 1942–1945," in Douglas et al., eds., *Imperialism on Trial* and Marika Sherwood, "'There Is No New Deal for the Black Man in San Francisco': African Attempts to Influence the Founding Conference of the United Nations, April-July 1945," *International Journal of African Historical Studies* 29, 1 (1996): 71–94.

52. Cited in Anderson, *Eyes,* 93

53. Citations from ibid., 140; and David Levering Lewis, *W. E. B. Du Bois: The Fight for Equality and the American Century, 1919–1963* (New York, 2000), 529; cf. 521–22, 528–34.

54. Du Bois, "Human Rights for All Minorities," rpt. in *W. E. B. Du Bois Speaks,* was a talk before Pearl Buck's East and West Association from November 1945. Du Bois's introduction to the appeal is rpt. in the same collection. For minor reporting, see George Streator, "Negroes to Bring Cause before U.N.," *New York Times,* October 12, 1947; and "U.N. Gets Charges of Wide Bias in U.S.," *New York Times,* October 24, 1947.

55. See von Eschen, *Race,* chap. 5; and Nikhil Singh, *Black Is a Country: Race and the Unfinished Struggle for Democracy* (Cambridge, Mass., 2004), chap. 4; as well as Mary Dudziak, *Cold War Civil Rights: Race and the Image of American Democracy* (Princeton, 2000), on the Cold War origins of the NAACP's legal strategy and the *Brown v. Board of Education* decision.

56. See Ralph Bunche, "The International Trusteeship System," in Trygve

Lie, ed., *Peace on Earth* (New York, 1949); and, for persuasive analysis, Lawrence S. Finkelstein, "Bunche and the Colonial World: From Trusteeship to Decolonization," in Benjamin Rivlin, ed., *Ralph Bunche: The Man and His Times* (New York, 1990).

57. On Shuttlesworth, see Marjorie L. White and Andrew M. Manis, eds., *Birmingham Revolutionaries: Fred Shuttlesworth and the Alabama Christian Movement for Human Rights* (Macon, 2000). On Kenyatta and Nkrumah, see Horne, *Black and Red*, 79.

58. Malcolm X, "The Ballot or the Bullet," in *Malcolm X Speaks: Selected Speeches and Statements*, ed. George Breitman (New York, 1965), 34–35; cf. "The Black Revolution," from the same month, in ibid., 52.

59. Malcolm X, "Letters from Abroad," in ibid., 61. Interestingly, Malcolm X complained of some of the very earliest stirrings of what would come to be a central human rights cause in the decade after his death. "I read in the paper yesterday where one of the Supreme Court justices, [Arthur] Goldberg, was crying about the violation of human rights of three million Jews in the Soviet Union. Imagine this. I haven't got anything against Jews, but that's their problem. How in the world are you going to cry about problems on the other side of the world when you haven't got the problems straightened out here? How can the plight of three million Jews in Russia be qualified to be taken to the United Nations by a man who is a justice in this Supreme Court, and is supposed to be a liberal, supposed to be a friend of black people, and hasn't opened up his mouth one time about taking the plight of black people down here to the United Nations?" Malcolm X, "The Black Revolution," 55.

60. See notably his July 1964 "Appeal to the African Heads of State," in ibid., esp. 75; cf. Malcolm X, *The Last Speeches*, ed. Bruce Perry (New York, 1989), 89, 181, and (with Alex Haley), *The Autobiography of Malcolm X* (New York, 1964), 207.

61. See Robert L. Harris, "Malcolm X: Human Rights and the United Nations," in James L. Conyers, Jr. and Andrew P. Smallwood, ed., *Malcolm X: A Historical Reader* (New York, 2008); and Thomas F. Jackson, *From Civil Rights to Human Rights: Martin Luther King, Jr., and the Struggle for Economic Justice* (Philadelphia, 2007).

62. Cf. Roland J. Burke, "'The Compelling Dialogue of Freedom': Human

Rights and the Bandung Conference," *Human Rights Quarterly* 28 (2006): 947–65.

63. "Final Communiqué of the Asian-African Conference," in George M. Kahin, *The Asian African Conference: Bandung, Indonesia, April 1955* (Ithaca, 1956), 80.

64. Malik, "The Spiritual Significance of the United Nations," *Christian Scholar* 38, 1 (March 1955), 30; rpt. in Walter Leibrecht, ed., *Religion and Culture: Essays in Honor of Paul Tillich* (New York, 1959), 353. Cf. Charles Malik, "Appeal to Asia," *Thought* 26, 100 (Spring 1951): 9–24 and Cary Fraser, "An American Dilemma: Race and Realpolitik in the American Response to the Bandung Conference, 1955," in Brenda Gayle Plummer, ed., *Window on Freedom: Race, Civil Rights, and Foreign Affairs, 1945–1988* (Chapel Hill, 2003), esp. 129–31.

65. See Carlos P. Romulo, *The Meaning of Bandung* (Chapel Hill, 1956), together with his *Crusade in Asia* (New York, 1955) on communist incursions, and *Contemporary Nationalism and the World Order* (New York, 1964), for liberal, pro-Western nationalism.

66. "In Christianity, the individual human person possesses an absolute value," Malik explained in 1951. "The ultimate ground of all our freedom is the Christian doctrine of the absolute inviolability of the human person." Charles Malik, "The Prospect for Freedom" (address at honorary rectorial convocation, University of Dubuque, February 19, 1951), unpaginated. See also Carlos Romulo, "Natural Law and International Law," *University of Notre Dame Natural Law Institute Proceedings* 3 (1949): 121, 126.

67. Kenneth Kaunda, *Speech by the Honorable Kenneth Kaunda, Fordham University* (Duquesne, 1963), 3.

68. Ullrich Lohrmann, *Voices from Tanganyika: Great Britain, the United Nations, and the Decolonization of a Trust Territory* (Berlin, 2008), esp. 28–38 and chaps. 4–6.

69. Andreas Eckert identifies Nyerere as the first-generation African statesman who "most frequently referred" to human rights, without noting the trusteeship background. Andreas Eckert, "African Nationalists and Human Rights, 1940s to 1970s," in Stefan-Ludwig Hoffmann, ed, *A History of Human Rights in the Twentieth Century* (Cambridge, 2010).

70. Julius Nyerere, "Individual Human Rights" (September 1959), in *Freedom and Unity: Uhuru na Umoja* (London, 1967), 70. However, the remainder of the speech makes clear that he intended this pre-Independence speech to respond to groups whom he cast as wrongly angling for regional autonomy as opposed to the individual rights his Tanganyika African National Union party promised.

71. Nyerere, "Independence Address to the United Nations" (December 1961), in ibid., 145–46. See also his Dag Hammerskjöld Memorial Lecture of January 1964, "The Courage of Reconciliation," in ibid., esp. 282–83.

72. See Nyerere, "The Arusha Declaration: Socialism and Self-Reliance," in *Freedom and Socialism: Uhuru na Ujamaa* (New York, 1968), 132–33.

73. See Boris Mirkine-Guetzévitch, *Les constitutions de l'Europe nouvelle* (Paris, 1928), 35–40; and Mirkine-Guetzévitch, *Les constitutions européennes* (Paris, 1951), chap. 8. Cf. Mirkine-Guetzévitch, *Les nouvelles tendances des Déclarations des Droits de l'homme* (Paris, 1930, 1936).

74. See the summary in M. G. Gupta, "Fundamental Rights and Directive Principles of State Policy," in Gupta, ed., *Aspects of the Indian Constitution,* 2nd ed. (Allahabad, 1964), esp. 114–21. For an early analysis of the large wave of litigation the bill enabled, see Alan Gledhill, *Fundamental Rights in India* (London, 1955). B. R. Ambedkar, *States and Minorities: What Are Their Rights and How to Secure Them in the Constitution of Free India* (Bombay, 1947).

75. Charles O. H. Parkinson, *Bills of Rights and Decolonization: The Emergence of Domestic Human Rights Instruments in Britain's Overseas Territories* (Oxford, 2007); Ivor Jennings, *The Approach to Self-Government* (Cambridge, 1956), chap. 6 at 103. Britain did formally extend the protection of the European Convention on Human Rights to its colonial territories. This made no difference in late colonial governance (the theory being that the convention was redundant, and in any event derogable in emergency), and the text of the European Convention did not normally influence bills of rights adopted in the constitution-making of former British possessions.

76. See Parkinson, *Bills of Rights,* 228–33; Ivo Ducachek, *Rights and Liberties in the World Today: Constitutional Promise and Reality* (Santa Barbara,

1973), chap. 1; and Dudziak, *Exporting American Dreams: Thurgood Marshall's African Journey* (Oxford, 2008), appendix.

77. Kim Lane Scheppele, "The Migration of Anti-Constitutional Ideas: The Post-9/11 Globalization of Public Law and the International State of Emergency," in Sujit Choudry, ed., *The Migration of Constitutional Ideas* (Cambridge, 2006), 350. Cf. Inis Claude, ed., *Comparative Human Rights* (Johns Hopkins, 1976).

78. See Stephen Howe, *Anticolonialism in British Politics: The Left and the End of Empire, 1918–1964* (Oxford, 1993), esp. chaps. 5–7. Vidal-Naquet, due to his contacts with Peter Benenson, published his classic account, *Torture, Cancer of Democracy: Algeria, 1954–1962* (London, 1963) as a Penguin special in English first.

79. Sartre, "Preface," in Fanon, 20–21.

80. See, e.g., Eqbal Ahmad, "Revolutionary Warfare and Counterinsurgency," in Norman Miller and Roderick Aya, eds., *National Liberation: Revolution in the Third World* (New York, 1971); Régis Debray, *A Revolution in the Revolution? Armed Struggle and Revolutionary Struggle in Latin America*, trans. Bobby Oritz (New York, 1967) and *Che's Guerilla War*, trans. Rosemary Sheed (Baltimore, 1975); then Gérard Chaliand, *Revolution in the Third World: Myths and Prospects* (1976; New York, 1977); and Pascal Bruckner, *The Tears of the White Man: Compassion as Contempt*, trans. William R. Beer (1983; New York, 1986). See also Rony Brauman, ed., *Le Tiers-mondisme en question* (Paris, 1986).

81. Emerson, *From Empire to Nation: The Rise to Self-Assertion of Asian and African Peoples* (Cambridge, Mass., 1960); and Gilbert Rist, *The History of Development: From Western Origins to Global Faith*, new ed., trans. Patrick Camiller (London, 2002), chap. 9.

82. David H. Bayley, *Public Liberties in the New States* (Chicago, 1964), 142; S. Prakash Sinha, "Is Self-Determination Passé?" *Columbia Journal of Transnational Law* 12 (1973): 260–73.

83. Emerson, "The Fate of Human Rights in the Third World," *World Politics* 27, 2 (January 1975): 223; Arthur Schlesinger, Jr., "Human Rights: How Far, How Fast?" *Wall Street Journal*, March 4, 1977; Louis Henkin, *The Rights of Man Today* (Boulder, 1978), 136; Daniel Patrick Moynihan, "The Politics of Human Rights," *Commentary* 64, 2 (August 1977): 22;

cf. Elizabeth Peterson Spiro, "From Self-Determination to Human Rights: A Paradigm Shift in American Foreign Policy," *Worldview*, January–February 1977; and Sidney Liskofsky, "Human Rights Minus Liberty?" *Worldview*, July 1978.

4 The Purity of This Struggle

1. Bronislaw Baczko, "The Shifting Frontiers of Utopia," *Journal of Modern History* 53, 3 (September 1981): 468, 475.
2. Interview with Moses Moskowitz, recorded November 7, 1979, AJC William E. Wiener Oral History Collection, New York Public Library, Dorot Jewish Division, 22.
3. Ibid., 25, 33, 35. I also draw on a typescript "Curriculum Vitae," and other documents, Moses Moskowitz Papers, White Plains, New York. Moskowitz, *Human Rights and World Order: The Struggle for Human Rights in the United Nations* (New York, 1958), *The Politics and Dynamics of Human Rights* (New York, 1968), *International Concern with Human Rights* (Leiden, 1972), *The Roots and Reaches of United Nations Decisions* (Aalphen an den Rijn, 1980). For the high commissioner, see esp. the original 1963 proposal of Jacob Blaustein, "Human Rights: A Challenge to the United Nations and to Our Generation," in Andrew W. Cordier and Wilder Foote, eds., *The Quest for Peace: The Dag Hammerskjöld Memorial Lectures* (New York, 1965).
4. Lyman Cromwell White, *International Non-Governmental Organizations: Their Purposes, Methods, and Accomplishments* (New Brunswick, 1951), vii, 261–66.
5. See Sandi E. Cooper, "Peace as a Human Right: The Invasion of Women into the World of High International Politics," *Journal of Women's History* 14, 2 (May 2002): 9–25 and, for an emblematic organizational study, Catherine Foster, *Women for All Seasons: The Story of the Women's International League for Peace and Freedom* (Athens, 1989).
6. As Moskowitz put it in an internal memo, "The whole program of the committee is based on a strategic conception that the best defense of the rights of the Jews is an attack on the sources of bias and prejudice and the promotion of democratic ideals and institutions. If there is any validity to this program, the UN, in the long run as well as in the short

run, is the best hope." "Evaluation of the United Nations Program of the American Jewish Committee" (February 1951), AJC RG 347.17.10, YIVO Archives, Center for Jewish History, New York, Gen-10, Box 173.

7. Cited in Jan Eckel, "'To Make the World a Slightly Less Wicked Place': The International League of the Rights of Man, Amnesty International USA and the Transformation of Human Rights Activism from the 1940s through the 1970s," unpublished, whose fine analysis converges with mine.

8. Baldwin's interest in international civil liberties, though he did not convince the ACLU to follow him then, dated back to the 1920s and his enthusiasm for Indian independence and the cause of political prisoners. See Robert C. Cottrell, *Roger Nash Baldwin and the American Civil Liberties Union* (New York, 2000), chap. 13. For Baldwin's UN focus, see Baldwin, "Some Techniques for Human Rights," *International Associations* 8 (1958): 466–69. See Roger S. Clark, "The International League of the Rights of Man," unpublished; and Clark, "The International League for Human Rights and South West Africa 1947–1957: The Human Rights NGO as Catalyst in the International Legal Process," *Human Rights Quarterly* 3, 4 (1981): 101–36. For an appraisal in the mid-1970s, shortly after its name change, see Harry Scoble and Laurie Wiseberg, "The International League for Human Rights: The Strategy of a Human Rights NGO," *Georgia Journal of International and Comparative Law* 7, Supp. (1977): 289–314, esp. 292–95, rpt. as "Human Rights as an International League," *Society* 15, 1 (November/December 1977): 71–75.

9. Tehran was very little covered. See Drew Middleton, "Israel Is Accused at Rights Parley," *New York Times,* April 24, 1968. Seán MacBride, "The Promise of Human Rights Year," *Journal of the International Commission of Jurists* 9, 1 (June 1968): ii. The ICJ had been founded in 1952, and worked with CIA funding to promote the rule of law. It slowly incorporated the human rights framework. See Howard B. Tolley, Jr., *The International Commission of Jurists: Global Advocates for Human Rights* (Philadelphia, 1994).

10. See Ethel C. Phillips, *You in Human Rights: A Community Action Guide for International Human Rights Year* (New York, 1968) and Stanley I. Stuber, *Human Rights and Fundamental Freedoms in Your Community*

(New York, 1968), the latter cosponsored by the American Association for the United Nations. For the commission, see its final pamphlet report, *To Continue Action for Human Rights* (Washington, 1969). Compare, at a more policy-oriented level, John Carey, ed., *The International Protection of Human Rights* (Twelfth Hammerskjöld Forum) (New York, 1968).

11. Morris B. Abram, "The UN and Human Rights," *Foreign Affairs* 47, 2 (January 1969): 363–74 at 363; Moskowitz, *International Concern*, chap. 2, "Disappointment at Tehran," 13, 23.

12. René Cassin, "Twenty Years of NGO Effort on Behalf of Human Rights," Charles Malik, "An Ethical Perspective," and O. Frederick Nolde, "The Work of the NGO's: Problems and Opportunities," in Conference of NGOs in Consultative Status, *Toward an NGO Strategy for the Advancement of Human Rights* (New York, 1968), 22, 99–100, 111. Similarly, Swiss philosopher Jeanne Hersch, who had put together the UNESCO publication *Birthright of Man* (Paris, 1969), rued the fact that "certain people, particularly ours, are seized with the virtuous fever of destruction, or brandishing destruction to make justice spring from a void. Such indignation is very fashionable." Hersch, "Man's Estate and His Rights," in ibid., 102. Cf. W. J. Ganshof van der Meersch, "Droits de l'homme 1968," *Droits de l'homme* 1, 4 (1968): 483–90 and Gerd Kaminski, "La jeunesse, facteur de la promotion et de la réalisation du respect universel des droits de l'homme," *Droits de l'homme* 4, 1 (1971): 153–90.

13. Sir Egerton Richardson, "The Perspective of the Tehran Conference," in *Toward an NGO Strategy,* 25; Germaine Cyfer-Diderich, "Report of the General Rapporteur," in ibid., 1.

14. H. G. Nicholas, *The United Nations as a Political Institution*, 5th ed. (Oxford, 1975), 148–49.

15. For an interesting barometer of the state of old-style American internationalism in the mid-1960s, see Richard N. Gardner, ed., *Blueprint for Peace: Being the Proposals of Prominent Americans to the White House Conference on International Cooperation* (New York, 1966), esp. 84–102 on human rights.

16. Cited in Tom Buchanan, "'The Truth Will Set You Free': The Making of

Amnesty International," *Journal of Contemporary History* 37, 4 (2002): 591.

17. On Pax Christi, see François Mabille, *Les catholiques et la paix au temps de la guerre froide* (Paris, 2004). On the WCC, see Edward Duff, *The Social Thought of the World Council of Churches* (London, 1956).

18. Archer, who was supposed to write a companion volume on human rights to Benenson's on prisoners, failed to do so at the time. Cf. later Archer, "Action by Unofficial Organizations of Human Rights," in Evan Luard, ed., *The International Protection of Human Rights* (London, 1967); and Archer, *Human Rights*, Fabian Research Series 274 (London, 1969). But it was on his suggestion that Benenson had the campaign culminate on December 10, the anniversary of the Universal Declaration's passage.

19. Peter Benenson, *Persecution 1961* (Harmondsworth, 1961), 152. One of the earliest Amnesty "godfathers," Andrew Martin, had been particularly concerned with East European clerics in the 1940s. For the best overall source on MacBride's human rights activities over the years, see MacBride (with Éric Laurent), *L'exigence de la liberté* (Paris, 1980), 163–70.

20. Arthur Danto, personal communication.

21. Jeremi Suri, *Power and Protest: Global Revolution and the Rise of Détente* (Cambridge, Mass., 2003).

22. Valery Chalidze, *To Defend these Rights: Human Rights in the Soviet Union*, trans. Guy Daniels (New York, 1974), 51.

23. On Volpin, see, brilliantly, Benjamin Nathans, "The Dictatorship of Reason: Aleksandr Volpin and the Idea of Rights under 'Developed Socialism,'" *Slavic Review* 66, 4 (Winter 2007): 630–63.

24. See the partial translation in Peter Reddaway, ed., *Uncensored Russia: Protest and Dissent in the Soviet Union* (New York, 1972), 53–54; cf. Mark Hopkins, *Russia's Underground Press: The Chronicle of Current Events* (New York, 1983), 1, 26–27.

25. The appeal's text is in George Saunders, ed., *Samizdat: Voices of the Soviet Opposition* (New York, 1974), 365–69. Chalidze also began researching United Nations law as part of his larger commitment at this moment to learn the law. Joshua Rubenstein, *Soviet Dissidents: Their*

Struggle for Human Rights (Boston, 1980), 128–29. Cf. Chalidze, *The Soviet Human Rights Movement: A Memoir* (New York, 1984).

26. See David Kowalewksi, "The Multinationalization of Soviet Dissent," *Nationalities Papers* 11, 2 (Fall 1983): 207.

27. Yakobson cited in Natalia Gorbanevskaya, *Red Square at Noon* (New York, 1972), 284; Orlov and Litvinov cited in Philip Boobbyer, *Conscience, Dissent, and Reform in Soviet Russia* (New York, 2005), 88, 75; and ibid., 89, for his comment. Later, Litvinov reflected, "The human-rights movement has focused its full attention on the defense of the individual against the arbitrary behavior of the government, not on questions of state and social structure. Devoting itself to this seemingly simple and practical mission, the revitalized intelligentsia is overcoming the old intelligentsia's vice of blind faith in utopian schemes." Litvinov, "The Human-Rights Movement in the Soviet Union," in David Sidorsky, ed., *Essays on Human Rights: Contemporary Issues and Jewish Perspectives* (Philadelphia, 1979), 124.

28. I cite the rapidly published book version *Progress, Coexistence, and Intellectual Freedom* (New York, 1968), 42. While Sakharov surely defended intellectual freedom, and even referred to the worth of the human personality (48), it is anachronistic to interpret his framework as one founded on human rights at this date. Cf. Joshua Rubenstein, "Andrei Sakharov, the KGB, and the Legacy of Soviet Dissent," in Rubenstein and Alexander Gribanov, eds., *The KGB File of Andrei Sakharov* (New Haven, 2005), 20.

29. See Sakharov, *Memoirs*, 319, where he recalled, "I knew little of the movement's history, I was uncomfortable with [Chalidze's] legalistic approach," and 336–37, ascribing his attention to the long-term suppression of religion he had ignored to the May 1971 trial of Anatoly Krasnov-Levitin; cf. Sakharov, *Sakharov Speaks*, 160–63 (New York, 1974), in which the text of his memo to Brezhnev is also reproduced. Aleksandr Solzhenitsyn, *The Nobel Lecture on Literature*, trans. F. D. Reeve (New York, 1972), 30.

30. In the era when anticolonialism had otherwise defined the idea in the 1960s, some Americans referred to domestic civil rights as "human rights"—without, like Malcolm X, understanding this linkage to imply the internationalization of civil rights. For example, the New York state

civil rights bureau, founded for the purposes of combating discrimination in housing and employment, was renamed the Division of Human Rights in 1968, and Columbia University law students simultaneously founded the *Columbia Survey of Human Rights Law* (it was renamed the *Columbia Human Rights Law Review* three years later). In these developments, the total absence of reference outside the domestic forum—and the perception that there was no need to make such reference—testify to how little impact international human rights had on the American scene to that point. I have excluded mention of the New York state agency from the chart in the appendix to this book.

31. Hedrick Smith, "The Intolerable Andrei Sakharov," *New York Times Magazine,* November 4, 1973, in which the only mention of human rights is the (mistaken) assertion that Sakharov's first act of public dissent in 1966 had been on International Human Rights Day rather than in observance of the Stalin constitution anniversary. Sakharov, "Peace, Progress and Human Rights," in *Alarm and Hope,* ed. Efrem Yankelevich and Alfred Friendly, Jr. (New York, 1978).

32. Sakharov, "How I Came to Dissent," trans. Guy Daniels, *New York Review of Books,* March 21, 1974.

33. See Radio Liberty, *Register of Samizdat* (Munich, 1971). See also Felix Corley, "Obituary: Peter Dornan," *The Independent,* November 17, 1999. For the Comité, an offshoot of the older Union internationale de la Résistance et de la Déportation, see its bulletin, *Droits de l'homme en U.R.S.S,* which ran 1972–1976, and the record of its fascinating symposium, *Human Rights in the U.S.S.R.: Proceedings and Papers of the International Symposium on the 50th Anniversary of the U.S.S.R.* (Brussels, 1972), held December 1972 with participation from Cassin, Reddaway, and others. For representative AI publications, see Christopher R. Hill, ed., *Rights and Wrongs: Some Essays on Human Rights* (London, 1969), which includes Peter Reddaway's piece on Soviet dissent, or *Prisoners of Conscience in the USSR: Their Treatment and Conditions* (London, 1975).

34. Kathleen Teltsch, "Human Rights Association Says Soviet Group Becomes Affiliate," *New York Times,* June 30, 1971. See, e.g., V. N. Chalidze, "Important Aspects of Human Rights in the Soviet Union," (a translation from *Social Problems*) (AJC pamphlet, 1972).

35. Michael Scammell, "Notebook," *Index of Censorship 1*, 1 (Spring 1972): 7; Sakharov, *Memoirs*, 288. Writers and Scholars International originated after Stephen Spender published his "With Concern for Those Not Free," *Times Literary Supplement*, October 1971, rpt. *Index of Censorship 1*, 1 (Spring 1972): 11–16; and in W. L. Webb and Rose Bell, eds., *An Embarrassment of Tyrannies: Twenty-Five Years of the Index of Censorship* (New York, 1998).

36. Cited in Kathryn Sikkink, "The Emergence, Evolution, and Effectiveness of the Latin American Human Rights Network," in Elizabeth Jelin and Eric Hershberg, eds., *Constructing Democracy: Human Rights, Citizenship, and Society in Latin America* (Boulder, 1996), 63. See, e.g., David F. Schmitz, *Thank God They're on Our Side: The United States and Right-Wing Dictatorships, 1921–1965* (Chapel Hill, 1999).

37. In an extensive literature, see J. Patrice McSherry, *Predatory States: Operation Condor and Covert War in Latin America* (Lanham 2005) and Jorge G. Castañeda, *Utopia Unarmed: The Latin American Left after the Cold War* (New York, 1993).

38. John Duffett, ed., *Against the Crime of Silence: Proceedings of the Russell International War Crimes Tribunal* (New York, 1968); William Jerman, ed., *Repression in Latin America: Report on the First Session of the Second Russell Tribunal* (Nottingham, 1975); cf. Arthur Jay and Judith Apter Klinghoffer, *International Citizens' Tribunals: Mobilizing Public Opinion to Advance Human Rights* (New York, 2002).

39. Cited in Vania Markarian, *Left in Transformation: Uruguayan Exiles and the Latin American Human Rights Networks, 1967–1984* (New York 2005), 99.

40. Ibid., 141, 177–78.

41. José Cabranes, "Human Rights and Non-Intervention in the Inter-American System," *Michigan Law Review* 65, 6 (April 1967): 1175; for Cuba, Anna P. Schreiber, *The Inter-American Commission on Human Rights* (Leyden, 1970), chap. 6; and Tom Farer, "The Rise of the Inter-American Human Rights Regime: No Longer a Unicorn, Not Yet an Ox," in David J. Harris and Stephen Livingstone, eds., *The Inter-American System of Human Rights* (Oxford, 1998), esp. 45 on Brazil. Dominican Republic president Rafael Trujillo's meddling in Venezuelan affairs also stimulated the erosion of the non-intervention norm.

Cf. Inter-American Human Rights Commission, *Ten Years of Activities: 1971–1981* (Washington, 1982).

42. See Markarian, *Left in Transformation*, 78–79, citation at 79.

43. See, e.g., Michel Bourdeaux, *Religious Ferment in Russia: Protestant Opposition to Soviet Religious Policy* (New York, 1968); Agostino Bono, "Catholic Bishops and Human Rights in Latin America," *Worldview,* March 1978; and Lawrence Weschler, *A Miracle, a Universe: Settling Accounts with Torturers* (New York, 1990), esp. 13, 26, 66. By the time the human rights movement coalesced, ironically, the Brazilian regime had scaled down its use of torture.

44. Pamela Lowden, *Moral Opposition to Authoritarian Rule in Chile, 1973–1990* (Houndmills, 1996). See also Brian H. Smith, "Churches and Human Rights in Latin America: Recent Trends," *Journal of Interamerican Studies and World Affairs* 21, 1 (1979): 89–128. Argentine clerics, by contrast, were notably passive towards or supportive of their regime in 1976 and after. See Margaret E. Crahan, "Catholicism and Human Rights in Latin America" (Institute for Latin American and Iberian Studies, Columbia University, 1989), and Emilio Mignone, *Witness to the Truth: The Complicity of Church and Dictatorship in Argentina, 1976–1983*, trans. Philip Berryman (Maryknoll, 1988).

45. Lowden, *Moral Opposition*, 146.

46. Eckel, "To Make the World," the best analysis, his citations omitted. Cf. Buchanan, "Amnesty International in Crisis, 1966–7," *Twentieth-Century British History* 15, 3 (2004): 267–89 and, for some of my factual information, Rubenstein, "Amnesty International," *The New Republic,* December 18, 1976.

47. See Amnesty International, *Amnesty International Report on Torture,* 1st ed. (London, 1973), 2nd ed. (London, 1975); it also published reports on torture in Brazil (1972) and Chile (1974) specifically, and ill-treatment more generally in several other countries. The ICJ and an ad hoc Chicago Commission of Inquiry into the Status of Human Rights in Chile (formed after young American Frank Teruggi, Jr. of Chicago was killed by the regime) also published reports. See *New York Review of Books,* May 30, 1974, which reprinted excerpts of the AI and Chicago Commission reports. See also Antonio Cassese, ed., *The International Fight against Torture* (Baden-Baden, 1991). For comment, see Ann

Marie Clark, *Diplomacy of Conscience: Amnesty International and Changing Human Rights Norms* (Princeton, 2001), chap. 3, and Barbara Keys, "Anti-Torture Politics: Amnesty International, the Greek Junta, and the Origins of the Human Rights 'Boom' in the United States," in Akira Iriye, et al, eds., *Human Rights in the Twentieth Century: An International History* (New York, forthcoming).

48. See, e.g., David B. Ottaway, "The Growing Lobby for Human Rights," *Washington Post*, December 12, 1976. On Chile, the Washington Office on Latin America was of some importance. See Lewis Diuguid, "Lobbying for Human Rights," *Worldview*, September 1978. For a contemporary study, Marc Bossuyt, "The United Nations and Civil and Political Rights in Chile," *International and Comparative Law Quarterly* 27, 2 (April 1978): 462–71; for the most nuanced recent analysis, Jan Eckel, "'Under a Magnifying Glass': The International Human Rights Campaign against Chile in the 1970s," in Stefan-Ludwig Hoffmann, *A History of Human Rights in the Twentieth Century* (Cambridge, forthcoming). For the earliest academic comment on 1970s human rights activism, see the bibliographical essay.

49. Jeri Laber, *The Courage of Strangers: Coming of Age with the Human Rights Movement* (New York, 2002), 7–8, 73. Rose Styron, "Torture," *The New Republic*, December 8, 1973; and later, "Torture in Chile," *The New Republic*, March 20, 1976. Though Laber had written journalistic pieces about Siniavsky and Solzhenitsyn in the later 1960s, by the mid-1970s she became known for harshly skeptical treatments of Solzhenitsyn for his illiberalism, just before American observers started to come to grips with it, and his polemics with Sakharov broke into the open. See Laber, "The Trial Ends," *The New Republic*, March 19, 1966; "Indictment of Soviet Terror," *The New Republic*, October 19, 1968; "The Selling of Solzhenitsyn," *Columbia Journalism Review* 13, 1 (May/June 1974): 4–7; "The Real Solzhenitsyn," *Commentary*, May 1974. Regarding her AI affiliation, see Laber, "The 'Wire Skeleton' of Vladimir Prison," *New York Times*, November 9, 1974; and later, Laber, "Torture and Death in Paraguay," *New York Times*, March 10, 1976.

50. Laber, *Courage*, 74.

51. Korey, "Good Intentions," *The New Republic*, August 2, 1975.

52. The journalist is cited in Floribert Baudet, "'It Was Cold War and We

Wanted to Win': Human Rights, 'Détente,' and the CSCE," in Andreas Wenger et al., eds., *Origins of the European Security System: The Helsinki Process Revisited, 1968–1975* (New York, 2008), 183. For Kissinger, Jussi M. Hanhimäki, "'They Can Write It in Swahili': Kissinger, the Soviets, and the Helsinki Accords, 1973–1975," *Journal of Transatlantic Studies* 1, 1 (2003): 37–58; cf. Michael Cotey Morgan, "The United States and the Making of the Helsinki Final Act," in Fredrik Logevall and Andrew Preston, eds., *Nixon in the World: American Foreign Relations, 1969–1977* (New York, 2008); and Jeremi Suri, "Détente and Human Rights: American and West European Perspectives on International Change," *Cold War History* 8, 4 (November 2008): 537–45. The Davignon Report is in James Mayall and Cornelia Navari, eds., *The End of the Post-War Era: Documents on Great Power Relations 1968–1975* (Cambridge, 1980); for perspectives on the interests of European states at Helsinki, see Oliver Bange and Gottfried Niedhart, *Helsinki 1975 and the Transformation of Europe* (New York, 2008).

53. See, e.g., Korey's views, which were caustic about the UN even as he threw himself into the Helsinki process he later chronicled. Korey, "The U.N.'s Double Standard on Human Rights," *Washington Post,* May 22, 1977, "Final Acts and Final Solutions," *Society* 15, 1 (November 1977): 81–86. Cf. Suzanne Bastide, "The Special Significance of the Helsinki Final Act," in Thomas Buergenthal, ed., *Human Rights, International Law, and the Helsinki Accord* (Montclair, 1977).

54. It was followed by similar groups in Ukraine, Lithuania, Georgia, and Armenia. Ludmilla Alexeyeva, *Soviet Dissent: Contemporary Movements for National, Religious, and Human Rights,* trans. Carol Pearce and John Glad (Middletown, 1987), 335–49.

55. Richard Bilder, "Human Rights and U.S. Foreign Policy: Short-Term Prospects," *Virginia Journal of International Law* 14 (1973–74): 601.

56. See U.S. House of Representatives, *International Protection of Human Rights: The Work of International Organizations and the Role of U.S. Foreign Policy* (Washington, D.C., 1974), and *Human Rights in Chile* (Washington, D.C., 1974–75). For the report, *Human Rights in the World Community: A Call for U.S. Leadership* (Washington, D.C., 1974) and David Binder, "U.S. Urged to Act on Human Rights," *New York Times,* March 28, 1974. For Fraser's verdict on the UN, see Donald M. Fraser,

"Human Rights at the U.N.," *The Nation,* September 21, 1974. The analyst memo was first cited in Patrick Breslin, "Human Rights: Rhetoric
or Action?" *Washington Post,* February 17, 1977. See also Barbara Keys,
"Kissinger, Congress, and the Origins of Human Rights Diplomacy,"
Diplomatic History (forthcoming), which supersedes early literature
like Howard Washawsky, "The Department of State and Human Rights
Policy: A Case Study of the Human Rights Bureau," *World Affairs* 142
(1980): 118–215.

57. Dorothy Fosdick, ed., *Henry M. Jackson and World Affairs: Selected
    Speeches, 1953–1983* (Seattle, 1990), 186, and the rest of Part V for his re-
    lated speeches. Sakharov endorsed the Jackson-Vanik amendment in a
    letter to the U.S. Congress in late 1973, rpt. in *Sakharov Speaks,* 211–15.

58. The best background history of the cause of Soviet Jewry is Albert D.
    Chernin, "Making Soviet Jews an Issue: A History," in Chernin and
    Murray Friedman, eds., *A Second Exodus: The American Movement to
    Free Soviet Jews* (Hanover, 1999). See also Yossi Klein Halevi, "Jacob
    Birnbaum and the Struggle for Soviet Jewry," *Azure* (Spring 2004): 27–
    57. For Uppsala, Karal Vasak and Sidney Liskofsky, *The Right to Leave
    and to Return: Papers and Recommendations of the International Collo-
    quium Held in Uppsala, Sweden, 19–20 June 1972* (New York, 1976); see
    also, e.g., Yoram Dinstein, "The International Human Rights of Soviet
    Jewry," *Israel Yearbook on Human Rights* 2 (1972): 194–210. "The treat-
    ment of Soviet Jewry gradually became a human rights problem," the
    movement's historian Henry Feingold puts it, "but that was not pre-
    cisely a change for the activists. It simply meant that their public rela-
    tions would now be couched in broader terms." Henry L. Feingold, *"Si-
    lent No More": Saving the Jews of Russia, the American Jewish Effort,
    1967–1989* (Syracuse, 2007), 200.

59. Daniel Patrick Moynihan, "The Politics of Human Rights," *Commen-
    tary* 64, 2 (August 1977): 22; David E. Rosenbaum, "Democrats Back
    Call in Platform for Soviet Amity," *New York Times,* June 14, 1976. True,
    it also mattered that Moynihan, a Jackson ally who served Gerald Ford
    as United Nations ambassador, discovered just before that human
    rights had become a third-worldist and antiracist language, not one
    protecting "liberty." However, there is no evidence that this outraged
    discovery of anticolonialist uses of the language at the United Na-

tions—uses which for him, were Soviet-driven and totalitarian—portended a grand new alternative American foreign policy lexicon. Moynihan, "The United States in Opposition," *Commentary* 59, 3 (March 1975): 31–45; and Daniel Sargent, "From Internationalism to Globalism: The United States and the Transformation of International Politics in the 1970s" (Ph.D. diss., Harvard University, 2008), 454–77, for the best treatment. Cf. Barry Rubin, "Human Rights and the Equal Time Provision," *Worldview* 23, 3 (March 1977): 27–28.

60. Elizabeth Drew, *American Journal: The Events of 1976* (New York, 1977), 291; cf. 296.

61. The minor exceptions were speeches before the B'nai Brith in September and at Notre Dame University in October. See the texts in *The Presidential Campaign 1976*, 3 vols. (Washington, 1978), 1: 709–14 and 993–98. Carter's own later accounts naturally downplay the contingencies of his discovery of human rights. See Carter, "The American Road to Human Rights Policy," in Samantha Power and Graham Allison, eds., *Realizing Human Rights: Moving from Inspiration to Impact* (New York, 2000).

62. "Henry has come a hell of a long way on human rights in the last 18 months," one American official put it, in a reflection on Kissinger's remarkably bold claims of the importance of human rights as "the very essence of a meaningful life" in his June 1976 speech at the Organization of American States meeting in Santiago, Chile. See "A Harsh Warning on Human Rights," *Time*, June 21, 1976. For Kissinger's increasing invocations, see Hugh M. Arnold, "Henry Kissinger and Human Rights," *Universal Human Rights* 2, 4 (1980): 57–71.

63. Gaddis Smith, *Morality, Reason, and Power: American Diplomacy in the Carter Years* (New York, 1986), 242.

64. See Arthur Schlesinger, "Human Rights and the American Tradition," *Foreign Affairs* 57, 3 (1979), 514; James Reston, "The Sakharov Letter," *New York Times*, February 20, 1977. Zbigniew Brzezinski claimed in his memoirs to have authored the crucial line, but I have seen no verification of this fact. Brzezinski, *Power and Principle: Memoirs of the National Security Adviser, 1977–1981* (New York, 1983), 125.

65. For Solzhenitsyn, interpreted as a reflection of the crisis of détente, see, e.g., Richard Steele, "What Price Détente?" *Newsweek*, July 28, 1977. For

the Sakharov exchange, see Bernard Gwertzman, "Sakharov Sends Letter to Carter Urging Help on Rights in Soviet [Union]," *New York Times*, January 29, 1977; and Christopher S. Wren, "Sakharov Receives Carter Letter Affirming Commitment on Rights," *New York Times*, February 18, 1977. Cf. Anthony Lewis, "A Craving for Rights," *New York Times*, January 31, 1977. William Safire, "Rejected Counsel," *New York Times*, February 3, 1977.

66. One skeptic, commenting on "boom time for human rights," called Owen's tones "somewhat prim . . . reminiscent of an up-and-coming curate." Alan Watkins, "Awkward People Insist on Rights," *The Observer*, June 5, 1977. See also Patrick Keatley, "Owen Champions Human Rights," *The Guardian*, March 4, 1977; Richard Norton-Taylor, "Foreign Office Seeks Human Rights Policy," *The Guardian*, May 4, 1977; "Stand on Rights by Owen," *The Guardian*, October 11, 1977; David Owen, *Human Rights* (London, 1978).

67. Drew, "A Reporter at Large: Human Rights," *The New Yorker*, July 18, 1977; Carter, "Human Rights and Foreign Policy," in *Public Papers of the Presidents: Jimmy Carter, 1977*, 2 vols. (Washington, 1977–78); Cyrus Vance, "Human Rights and Foreign Policy," *Georgia Journal of International and Comparative Law* 7 (1977): 223–229; Cohen cited in Teltsch, "Human Rights Groups Are Riding a Wave of Popularity," *New York Times*, February 28, 1977. For comment, C. L. Sulzberger, "Where Do We Go Now?" *New York Times*, February 20, 1977 and Robert G. Kaiser, "Administration Still Groping to Define 'Human Rights,'" *Washington Post*, April 16, 1977. The *Boston Globe* ran a large special section ("The Carter Crusade for Human Rights," March 13, 1977), and *Time* followed suit ("The Push for Human Rights," June 20, 1977), while by summer numerous intellectual fora were debating the issue.

68. Chalidze, recognizing this risk in the Sakharov correspondence, immediately counseled evenhanded policy. See Chalidze, "Dealing with Human Rights on a Global Scale," *Washington Post*, Feburary 23, 1977. Graham Hovey, "Carter Denies U.S. Singles Out Soviet in Rights Protests," *New York Times*, February 24, 1977. See also "Human Rights: Other Violators," *Time*, March 7, 1977; and Henry Fairlie, "'Desaparecidos,'" *The New Republic*, April 9, 1977. Cf. Breslin, "Human Rights," noting

the paucity of public attention to the non-communist world by the same moment. Later this would shift palpably, even within the larger deemphasis of human rights by 1978. Compare the very illuminating study by Robert A. Strong, *Working in the World: Jimmy Carter and the Making of American Foreign Policy* (Baton Rouge, 2000), chap. 3, "A Tale of Two Letters: Human Rights, Sakharov, and Somoza."

69. Walter Laqueur, "The Issue of Human Rights," *Commentary,* May 1977; Noam Chomsky, *"Human Rights" and American Foreign Policy* (Nottingham, 1978), ix (dating), 67 (quotation). See also Chomsky and Edward Herman, "The United States versus Human Rights," *Monthly Review,* August 1977. Cf. Wm. F. Buckley, Jr., "Mr. Carter's Discovery of Human Rights," *National Review,* April 1, 1977.

70. Richard Steele, "The Limits of Morality," *Newsweek,* March 7, 1977; "The Soviets Hit Back on Human Rights," *Time,* March 14, 1977; Richard Steele, "Testing Carter," *Time,* April 11, 1977; David Binder, "Carter Said to See No Immediate Gains in Ties with Soviets," *New York Times,* June 26, 1977.

71. Christopher Whipple, "Human Rights: Carter Backs Off," *Newsweek,* October 10, 1977; Tracy Early, "A Campaign Quickly Canceled," and Patricia Derian, "A Commitment Sustained," both in *Worldview,* July–August 1978. See later Derian, "Human Rights and American Foreign Policy," *Universal Human Rights* 1, 1 (January 1979): 1–9.

72. Notre Dame president and Commission on Civil Rights member Theodore Hesburgh—who had represented the Vatican at the Tehran conference in 1968—suggested in 1971 Congressional testimony that, given the necessary socioeconomic basis of civil rights, "we are coming to a kind of watershed in this country in the matter of civil rights that might [better] be faced in terms of human rights." Cited in Hesburgh, "The Commission on Civil Rights—and Human Rights," *Review of Politics* 34, 3 (July 1972): 303. This style of argument, however, didn't define the meaning of human rights five years later. Cf. Hesburgh, *The Humane Imperative* (New Haven, 1974), chap. 3, "Human and Civil Rights." On social rights, cf. Cass Sunstein, *The Second Bill of Rights: FDR's Unfinished Revolution and Why We Need It More Than Ever* (New York, 2006), chap. 9.

73. Sean Wilentz, *The Age of Reagan, 1974–2008* (New York, 2008), chap. 3.

74. Ronald Steel, "Motherhood, Apple Pie, and Human Rights," *The New Republic*, June, 4, 1977.

75. Carter, "Human Rights," 1: 956; Drew, "A Reporter."

76. Václav Havel, "The Power of the Powerless," in *Open Letters: Selected Writings, 1965–1990* (New York, 1992), 127.

77. Havel's April 1968 intervention is "On the Theme of an Opposition," in *Open Letters*, esp. 31. Strangely, he remarked later in the summer of 1968 that it was right to replace Dubček with more conformist Gustáv Husák, for reasons that remain unclear. See John Keane, *Václav Havel: A Political Tragedy in Six Acts* (New York, 2000), 221.

78. Havel, *Disturbing the Peace: A Conversation with Karel Hvízdala*, trans. Paul Wilson (New York, 1990) 119–22; Havel, "Second Wind" (1976), in *Open Letters*, 8. On the repression that went by the name of "normalization," see Vladimir V. Kusin, *From Dubček to Charter 77: A Study of "Normalization" in Czechoslovakia, 1968–1978* (New York, 1978). Cf. Havel, "Letter to Dr. Husák," in *Open Letters* and, for sources, Alexandra Laignel-Lavastine, *Jan Patočka: l'esprit de la dissidence* (Paris, 1998); or Aviezer Tucker, *The Philosophy and Politics of Czech Dissidence* (Pittsburgh, 2000).

79. Havel, "The Power of the Powerless," in *Open Letters*, 202–3, 159, 165, 183.

80. Ibid., 207–208. These themes are even more pronounced in Havel's "Politics and Conscience," from a few years later, also in *Open Letters*. I have substituted "totalitarianism" for Havel's usage of "post-totalitarianism."

81. Ibid., 136, 188–89, 191. For good measure, Havel added: "The struggle for what is called 'legality' must constantly keep this legality in perspective against the background of life as it really is" (192).

82. Havel, "Power," 148, 152, 154, 164, 157, 152, 197; cf. 149. For Michnik, see "The New Evolutionism," *Survey* 22 (Summer/Autumn 1976), rpt. in Michnik, *Letters from Prison and Other Essays* (Berkeley, 1985). For Benda, see "The Parallel 'Polis,'" in H. Gordon Skilling and Paul Wilson, eds., *Civic Freedom in Central Europe: Voices from Czechoslovakia* (Basingstoke, 1991). For Hájek, see "Human Rights, Peaceful Coexistence, and Socialism," in Skilling, ed., *Charter 77 and Human Rights*

in Czechoslovakia (London, 1981), 226; cf. Hájek, "The Human Rights Movement and Social Progress," in Keane, ed., *The Power of the Powerless: Citizens against the State in Central-Eastern Europe* (Armonk, 1985). On the Polish case, compare the similar analysis of David Ost, *Solidarity and the Politics of Antipolitics: Opposition and Reform in Poland since 1968* (Philadelphia, 1990).

83. Havel, "Power," 180–81, 161, 148. Jan Patočka, "What Charter 77 Is and What It Is Not," in Skilling, ed., *Charter 77*, 218.

84. Havel, "Power," 157, 162, 151, 205; George Konrád, *Antipolitics: An Essay* (New York, 1984), and Tony Judt, "The Dilemmas of Dissidence: The Politics of Opposition in East-Central Europe," *East European Politics and Society* 2, 2 (1988): 240.

85. On the peculiarities of Czech (as opposed to Slovak) Catholicism, see Benda, "Catholicism and Politics," in Keane, ed., *Power*; on Poland, see Jacques Rupnik, "Dissent in Poland, 1968–1978: The End of Revisionism and the Rebirth of Civil Society," in Rudolf L. Tökés, ed., *Opposition in Eastern Europe* (Baltimore, 1979), 90, 78–79; Michnik, *The Church and the Left*, ed. and trans. David Ost (Chicago, 1993). Fascinatingly, the Helsinki Accords were cited not just for human rights but because the constitutional revisions ran afoul of the treaty's affirmation of sovereignty in an era of anticolonialism. See *Dissent in Poland: Reports and Documents in Translation* (London, 1977), 15–17.

86. The link was forged already during the campaign, when Carter accepted the invitation of Notre Dame's Center for Civil Rights, founded in 1972 but with a new director, German law specialist Donald Kommers, in 1976, who resolved to move the center in the direction of international human rights thanks to a large Ford Foundation grant. As he explained to Theodore Hesburgh, Notre Dame's president (and high-profile Democrat nationally), "After more than thirty years of public debate in the United Nations and abroad, the subject of international concern with human rights, and its aims and purposes remains largely unfamiliar terrain on the frontier of thought. The search for its mainsprings as an ideological force has barely begun." When Carter swung through that October, he gave an informal talk to the Center and the law faculty, saying, "There are many things that we can do. And I believe that this Center here that shifts its goals from strictly domestic

civil rights, which is still very important, to a broader concept of all human rights, and I hope this will be done expeditiously, and I'll help if I am elected President, can be a beacon to our own country and to the world for a constant reassessment of what can be done in a world that we acknowledge to be imperfect." Kommers then moved to organize a landmark conference on human rights in April 1977, which Carter then referenced the next month in his commencement speech. See Notre Dame Archives, UDIS 39/1–3. For Carter's public talk in October, see *The Presidential Campaign 1976*, 996. For the conference, see Donald P. Kommers and Gilburt D. Loescher, eds., *Human Rights and American Foreign Policy* (Notre Dame, 1979).

87. For other religious affiliations and survivals, one must mention theologian Jürgen Moltmann's liberationist affiliation with human rights; see Jan Milic Lochman and Jürgen Moltmann, eds., *Gottes Recht und Menschenrechte* (Neukirchen, 1976), in English as Allen O. Miller, ed., *A Christian Declaration of Human Rights* (Grand Rapids, 1977). Also notable in American and Britain were David Hollenbach, *Claims in Conflict: Retrieving and Renewing the Catholic Human Rights Tradition* (New York, 1979) and Edward Norman, *Christianity and the World Order* (Oxford, 1979), chap. 3, "A New Commandment: Human Rights." Cf. Lowell Livezey, *Non-Governmental Organizations and the Ideas of Human Rights* (Princeton, 1988) for concrete Christian activism on the American scene.

88. See, e.g., Callum G. Brown, "The Secularisation Decade: What the 1960s Have Done to the Study of Religious History," in Hugh McLeod and Werner Usdorf, eds., *The Decline of Christendom in Western Europe, 1750–2000* (Cambridge, 2003) and McLeod, *The Religious Crisis of the 1960s* (New York, 2007).

89. For Czechoslovakia, Vladimir V. Kusin, "Challenge to Normalcy: Political Opposition in Czechoslovakia, 1968–1977," in Tökés, ed., *Opposition*, 44–51; for Eurocommunism more broadly, Tökés, ed., *Eurocommunism and Détente* (New York, 1978); Wolfgang Leonhard, *Eurocommunism: Challenge for East and West*, trans. Mark Vecchio (New York, 1978); Leszek Kołakowski, *Towards a Marxist Humanism: Essays on the Left Today*, trans. Jane Zielonko Peel (New York, 1968), 70–71; and "Marxism and Human Rights," *Daedalus* 112, 4 (Fall 1983): 81–92. Consider Ray-

mond Taras, ed., *The Road to Disillusion: From Critical Marxism to Postcommunism in Eastern Europe* (Armonk, 1992).

90. Cf. Robert Horvath, "'The Solzhenitsyn Effect': East European Dissidents and the Demise of the Revolutionary Privilege," *Human Rights Quarterly* 29 (2007): 879–907.

91. This account is based on Michael Scott Christofferson's *French Intellectuals against the Left: The Antitotalitarian Moment of the 1970s* (New York, 2004), chap. 4. Besides media coverage, see Tania Mathon and Jean-Jacques Marie, eds., *L'affaire Pliouchtch* (Paris, 1976); *The Case of Leonid Plyushch,* trans. Marite Spiets et al. (Boulder, 1976); and his later memoirs, which appeared in 1977 in France and 1979 in the United States. Though he testified before the U.S. Congress in 1976, where leftist excitement about dissent had been far more minor, Plyushch struck a high-profile in France for obvious reasons. Compare, e.g., Roy Medvedev et al., *Détente and Socialist Democracy* (London, 1975), and his critique of the liberalization of dissent included in the *Newsweek* dossier, Fred Coleman, "Loyal Opposition," *Newsweek,* June 20, 1977.

92. See André Glucksmann, "Le Marxisme rend sourd," *Le Nouvel Observateur,* March 4, 1974; *La cuisinière et le mangeur d'hommes* (Paris, 1975); and *Les maîtres-penseurs* (Paris, 1977). Bernard-Henri Lévy, "Le vrai crime de Soljenitsyne," *Le Nouvel Observateur,* June 30, 1975; Lévy, *Barbarism with a Human Face,* trans George Holoch (1977; New York, 1979), 197.

93. See Arnaud de Borchgrave, "Giscard Speaks Out," *Newsweek,* July 25, 1977. Andrei Amalrik was rebuffed in European capitals simultaneously with Bukovsky's welcome in America. See Craig R. Whitney, "Carter Rights Stand Worries Europe," *New York Times,* March 5, 1977 and Hella Pick, "Europe Wants Cooler Carter," *The Guardian,* March 9, 1977.

94. Julia Kristeva, "Un nouveau type d'intellectual: le dissident," *Tel Quel* 74 (Winter 1977): 3–8; Dominique Lecourt, *Dissidence ou révolution* (Paris, 1978); Marcel Gauchet, "Les droits de l'homme ne sont pas une politique," *Le Débat* 3 (July–August 1980): 3.

95. Milan Simecka, "A World with Utopias or Without Them," in Peter Alexander and Roger Gill, eds., *Utopias* (London, 1984), 175, cited in Henri Vogt, *Between Utopia and Disillusionment: A Narrative of Political Transformation in Eastern Europe* (New York, 2005), 77.

96. "Doing without Utopias: An Interview with Václav Havel," *Times Literary Supplement,* January 23, 1987. Cf. Kołakowski, "The Death of Utopia Reconsidered" (1982), in *Modernity on Endless Trial* (Chicago, 1997).

97. See Laber, *Courage,* for a narrative of the origins; for Aryeh Neier's belated move into the human rights movement, see his memoir, *Taking Liberties: Four Decades in the Struggle for Rights* (New York, 2003), in which there is little reflection on the historical conditions for his switch from domestic to international rights. On the Ford Foundation, see Korey, *Taking on the World's Repressive Regimes: The Ford Foundation's International Human Rights Policies and Practices* (New York, 2007).

98. See analyses by those involved in governmental human rights in the 1970s in Peter G. Brown and Douglas MacLean, *Human Rights and U.S. Foreign Policy* (Lexington, 1979); as well as policy planning staffer Sandy Vogelgesang, "What Price Principle? U.S. Policy on Human Rights," *Foreign Affairs* 56, 4 (July 1978): 819–41 and Vogelgesang, *American Dream, Global Nightmare: The Dilemmas of U.S. Human Rights Policy* (New York, 1980). See also Natalie Kaufman Hevener, ed., *The Dynamics of Human Rights in U.S. Foreign Policy* (New Brunswick, 1981); and since, in an endless literature, Joshua Muravchik, *The Uncertain Crusade: Jimmy Carter and the Dilemmas of Human Rights Policy* (New York, 1986). Irving Kristol, "The 'Human Rights' Muddle," *Wall Street Journal,* March 20, 1978.

99. The Indonesian case thus must be read in a moment when human rights were *new,* while optics favoring self-determination which had been so influential even in the West were failing. See Bradley Simpson's pioneering "Denying the 'First Right': The United States, Indonesia, and the Ranking of Human Rights by the Carter Administration, 1976–1980," *International History Review* 31, 4 (December 2009): 788–826. For a similar indictment of Carter's subordination of human rights to Cold War imperatives, see Kenton Clymer, "Jimmy Carter, Human Rights, and Cambodia," *Diplomatic History* 27, 2 (April 2003): 245–78. Håkan Thörn, *Anti-Apartheid and the Emergence of a Global Civil Society* (New York, 2006), chap. 7.

100. See Fox Butterfield, "Peking's Poster Warriors Are Not Just Paper Tigers," *New York Times,* November 26, 1978. But attention to China, and indigenous human rights resistance, were by and large a later develop-

ments. See Rosemary Foot, *Rights Beyond Borders: The Global Community and the Struggle over Human Rights in China* (New York, 2000). For Milk's invocations, see, e.g., *The Times of Harvey Milk*, dir. Rob Epstein (1984); for a name change, see "Battle over Gay Rights," *Newsweek*, June 6, 1977.

101. Sakharov, "The Human Rights Movement in the USSR and Eastern Europe: Its Goals, Significance, and Difficulties," *Trialogue*, January 1979, rpt. in Alexander Babyonyshev, ed., *On Sakharov* (New York, 1982), 259. Jerome J. Shestack, "Sisyphus Endures: The International Human Rights NGO," *New York Law School Law Review* 24, 1 (1978): 89.

5 International Law and Human Rights

1. Paul W. Kahn, *Sacred Violence: Torture, Terror and Sovereignty* (Ann Arbor, 2008), 49.

2. Consider, e.g., Jack Goldsmith and Eric Posner, *The Limits of International Law* (Oxford, 2005); Oona Hathaway, "Do Human Rights Treaties Make a Difference?" *Yale Law Journal* 111, 8 (June 2002): 1870–2042; and Richard Burchill, "International Human Rights Law: Struggling between Apology and Utopia," in Alice Bullard, ed., *Human Rights in Crisis* (New York, 2008).

3. Martti Koskenniemi, *From Apology to Utopia: The Structure of International Legal Argument* (1989; Cambridge, 2005); and *The Gentle Civilizer of Nations: The Rise and Fall of International Law* (Cambridge, 2002). I adopt the framework of these classics, while departing very substantially from Koskenniemi's reading of American international law in the postwar era.

4. Reva Siegel, "The Jurisgenerative Role of Social Movements in U.S. Constitutional History," Seminario en Latino América de Teoria Constitucional y Politica, 2004.

5. See, for example, William B. Ziff, *The Gentlemen Talk of Peace* (New York, 1944). Hans Kelsen, *Law and Peace in International Relations* (Oliver Wendell Holmes Lecture, 1940–41) (Cambridge, Mass., 1942); and Kelsen, *Peace through Law* (Chapel Hill, 1944).

6. See "Future of International Law," *Transactions of the Grotius Society* 27 (1941): 289–312; Carnegie Endowment, *The International Law of the*

Future (Washington, 1944), also in *American Journal of International Law Supplement* 38, 2 (1944): 41–139 and *International Conciliation* 399 (April 1944): 251–381. For an interesting commentary, see P. E. Corbett, "World Order: An Agenda for Lawyers," *American Journal of International Law* 37, 2 (April 1943): 207–21; and Manley O. Hudson, "'The International Law of the Future,'" *American Journal of International Law* 38, 2 (April 1944): 278–81. It is highly revealing that this American proposal does not foreground any concept of human rights; the same is true of the later "Design for a Charter of the General International Organization," to which Hudson, Philip Jessup, and Louis Sohn contributed. "Design," *American Journal of International Law Supplement* 38, 4 (October 1944): 203–16.

7. See André Mandelstam, "La Déclaration des droits internationaux de l'homme, adoptée par l'Institut de droit international," *Revue de droit international* 5 (1930): 59–78; Mandelstam, *Les Droits internationaux de l'homme* (Paris, 1931); George A. Finch, "The International Rights of Man," *American Journal of International Law* 35, 4 (October 1941): 662–65. On Mandelstam, see, e.g., Dzovinar Kévonian, "Exilés politiques et avènement du 'droit humain': La pensée juridique d'André Mandelstam (1869–1949)," *Revue d'histoire de la Shoah* 177–178 (January–August 2001): 245–273.

8. J. C. Brierly, *The Outlook for International Law* (Oxford, 1944); Cecil J. B. Hurst, "Foreword," *International Law Quarterly* 1, 1 (Spring 1947): 1.

9. Philip C. Jessup, "International Law in the Post-War World," *Proceedings of the American Society of International Law* 36 (1942): 46–50; Quincy Wright, "Human Rights and World Order," *International Conciliation* 389 (April 1943): 238–62; Clyde Eagleton, *Proceedings of the American Society of International Law* 40 (1946): 29.

10. UN Charter, Art. 13; William Jowitt, "The Value of International Law," *International Law Quarterly* 1, 3 (Autumn 1947): 299; Eagleton, "International Law and the Charter of the United Nations," *American Journal of International Law* 39, 4 (October 1945): 752.

11. On natural law, see Ulrich Scheuner, "Naturrechtliche Strömungen im heutigen Völkerrecht," *Zeitschrift für ausländisches Öffentliches Recht und Völkerrecht* 13 (1950–51): 556–614. Even in Germany and Austria,

where renewed naturalism was most marked, its ascendancy was brief. See Johannes Messner, "The Postwar Natural Law Revival and Its Outcome," *Natural Law Forum* 4 (1959): 101–5. See, e.g., René Dollot, "L'organisation politique mondiale et le déclin de la souveraineté," *Revue générale de droit international public* 51 (1947): 28–47. For remarkable evidence of the accumulated difficulty of advocating individualistic conceptions in politics or law, see Marcel Waline, *L'individualisme et le droit* (lectures given 1943–44) (Paris, 1945). Morris Ginsberg, "The Persistence of Individualism in the Theory of International Relations" (lecture of December 1944), *International Affairs* 21, 2 (April 1945): 155–67 at 163.

12. George W. Keeting and Georg Schwarzenberger, *Making International Law Work,* 2nd ed. (London, 1946), 109–110; W. Harvey Moore, "The International Guarantee of the Rights of Man," *International Law Quarterly* 1, 4 (Winter 1947): 516; compare Corbett, "Next Steps after the Charter: An Approach to the Enforcement of Human Rights," *Commentary* 1 (November 1945): 21–29.

13. Hudson, "Integrity of International Instruments," *American Journal of International Law* 42, 1 (January 1948): 105. He was reacting specifically to the attempt by the American Association for the United Nations to intervene in the famous case of *Shelley v. Kraemer,* 334 U.S. 1 (1948), by suggesting that Charter language about human rights impacted constitutional law (the case challenged racially exclusionary real estate covenants). Compare Paul Sayre, "*Shelley v. Kraemer* and United Nations Law," *Iowa Law Review* 34, 1 (November 1948): 1–12. After the Declaration, see Hudson, "Charter Provisions on Human Rights in American Law," *American Journal of International Law* 44, 3 (July 1950): 543–48. Mintauts Chakste, "Justice and Law in the Charter of the United Nations," *American Journal of International Law* 42, 3 (July 1948): 590–600.

14. Hersch Lauterpacht, *An International Declaration on the Rights of Man* (New York, 1945). The materials were drafted in 1943. Lauterpacht, comments on Vladimir C. Idelson, "The Law of Nations and the Individual," *Transactions of the Grotius Society* 30 (1944): 68. Compare A. W. B. Simpson, "Hersch Lauterpacht and the Genesis of the Age of Human Rights," *Law Quarterly Review* 120 (January 2004): 49–80 at 69–74. See also Koskenniemi, *Gentle Civilizers,* chap. 5 and "Hersch

Lauterpacht (1897–1960)," in Jack Beatson and Reinhard Zimmerman, *Jurists Uprooted: German-speaking Émigré Lawyers in Twentieth-Century Britain* (Oxford, 2004).

15. Lauterpacht, *International Law and Human Rights* (New York, 1950), 412, 166. Lauterpacht, "Towards an International Bill of Rights," *The Listener* 42, 1084 (3 November 1949), rpt. in *International Law: Being the Collected Papers of Hersch Lauterpacht*, 5 vols. (Cambridge, 1970–2004), 3: 410–15 at 415: "A Bill of Rights is of the greatest importance—but it is not essential—for the fulfillment of that object [of legalization]. Enlightened public opinion may assist and encourage Governments in making the most of the instrument already at hand, namely, the Charter." See also Karl Josef Partsch, "Internationale Menschenrechte," *Archiv des öffentlichen Rechts* 74 (1948): 158–90. For guarded optimism, see André Salomon, *Le préambule de la Charte, base idéologique de l'O.N.U.* (Geneva, 1946); and Lawrence Preuss, "Article 2, Paragraph 7 of the United Nations and Matters of Domestic Jurisdiction," *Recueil des cours de l'Académie du droit international* [hereafter *Recueil des cours*] 74 (1949): 557–653. For the best survey of opinion about the legality of the declaration in the years immediately after its adoption, see Nehemiah Robinson, *The Universal Declaration of Human Rights: Its Origin, Significance, Application, and Interpretation*, rev. ed. (New York, 1958), Part II.

16. L. B. Schapiro, review of Brunet, *International Law Quarterly* 1, 3 (Autumn 19947): 398. Lauterpacht's comparatively enthusiastic remarks on the Stalin Constitution are to be found in his 1945 study. See, e.g., L. C. Green, review of Lauterpacht, *International Law Quarterly* 4, 1 (January 1951): 126–29.

17. Lauterpacht, "The Grotian Tradition in International Law," *British Year Book of International Law* 23 (1946), rpt. in *International Law*, 2: 354–55, where he also called Grotius' lapse "foreign to the spirit of his teaching and personal condition." The tercentenary of Grotius' death had been in 1945. H. A. Smith, *The Crisis in the Law of Nations* (London, 1947), 1. For continuing wrestling with Grotius as alleged founder, see Rosalyn Higgins, "Grotius and the Development of International Law in the United Nations Period," in Hedley Bull, et al., eds., *Hugo Grotius and International Relations* (Oxford, 1990).

18. See Editorial Notes, "Human Rights," *International Law Quarterly* 2, 2 (Summer 1948): 228–30. See also Hans Kelsen, *The Law of the United Nations: A Critical Analysis of Its Fundamental Problems* (London, 1950), 39–42, deeming the UDHR "almost worthless" (41) due to its lack of enforceability. See also Josef L. Kunz, "The United Nations Declaration of Human Rights," *American Journal of International Law* 43, 2 (April 1949): 316–23 at 322.

19. "Les droits fondamentaux de l'homme, base d'une restauration du droit international," *Annuaire de l'Institut de Droit International* 41 (1947): 1–13 (travaux préparatoires by Charles de Visscher), 142–90 (discussion), 258–60 (declaration), at 153. The text of the declaration is in English as "Fundamental Rights of Man, as the Basis of a Restoration of International Law," *International Law Quarterly* 2, 2 (Summer 1948): 231–32. See "The International Protection of Human Rights," *Proceedings of the American Society of International Law* 43 (1949): 46–89. Compare Stevan Tscirkovitch, "La déclaration universelle des Droits de l'homme et sa portée internationale," *Revue générale de droit international public* 53 (1949): 341–58. Simultaneously, American lawyers did consider the promise or, more likely, threat a human rights covenant would pose, especially in relation to U.S. constitutional law. See esp. Zechariah Chafee, Jr., "Some Problems of the Draft International Covenant on Human Rights," *Proceedings of the American Philosophical Society* 95, 5 (1951): 471–89. In these years, Chafee taught a Harvard Law School course on "fundamental human rights" which dwelled for 900 of its 1,000 pages on the American constitutional tradition. See Chafee, *Documents on Fundamental Human Rights,* 3 vols. (Cambridge, Mass.: Mimeo distributed by Harvard University Press, 1951–52).

20. Kunz, "Present-Day Efforts at International Protection of Human Rights," *Proceedings of the American Society of International Law* 45 (1951): 110, 117.

21. Jessup, *A Modern Law of Nations* (New York: Macmillan, 1950), chap. 4, "Nationality and the Rights of Man." Jessup, "International Law in 1953 A.D.," *Transactions of the American Society for International Law* 47 (1953): 8–9.

22. Lauterpacht, "International Law after the Second World War," in *International Law,* 2: 163. Georg Schwarzenberger, *International Law*

and Totalitarian Lawlessness (London, 1943); compare Stephanie Steinle, *Völkerrecht und Machtpolitik: Georg Schwarzenberger (1908–1991)* (Baden-Baden, 2002); "'Plus ça change, plus c'est la meme chose': Georg Schwarzenberger's *Power Politics,*" *Journal of the History of International Law* 5, 2 (2003): 387–402; and her chapter in Beatson and Zimmerman, *Jurists.*

23. Schwarzenberger, "The Impact of the East-West Rift on International Law," *Transactions of the Grotius Society* 36 (1950): 244.

24. Schwarzenberger, *Power Politics: A Study of International Society,* 2nd ed. (London, 1951), 644, 640, and chap. 30 generally. Of Lauterpacht's 1945 optimism about the Soviet potential to live up to the "Stalin" Constitution, Schwarzenberger acidly commented, "Words were taken for deeds or, at least, as a cheque drawn on a brighter future" (646). For Lauterpacht's angry response to the *non possumus* decision, see *International Law and Human Rights,* chap. 11.

25. Max Radin, "Natural Law and Natural Rights," *Yale Law Journal* 59, 2 (January 1950): 214–37; Stanley Hoffmann, "Implementation of International Instruments on Human Rights," *Proceedings of the American Society for International Law* 53 (1959): 235–45 at 236, 241.

26. Smith, *The Crisis in the Law of Nations,* 18; Cyril Radcliffe, "The Rights of Man," *Transactions of the Grotius Society* 36 (1950): 8; Clive Parry, "Climate of International Law in Europe," *Transactions of the Grotius Society* 47 (1953): 40; Corbett, *The Individual and World Society* (Princeton, 1953), 50. Compare Kurt Wilk, "International Law and Global Ideological Conflict: Reflections on the Universality of International Law," *American Journal of International Law* 45, 4 (October 1951): 648–70; and Ernst Sauer, "Universal Principles in International Law," *Transactions of the Grotius Society* 42 (1956): 181–91; as well as the melancholy assessment of Ernest Hamburger, German-trained international lawyer who fled to France in 1933 and America in 1940, where he became a UN functionary: Hamburger, "Droits de l'homme et relations internationales," *Recueil des cours* 97 (1959): 442–43.

27. See, e.g., René Cassin, "L'homme, sujet de droit international et la protection des droits de l'homme dans la société universelle," in *La technique et les principes du droit public: Études en l'honneur de Georges Scelle,* 2 vols. (Paris, 1950); Max Huber, "Das Völkerrecht und der

Mensch," *Schweizerisches Jahrbuch für internationales Recht* 8 (1951): 9–30; Boris Mirkine-Guetzévitch, "L'O.N.U. et la doctrine moderne des droits de l'homme," *Revue générale de droit international public* 55 (1951): 161–198; and Alfred Verdross, "Die Würde des Menschen als Gundlage der Menschenrechte," in *René Cassin: Amicorum Discipulorumque Liber*, 4 vols. (Paris, 1969).

28. "Les droits fondamentaux de l'homme," at 153–54. One of Thomas Buergenthal's early articles, however, persuasively argued that "the voluminous literature dealing with the European Convention . . . does little to point out the practical weakness of the system established by it." Buergenthal, "The Domestic Status of the European Convention on Human Rights: A Second Look," *Journal of the International Commission of Jurists* 7, 1 (Summer 1966): 55–96 at 55.

29. See, for example, Louis B. Sohn et al., "Human Rights," in Commission to Study the Organization of Peace, *Strengthening the United Nations* (New York, 1957); Grenville Clark and Sohn, *World Peace through World Law* (Cambridge, Mass., 1958), xxvi, 350–351. "It may be argued that the time has come for a world organization to guarantee to every person in the world and against any authority whatever a few fundamental rights, such as exemption from slavery, freedom from torture and the right to be heard before criminal condemnation," Clark and Sohn wrote. "We have not, however, thought it wise to attempt so vast a departure; and the proposed guarantees relate solely to the possible infringements by the United Nations itself" (xxvi-xxvii). Compare Sohn, "The New International Law: Protection of the Rights of Individuals Rather than States," *American University Law Review* 32 (1982): 1–16; and Sohn, "The Human Rights Movement: From Roosevelt's Four Freedoms to the Interdependence of Peace, Development and Human Rights," Edward A. Smith Visiting Lecture, Harvard Law School Human Rights Program, 1995. Compare Jo M. Pasqualucci, "Louis Sohn: Grandfather of International Human Rights Law in the United States," *Human Rights Quarterly* 20, 4 (1998): 924–44; as well as the series of tributes to Sohn in the *Harvard International Law Journal* 48, 1 (Winter 2007).

30. Oscar Schachter, "The Charter and the Constitution: The Human Rights Provisions in American Law," *Vanderbilt Law Review* 4, 3 (April 1951): 643–59; Schachter, "The Invisible College of International Law-

yers," *Northwestern University Law Review* 72 (1977): 217–226. Compare David Kennedy, "Tom Franck and the Manhattan School," *New York University Journal of International Law and Politics* 35, 2 (Winter 2003): 397–435.

31. Louis Henkin, *Arms Control and Inspection in American Law*, pref. Jessup (New York, 1958), "Toward a 'Rule of Law' Community," in Harlan Cleveland, ed., *The Promise of World Tensions* (New York, 1961). Henkin, "The Treaty Makers and the Law Makers: The Niagara Reservation," *Columbia Law Review* 56, 8 (December 1956): 1151–82 and esp. "The Treaty Makers and the Law Makers: The Law of the Land and Foreign Relations," *University of Pennsylvania Law Review* 107 (May 1959): 903–936, esp. 922–23. For an argument against utopian hopes in the United Nations, see Henkin, "The United Nations and Its Supporters: A Self-Examination," *Political Science Quarterly* 78, 4 (December 1963): 504–36. Compare Catherine Powell, "Louis Henkin and Human Rights: A New Deal at Home and Abroad," in Cynthia Soohoo et al., eds., *Bringing Human Rights Home*, vol. 1, *A History of Human Rights in the United States* (Westport, 2008).

32. Henkin, "The United Nations and Human Rights," *International Organization* 19, 3 (Summer 1965): 504–17 at 508, 514. In Stanley Hoffmann's words, "order will serve human dignity rather than a deliberate offensive for human dignity will serve order." Hoffmann, "Implementation," 244. Henkin, "International Law and the Behavior of Nations," *Recueil des cours* 114 (1965): 167–281; and *How Nations Behave: Law and Foreign Policy* (New York, 1968). Only the second edition of the book (1979) added a chapter on human rights. Henkin, "International Human Rights as 'Rights,'" *Cardozo Law Review* 1, 2 (Fall 1979): 425–48, rpt. in J. Roland Pennock and John W. Chapman, eds., *Human Rights* (Nomos XXIII) (New York, 1981); and Henkin, *The Age of Rights* (New York, 1990), chap. 2.

33. Wolfgang Friedmann, "The Disintegration of European Civilisation and the Future of International Law," *Modern Law Review* 2 (1938–39): 194; *What's Wrong with International Law?* (London, 1941); *Law in a Changing Society* (London, 1959), chap. 14; *The Changing Structure of International Law* (New York, 1964); "General Course in Public International Law," *Recueil des cours* 127 (1969): 124–25, 127; "Human Welfare

and International Law," in Friedmann et al., eds., *Transnational Law in a Changing Society: Essays in Honor of Philip C. Jessup* (New York, 1972), 124. Compare John Bell, "Wolfgang Friedmann (1907–1972)," in Beatson and Zimmerman, eds., *Jurists Uprooted.*

34. Koskenniemi, *Gentle Civilizers,* 476. Myres S. McDougal and Gertrude Leighton, "The Rights of Man in the World Community: Constitutional Illusions versus Rational Action," *Law and Contemporary Problems* 14, 3 (Summer 1949): 490–536, rpt. in McDougal et al., *Studies in World Public Order* (New Haven, 1960). See also, e.g., McDougal, "Perspectives for an International Law of Human Dignity," *Proceedings of the American Society for International Law* 53 (1959): 107–36. Compare McDougal, review of Lauterpacht, *International Law and Human Rights, Yale Law Journal* 60, 6 (June 1951): 1051–56. The president of the German Bundestag went so far in 1978 as to declare that "few men have contributed more to this new branch of international law than Myres S. McDougal." Karl Carstens, "The Contribution of Myres S. McDougal to the Development of Human Rights in International Law," *New York Law School Law Review* 24, 1 (1978): 1.

35. Henri Rolin, "Les principes de droit international public," *Recueil des cours* 77 (1950): 353–60 ("Les droits fondamentaux des États"); *Yearbook of the International Law Commission* (1949): 287–90; compare, e.g., Ricardo J. Alfaro, "The Rights and Duties of States," *Recueil des cours* 97 (1959): 91–202.

36. Jessup, "Non-Universal International Law," *Columbia Journal of International Law* 12 (1973): 415–29 at 429. I mean the phrase sociologically and ideologically, but compare Matthew Craven, *The Decolonization of International Law: State Succession and the Law of Treaties* (Oxford, 2007) and the materials listed in the bibliographical essay.

37. Charles de Visscher, *Theory and Reality in Public International Law,* trans. Corbett (1953; Princeton, 1957), 128; Hoare in UN Doc. A/C.3/SR. 643, para. 13 (October 25, 1955); J. E. S. Fawcett, "The Role of the United Nations in the Protection of Human Rights—Is It Misconceived?," in Asbjörn Eide and August Schou, *International Protection of Human Rights: Proceedings of the Seventh Nobel Symposium, Oslo, September 25–27, 1967* (New York, 1968), 96.

38. Eagleton, "Excesses of Self-Determination," *Foreign Affairs* 31, 4 (July

1953): 596, 604; Wright, "Freedom and Human Rights under International Law," in Milton R. Konvitz and Clinton Rossiter, eds., *Aspects of Liberty: Essays Presented to Robert E. Cushman* (Ithaca, 1958), 185–86.

39. Schwelb, *Human Rights and the International Community: The Roots and Growth of the Universal Declaration of Human Rights* (Chicago, 1964), 10, 26–29, 35–37, 54–55, 66–71 at 68; and "The United Nations and Human Rights," *Howard Law Journal* 11, 2 (Spring 1965): 361–62, 366–68. Schwelb's arguments stretched back to "Die Kodifikationsarbeiten der Vereinten Nationen auf dem Gebiet der Menschenrechte," *Archiv des Völkerrechts* 8 (1959–1960): 16–49 at 24–25; and "The Influence of the Universal Declaration of Human Rights on International and National Law," *Proceedings of the American Society for International Law* 53 (1959): 217–29 at 217–18. In reporting Lauterpacht's shift, he even reported that the two of them had planned to prepare a new edition of *International Law and Human Rights,* a project he did not continue after Lauterpacht's death (*Human Rights,* 75). See also his verbatim remarks at a May 1963 conference in American Jewish Committee Archives, FAD-IO, Unnumbered Box, summarized as comments on John Humphrey, "Human Rights," *Annual Review of United Nations Affairs* (1962–1963): 114–17. On Schwelb, see the *Festschrift* in *Revue de droits de l'homme* 4, 2–3 (June-July 1971).

40. The earliest strong statement of the Universal Declaration as customary law is in Humphrey Waldock, "Human Rights in Contemporary International Law and the Significance of the European Convention," in *The European Convention of Human Rights* (*International and Comparative Law Quarterly* Supplementary Publication 11) (London, 1965), 15. Yet surveying such propositions in 1965, Thomas Buergenthal noted: "The legal significance of the Universal Declaration, in the light of the actual practice, may thus be considerably more limited than recent scholarly claims would make us believe." Buergenthal, "The United Nations and the Development of Rules Relating to Human Rights," *Proceedings of the American Society for International Law* 59 (1965): 134. The evolution in confidence in this argument clearly occurred around the turn of the 1970s, as the differences between two articles by John Humphrey make clear. Humphrey, "The UN Charter and the Universal Declaration of Human Rights," in Evan Luard, ed., *The International*

Protection of Human Rights (London, 1967); and Humphrey, "The Universal Declaration of Human Rights: Its History, Impact, and Juridical Character," in B. G. Ramcharan, ed., *Human Rights: Thirty Years after the Universal Declaration* (The Hague, 1979). Sohn, "The Universal Declaration of Human Rights: A Common Standard of Achievement? (The Status of the Universal Declaration in International Law)," *Journal of the International Commission of Jurists* 8, 2 (December 1967): 17–26; also in L. M. Singhvi, ed., *Horizons of Freedom* (New Delhi, 1969); *Montreal Statement of the Assembly for Human Rights* (1968), 2; also "Montreal Statement of the Assembly for Human Rights," *Journal of the International Commission of Jurists* 9, 1 (June 1968): 94–112 at 95.

41. Richard B. Bilder, "Rethinking International Human Rights: Some Basic Questions," *Wisconsin Law Review* 1969, 1 (1969): 172, 217.

42. Newman deserves much further study. See his articles "Natural Justice, Due Process, and the New International Covenants on Human Rights," *Public Law* (1967): 274–313; "Interpreting the Human Rights Clauses of the UN Charter," *Revue des droits de l'homme* 5, 2/3 (1972): 283–91; and "The International Bill of Rights: Does It Exist?," in Antonio Cassese, ed., *Current Problems of International Law* (Milan, 1975). Most important, see Theo van Boven, "Creative and Dynamic Strategies for Using United Nations Institutions and Procedures: The Frank Newman File," in Ellen L. Lutz et al., eds., *New Directions in Human Rights* (Philadelphia, 1989). Newman, like Richard Falk and Tom Farer, also testified at Donald Fraser's landmark 1973 congressional hearings.

43. Henkin, "The United Nations and Human Rights," 513. Compare Henkin, "International Law and the Behavior of Nations," 216–20.

44. The full remarks are in the American Jewish Committee Archives, FAD-IO, Unnumbered Box, and summarized in the discussion after Humphrey, "Human Rights," 122–24.

45. [Louis Henkin], "The World of the 1970s: A Jewish Perspective," Task Force Report, American Jewish Committee, 1972, 32, 34, 36 and Henkin, ed., *World Politics and the Jewish Condition* (New York, 1972).

46. "International Institute of Human Rights (René Cassin Foundation)," *Revue de droits de l'homme* 2, 1 (1969): 4–19; Henkin, "The United States Institute of Human Rights," *American Journal of International Law* 64, 4 (October 1970): 924–25 (I have been unable to determine when and

how this connection and appointment occurred; unlike Schwelb and Sohn, Henkin did not participate in Cassin's 1969 *Festschrift*); U.S. House of Representatives, *International Protection of Human Rights: The Work of International Organizations and the Role of U.S. Foreign Policy* (Washington, 1974), 355, 357. The casebook is Sohn and Buergenthal, *International Protection of Human Rights* (Indianapolis, 1973); compare Sohn and Buergenthal, *Basic Documents on International Protection of Human Rights* (Indianapolis, 1973). A couple of years earlier, Ian Brownlie had collected the first edition of his *Basic Documents on Human Rights* (Oxford, 1971); a bit later, see Richard B. Lillich and Frank B. Newman, *International Human Rights: Problems of Law and Policy* (Boston, 1979) and the New Haven school's answer, McDougal, Lasswell, and Lung-Chu Chen, *Human Rights and World Public Order: The Basic Policies of an International Law of Human Dignity* (New Haven, 1980).

47. The draft papers of the McGill conference, which I have from the Moses Moskowitz Papers, White Plains, New York, are in my possession; another version appears as Henkin, "The United States and the Crisis in Human Rights," *Virginia Journal of International Law* 14, 4 (1973–74): 653–71.

48. Henkin, "The Internationalization of Human Rights," *Proceedings of the General Education Seminar*, 6, 1 (1977): 1–16; Alice H. Henkin, ed., *Human Dignity: The Internationalization of Human Rights* (New York, 1978); Louis Henkin, "Human Rights: Reappraisal and Readjustment," in David Sidorsky, ed., *Essays on Human Rights: Contemporary Issues and Jewish Perspectives* (New York, 1979), 86, an essay which in general provides the best barometric reading of change in Henkin's outlook. See also his response to the Helsinki process, "Human Rights and 'Domestic Jurisdiction,'" in Buergenthal, ed., *Human Rights, International Law, and the Helsinki Accords* (Montclair, 1977). Humphrey, "The Implementation of International Human Rights Law," and esp. Schachter, "International Law Implications of U.S. Human Rights Policies," in *New York Law School Law Review* 24 (1978–79): 31–61, 63–87.

49. Henkin, *The Rights of Man Today* (Boulder, 1978).

50. "The Case for U.S. Ratification," *New York Times*, April 1, 1977. Inci-

dentally, Henkin's letter includes the first use of the phrase "international human rights movement" in the history of the newspaper.

51. See Schwelb, "The Teaching of the International Aspects of Human Rights," *Proceedings of the American Society of International Law* 65 (1971): 242–46. UNESCO had entered the field in 1973, with its support of the Cassin institute's Karal Vasak, ed., *Human Rights Studies in Universities* (1973), also available in *Revue des droits de l'homme* 6, 2 (1973). Then, in 1978, it held a major conference on human rights education—the first focusing on the project of pedagogy—in Vienna and, two years later, the major American event took place at New York University's law school, supported by the Rockefeller Foundation. See UNESCO, *The Teaching of Human Rights: Proceedings of the International Congress of the Teaching of Human Rights* (Vienna, 1980) and Theodor Meron, "A Report on the N.Y.U. Conference on Teaching International Protection of Human Rights," *New York University Journal of International Law and Policy* 13, 4 (Spring 1981): 881–960; and also the landmark collection that Meron edited shortly after based on the conference, *Human Rights and International Law: Legal and Policy Issues* (New York, 1984), which includes teaching guides and syllabi on different topics by leaders in the field.

52. See Henkin, ed., *The International Bill of Rights: The Covenant on Civil and Political Rights* (New York, 1981); and Henkin, "International Law: Politics, Values and Functions," *Recueil des cours* 216 (1989), Part I, balancing a critique of the "mythology" of sovereignty with the building blocks of states.

53. Theodor Meron, *Human Rights and Humanitarian Norms as Customary Law* (Oxford, 1989), 99.

54. Antonio Cassese, "The Helsinki Declaration and Self-Determination," in Buergenthal, ed., *Human Rights, International Law, and the Helsinki Accords.*

Epilogue

1. See Rex Martin and James W. Nickel, "A Bibliography on the Nature and Foundations of Rights, 1947–1977," *Political Theory* 6, 3 (August

1978): 395–413. By far the most interesting and significant philosophical engagements in the postwar era through the 1970s are to be found in Institut International de Philosophie, *Le Fondement des droits de l'homme* (Florence, 1966), with contributions from a number of European luminaries as well as American Richard McKeon.

2. Cranston's best known position was the critique of social and economic rights. See Maurice Cranston, *Human Rights To-day* (London, 1955, 1962), entitled in the American edition (and the new third British edition), *What Are Human Rights?* (New York, 1962; London, 1973). See also his "Pope John XXIII on Peace and Human Rights," *Political Quarterly* 34, 4 (October 1963): 380–90; and his roles in D. D. Raphael, ed., *Political Theory and the Rights of Man* (Bloomington, 1967); and head-lining the *Daedalus* special issue 112, 4 (Fall 1983).

3. From the editor's introduction to J. Roland Pennock and John W. Chapman, eds., *Human Rights: Nomos XXIII* (New York, 1981), vii. See also Stephen R. Graubard's preface to the *Daedalus* special issue: "Is the term 'human rights' simply a late twentieth century equivalent for the eighteenth century concept of the 'rights of man'? If so, why was the earlier formulation ever abandoned?" (v).

4. See, e.g., Walter Laqueur and Barry Rubin, eds., *The Human Rights Reader* (New York, 1979).

5. Ronald Dworkin, "Human Rights," in *Human Rights: A Symposium, Proceedings of the General Education Seminar* 6, 1 (Fall 1977): 40–51.

6. Compare the paper originally presented at a conference on decision theory at Schloss Reisensburg in Germany in June 1976 and first published as T. M. Scanlon, "Rights, Goals, and Fairness," *Erkenntnis* 11, 1 (May 1977): 81–95 with Scanlon, "Human Rights as a Neutral Concern," in Peter Brown and Douglas Maclean, eds., *Human Rights and U.S. Foreign Policy* (Lexington, 1979), a hiatus which clearly reflects the intervening explosion. Both are rpt. in Scanlon, *The Difficulty of Tolerance: Essays in Political Philosophy* (Cambridge, 2003).

7. See, e.g., Hans J. Morgenthau, "Human Rights and Foreign Policy," Distinguished Council of Religion and International Affairs Lecture on Morality and Foreign Policy (New York, 1979) and Raymond Aron, "The Politics of Human Rights," in Myres S. McDougal and W. Michael

Reisman, eds., *Power and Policy in Quest of Law: Essays in Honor of Eugene Victor Rostow* (Dordrecht, 1985).

8. For an apt prediction as Reagan was about to come to power, see Ronald Steel, "Are Human Rights Passé?" *The New Republic*, December 27, 1980.

9. Nicolas Guilhot, *The Democracy Makers: Human Rights and the Policy of Global Order* (New York, 2005); Guilhot, "Limiting Sovereignty or Producing Governmentality: Two Human Rights Regimes in U.S. Political Discourse," *Constellations* 15, 4 (2008): 502–16.

10. Some examples to ponder are Jacques Rancière, "Who Is the Subject of the Rights of Man?" *South Atlantic Quarterly* 103, 2/3 (Spring/Summer 2004): 297–310; Slavoj Žižek, "Against Human Rights," *New Left Review* 34 (July-August 2005): 115–31; and Alain Supiot, *Homo Juridicus: On the Anthropological Function of Law*, trans. Saskia Brown (New York, 2007), chap. 6.

11. See, for example, Mitchel Lasser, *Judicial Revolutions: The Rights Revolution in the Courts of Europe* (New York, 2009).

12. Compare Bradley R. Simpson, "Denying the 'First Right': The United States, Indonesia, and the Ranking of Human Rights by the Carter Administration, 1976–1980," *International History Review* 31, 4 (December 2009): 788–826 on how Indonesian activists were educated to speak human rights, to Sally Engle Merry's work on translation of claims, including Mark Goodale and Merry, eds., *The Practice of Human Rights: Tracking Law between the Global and the Local* (New York, 2007).

13. For contending presentations of the lived experience and moral significance of human rights work in the field, see James Dawes, *That the World May Know: Bearing Witness to Atrocity* (Cambridge, Mass., 2007); and David Kennedy, *The Rights of Spring* (Princeton, 2009).

14. See, e.g., Thomas M. Franck and Nigel S. Rodley, "The Law, the United Nations, and Bangla Desh," *Israel Yearbook for Human Rights* 2 (1972): 142–75 and "After Bangladesh: The Law of Humanitarian Intervention by Military Force," *American Journal of International Law* 67 (1973): 275–305; Richard B. Lillich, ed., *Humanitarian Intervention and the United Nations* (Charlottesville, 1973).

15. For sociological theses that show the need for much more historical re-

search, see Daniel Levy and Natan Sznaider, *The Holocaust and Memory in Global Age*, trans. Assenka Oksiloff (Philadelphia, 2005); compare Jeffrey Alexander, *Remembering the Holocaust: A Debate* (New York, 2009).

16. See Samantha Power, *"A Problem from Hell": America and the Age of Genocide* (New York, 2002), for a vivid presentation that fails to reflect on the very recent conditions for the possibility of its own moral position and energy.

17. In legal doctrine, as well, the once secure border between old, so-called humanitarian law and new human rights law seriously eroded; see, e.g., Theodor Meron, "The Humanization of Humanitarian Law," *American Journal of International Law* 94, 2 (April 2000): 239–289 and *The Humanization of International Law* (Dordrecht, 2006).

18. The phrase is from Kennedy, "The International Human Rights Movement: Part of the Problem?" *Harvard Human Rights Journal* 15 (2002): 101–26, esp. 108–9, rpt. as *The Dark Sides of Virtue: Reassessing International Humanitarianism* (Princeton, 2004), chap. 1.

19. Paige Arthur, "How 'Transitions' Reshaped Human Rights," *Human Rights Quarterly* 31, 2 (May 2009): 321–67.

20. See Aryeh Neier, *Taking Liberties: Four Decades in the Struggle for Rights* (New York, 2005), xxix–xxxii.

21. See, e.g., Catharine MacKinnon, *Are Women Human? And Other International Dialogues* (Cambridge, Mass., 2006).

22. See, e.g., Balakrishnan Rajagopal, *International Law from Below: Development, Social Movements, and Third-World Resistance* (New York, 2003) and Sandra Fredman, *Human Rights Transformed: Positive Rights and Positive Duties* (New York, 2008).

23. In a huge literature, see, e.g., Nira Wickramasinghe, "From Human Rights to Good Governance," in Mortimer Sellers, ed., *The New World Order: Sovereignty, Human Rights, and the Self-Determination of Peoples* (Oxford, 1996); Paul F. Diehl, *The Politics of Global Governance: International Organizations in an Interdependent World* (Boulder, 1997); the journal *Global Governance* began to appear in 1995.

24. Kéba M'Baye, "Le droit au développement comme un droit de l'homme," *Revue des droits de l'homme* 5 (1972): 505–34; U.N. Gen. Ass. Res. 41/128 (December 4, 1986); and René-Jean Dupuy, ed., *Le droit au*

développement au plan international (Alphen aan den Rijn, 1980); compare Roger Normand and Sarah Zaidi, *Human Rights at the UN: The Political History of Universal Justice* (Bloomington, 2008), chap. 9.

25. In light of the post-9/11 war on terror and integrated with a new notion of "human security," see Mary Robinson, "Connecting Human Rights, Human Development, and Human Security," in Richard Ashby Wilson, ed., *Human Rights in the "War on Terror"* (Cambridge, 2005).

26. The leading legal doctrinalist is clearly Philip Alston, who has pursued the topic since the late 1970s; more recently, philosophers, with Thomas Pogge in the lead, have crafted arguments for "poverty as a human rights violation." See Alston, "The Right to Development at the International Level," in Dupuy, ed., *Le droit,* rpt. in Frederick E. Snyder and Surakiart Sathirathai, eds., *Third World Attitudes towards International Law* (Dordrecht, 1987); "Making Space for New Human Rights: The Case of the Right to Development," *Harvard Human Rights Yearbook* 1 (1988): 1–38; and later Alston and Mary Robinson, eds., *Human Rights and Development: Toward Mutual Reinforcement* (Oxford, 2005); compare Jack Donnelly, "The 'Right to Development': How Not to Link Human Rights and Development," in Claude E. Welch, Jr. and Roland I. Meltzer, eds., *Human Rights and Development in Africa* (Albany, 1984). Thomas Pogge, ed., *Freedom from Poverty as a Human Right: Who Owes What to the Very Poor?* (Oxford, 2007).

27. Willem van Genugten and Camilo Perez-Bustillo, *The Poverty of Rights: Human Rights and the Eradication of Poverty* (London, 2001).

28. These comments are to be found in Harvard Human Rights Program, *Religion and State: An Interdisciplinary Roundtable Discussion Held in Vouliagmeni, Greece, October 1999* (Cambridge, Mass., 2004), 52.

Bibliographical Essay

In interpreting the place of human rights in the history of moral opinions and modern schemes of progressive reform, this book relies on a large body of excellent scholarship. It is a distilled account of this research, but by no means a neutral one. As a guide to readers and scholars, these pages offer an overview of the main treatments and—after the 1940s where few professional historians have ventured so far—some valuable sources on specific historical problems or topics yet to be seriously investigated. Mainly, I hope to give a sense of how far back in history the emerging attention to "human rights" currently rests. It makes especially vivid the mismatch between scrutiny of earlier eras in the quixotic search for deep roots, on the one hand, and of recent but more relevant periods about which too little is still known, on the other.

Books that have attempted synthesis fall into teleology, tunnel vision, and triumphalism, focusing on the background or, at the latest, the 1940s. See Micheline Ishay, *The History of Human Rights: From the Stone Age to the Globalization Era* (Berkeley, 2004); and especially Paul Gordon Lauren, *The Evolution of International Human Rights: Visions Seen,* new ed. (Philadelphia, 2003). Essays by contributors in two recent volumes are helpful: Mark P. Bradley and Patrice Petro, *Truth Claims: Representation and Human Rights* (New Brunswick, 2002); and Jeffrey N. Wasserstrom, Greg Grandin, and Lynn Hunt, eds., *Human Rights and Revolution,* 2nd ed. (Lanham, 2007). Forthcoming volumes edited by Stefan-Ludwig Hoffmann, *A History of Human Rights in the Twentieth Century* (Cambridge University Press); and Akira Iriye et al., eds., *Human Rights in the Twentieth Century: An International History* (Oxford University Press) promise to be cutting-edge. Kenneth Cmiel died too soon to complete his promised work in the field, but his essays set the standard, notably "The Recent History of Human Rights,"

American Historical Review 109, 1 (February 2004): 117–34. Jan Eckel's emerging work is also of the highest quality; see his overview of the field, "Utopie der Moral, Kalkül der Macht: Menschenrechte in der globalen Politik seit 1945," *Archiv für Sozialgeschichte* 49 (2009): 437–84.

In recent decades, the deep past has faced the challenge of affording a lineage to a recent project. For claims about early Jewish sources, consider Louis Henkin, "Judaism and Human Rights," *Judaism* 25, 4 (Fall 1976): 435–46; and David Sidorsky, ed., *Essays in Human Rights* (Philadelphia, 1979); as well as Lenn E. Goodman, *Judaism, Human Rights, and Human Values* (New York, 1998). For deep Christian sources, see Nicholas Wolterstorff, *Justice: Rights and Wrongs* (Princeton, 2008). For Stoic sources, see especially Philip Mitsis, "Stoic Origins of Natural Rights," in Katerina Ierodiakonou, ed., *Topics in Stoic Philosophy* (New York, 1999); and, to evaluate how different Stoic beliefs really were, Malcolm Schofield, *The Stoic Idea of the City* (Cambridge, 1991); or Eric Brown, "Hellenistic Cosmopolitanism," in Mary Louise Gill and Pierre Pellegrin, eds., *A Companion to Ancient Philosophy* (Oxford, 2006). On Roman law, see Richard A. Bauman, *Human Rights in Ancient Rome* (New York, 2000); and Tony Honoré, *Ulpian: Pioneer of Human Rights,* 2nd ed. (New York, 2002).

The best materials for considering the prehistory of specific rights are due to German and Austrian research programs of the 1980s. See Günter Birtsch, ed., *Grund- und Freiheitsrechte im Wandel von Gesellschaft und Geschichte* (Göttingen, 1981); *Grund- und Freiheitsrechte von der ständischen zu spätbürgerlichen Gesellschaft* (Göttingen, 1987); and the truly mammoth bibliography: Birtsch et al., eds., *Grundfreiheiten, Menschenrechte, 1500–1850: eine internationale Bibliographie,* 5 vols. (Stuttgart, 1991–92). See also Wolfgang Schmale, *Archäologie der Grund- und Menschenrechte in der frühen Neuzeit: ein deutsch-französisches Paradigma* (Munich, 1997); and Margarete Grandner et al., eds., *Grund- und Menschenrechte: Historische Perspektiven— Aktuelle Problematiken* (Vienna, 2002), especially Schmale's synthetic essay. Consider also Peter Blickle's remarkable *Von der Leibeigenschaft zu den Menschenrechten: eine Geschichte der Freiheit in Deutschland* (Munich, 2003).

The now large literature on the origins of "natural" rights falls into four broad schools. The first two schools debate the role of the medieval developments that both consider formative, while the third and fourth stress the importance of subversive Renaissance humanists and the seventeenth-century school of "modern" natural law thinkers respectively. In the first, often Thomistic school, targeting late medieval nominalism for "subjectivism" in the origins of rights, see Michel Villey's series of publications beginning in the 1940s and leading through "La genèse du droit subjectif chez Guillaume d'Occam," *Archives de philosophie du droit* 9 (1964): 97–127; and *Le droit et les droits de l'homme* (Paris, 1983); compare Heinrich Rommen, "The Genealogy of Natural Rights," *Thought* 29, 114 (Autumn 1954): 403–25. Later, consult Richard Tuck, *Natural Rights Theories: Their Origin and Development* (Cambridge, 1979); and Arthur Stephen McGrade, "Ockham and the Birth of Individual Rights," in Brian Tierney and Peter Linehan, *Authority and Power: Studies on Medieval Law and Government Presented to Walter Ullmann* (Cambridge, 1980). The second school, in response, stresses continuity in Christian natural law, which it then traces forward into early modern developments: see Brian Tierney, *The Idea of Natural Rights* (Atlanta, 1997); and Annabel Brett, *Liberty, Right, and Nature: Individual Rights in Later Scholastic Thought* (Cambridge, 1997). For the third school, see Leo Strauss, *Natural Right and History* (Chicago, 1953); Tuck, "The 'Modern' Theory of Natural Law," in Anthony Pagden, ed., *The Languages of Political Theory in Early Modern Europe* (Cambridge, 1990); and Tuck, *Philosophy and Government, 1572–1651* (Cambridge, 1993). For the fourth, see Blandine Barret-Kriegel, *Les droits de l'homme et le droit naturel* (Paris, 1989); and many studies of modern natural law figures. No matter who is correct, of course, the results for a history of human rights are a matter of background precondition, not immediate causation.

On the rights of the Enlightenment and revolution, the most prominent work is surely Lynn Hunt, *Inventing Human Rights: A History* (New York, 2007); compare my review, "On the Genealogy of Morals," *The Nation*, April 17, 2007. Other valuable works on the American scene include Knud Haakonssen, "From Natural Law to the Rights of Man: A European Perspective on American Debates," in Haakonssen and Michael J. Lacey, eds., *A Culture of Rights: The Bill of Rights in Philosophy, Politics, and Law* (Cambridge, 1991); several essays in Robert Fatton Jr. and R. K. Ramazani, eds., *The Future of Liberal Democracy: Thomas Jefferson and the Contemporary World* (New York, 2004); and Barry Alan Shain, ed., *The Nature of Rights at the American Founding and Beyond* (Charlottesville, 2007). For France, see Marcel Gauchet, *La Révolution des droits de l'homme* (Paris, 1989); Stéphane Rials, *La declaration des droits de l'homme et du citoyen* (Paris, 1989); and Keith Michael Baker, "The Idea of a Declaration of Rights," in Dale van Kley, ed., *The French Idea of Freedom: The Old Regime and the Declaration of Rights of 1789* (Stanford, 1994).

The progressive assault on laissez-faire, on which I lay special emphasis in Chapter 1 as the most significant interruption in the trajectory of "individual rights" and formalist abstraction in the later nineteenth century, is best explored in classics ranging from Morton White, *Social Thought in America: The Revolt against Formalism* (New York, 1947); to James T. Kloppenberg, *Uncertain Victory: Progressivism and Social Democracy in Anglo-American Thought* (Oxford, 1986); as well as legal scholarship such as P. S. Atiyah, *The Rise and Fall of Freedom of Contract* (Oxford, 1987); and Barbara J. Fried's excellent *The Progressive Assault against Laissez-Faire: Robert Hale and the First Law and Economics Movement* (Cambridge, Mass., 1998). Works that do not restrict themselves to the Anglo-American sector of this revolt include Daniel Rodgers, *Atlantic Crossings: Social Politics in a Progressive Age* (Cambridge, Mass., 2000); and Janet Horne, *A Social Laboratory for Modern France: The Musée Social and the Rise of the Welfare State* (Raleigh, 2002). The sense of uncertainty around the meaning of rights talk after the New Deal overcame free labor thought is well captured in Risa Goluboff, *The Lost Promise of Civil Rights* (Cambridge, Mass., 2007), chap. 1.

On internationalism, the best work remains F. S. L. Lyons, *Internationalism in Europe, 1815–1914* (Leyden, 1963). On women's internationalism, the pioneering study is Leila Rupp, *Worlds of Women: The Making of an International Women's Movement* (Princeton, 1997); see also Rupp, "The Making of International Women's Organizations," in Martin Geyer and Johannes Paulmann, eds., *The Mechanics of Internationalism: Culture, Society and Politics from the 1840s to World War I* (Oxford, 2001); and Nitzka Berkovitch, "The Emergence and Transformation of the International Women's Movement," in John Boli and George M. Thomas, eds., *Constructing World Culture: International Non-Governmental Organizations since 1875* (Stanford, 1999).

Given the difficulty of writing the history of human rights about the period prior to the 1940s, much more responsible attention now focuses on that era, when Franklin Delano Roosevelt and then the United Nations made the phrase—essentially new in the English language—central to international organization for the first time. Most studies, unfortunately, are set on a story of breakthrough, triumph, and uplift that screens out the most interesting features of the period. Most illustrative is Mary Ann Glendon, *A World Made New: Eleanor Roosevelt and the Universal Declaration of Human Rights* (New York, 2001). See also Elizabeth Borgwardt, *A New Deal for the World: America's Vision for Human Rights* (Cambridge, Mass., 2006). I have tried to apply Borgwardt's passing complaint that scholars "ransack the past for early expressions of familiar-sounding political concepts" far more thoroughly to the 1940s than Borgwardt herself is willing to do (58–59). Consider also J. M. Winter's chapter on René Cassin in *Dreams of Peace and Freedom: Utopian Moments in the Twentieth Century* (New Haven, 2006); and his forthcoming biographical study, co-authored with Antoine Prost, of this important figure. A fine drafting history of the Universal Declaration of Human Rights is Johannes Morsink, *The Universal Declaration of Human Rights: Origins, Drafting, and Intent* (Philadelphia, 1999). In my chapter, I place more stress than these historians have on transnational Christianity, which I have also explored in my "The First Historian of Human Rights," *American Historical Review*, forthcoming; "Personalism, Community, and the Origins of Human Rights," in Hoffmann, ed., *A History*; and "Jacques Maritain: le origini dei Diritti umani e il pensiero politico cristiano," in Luigi Bonanate and Roberto Papini, eds., *Dialogo interculturale e diritti umani: La Dichiarazione Universale dei Diritti Umani, Genesi, evoluzione, e problemi odierni (1948–2008)* (Bologna, 2008).

But by far the richest book on the era, full of impressive detail, is A. W. B. Simpson, *Human Rights and the End of Empire: Britain and the Genesis of the European Convention* (Oxford, 2001), which—in spite of the restricted title—also provides the fullest story of origins of human rights in wartime and early United Nations processes. Like many other treatments, Simpson's is motivated by patriotic desire to award credit for human rights. His own voluminous evidence, however, proves against his intention the nonlegal and symbolic role of the relative ascendancy of rights involved. Marco Duranti's forthcoming study of the origins of the European Convention will restore it to its time very persuasively; for sociological insight, see Mikael Rask Madsen, *La genèse de l'Europe des droits de l'homme: Enjeux juridiques et stratégies d'État (1945–1970)* (Strasbourg, forthcoming). Valuable early legal commentaries on the Convention include Hersch Lauterpacht, *International Law and Human Rights* (New York, 1950), appendix; A. H. Robertson, "The European Convention for the Protection of Human Rights," *British Year Book for International Law* 27 (1950): 145–63; and Karl Josef Partsch,

"Die Entstehung der europäischen Menschenrechtskonvention," *Zeitschrift für ausländisches öffentliches Recht und Völkerrecht* 15 (1953–54): 631–60. In a more general literature over the decades, the place to start in English is Robertson's *Human Rights in Europe* (Manchester, 1963), whose later editions (1977, 1993) provide a sense of change.

While earlier general works treat anticolonialism and decolonization as if their inclusion in the history of human rights were obvious—a premise I dispute in this book—in reality scholars have only begun to analyze the topics in detail. Roland Burke, in *Decolonization and the Evolution of International Human Rights* (Philadelphia, 2010), has written a pioneering work championing liberal anticolonialism as the version that remained true to human rights (by comparison I treat human rights as more up for grabs, rather than a stable concept that anticolonialism could betray). Fabian Klose, *Menschenrechte im Schatten kolonialer Gewalt: Die Dekolonisierungskriege in Kenia und Algerien 1945–1962* (Munich, 2009) explores two prominent colonial counterinsurgencies. At the level of the United Nations, Roger Normand and Sarah Zaidi, *Human Rights at the UN: The Political History of Universal Justice* (Bloomington, 2007), is worth reading.

The history of nongovernmental organizations is also barely assayed. The pioneering student, Lyman Cromwell White, remains the starting point. White, who had originated this topic already in the interwar period with a Ph.D. thesis at Columbia University and later served in the UN secretariat, did not find many followers until a half century later. See his *Structure of Private International Organizations* (Philadelphia, 1933); "Nouvelles méthodes pour l'organisation de la paix internationale," *Revue de droit international, de sciences diplomatiques, politiques, et sociales* 27 (1949): 237–46; and *International Non-Governmental Organizations: Their Purposes, Methods, and Accomplishments* (New Brunswick, 1951). Of recent literature, Margaret E. Keck and Kathryn Sikkink, *Activists Beyond Borders: Advocacy Networks in International Politics* (Ithaca, 1998) is crucial; see also Jeremi Suri, "Non-Governmental Organizations and Non-State Actors," in Patrick Finney, ed., *Palgrave Advances in International History* (New York, 2005). At the United Nations, see Peter Willetts, ed., *"The Conscience of the World": The Influence of Non-Governmental Organisations in the United Nations* (Washington, 1996). It seems rather clear that blinders continue to exclude the early, striking, and persisting relevance of religious groups among NGOs generally. See Bruno Duriez et al., eds., *Les ONG confessionnelles: Religion et action internationale* (Paris, 2007). On human rights NGOs, see the rich but uncritical chapters in William Korey, *NGOs and the Universal Declaration of Human Rights: "A Curious Grapevine"* (Basingstoke, 1998). On Amnesty International, Egon Larsen, *A Flame in Barbed Wire: The Story of Amnesty International* (London, 1978); Jonathan Power, *Against Oblivion: Amnesty International's Fight for Human Rights* (Glasgow, 1981), and Power, *Like Water on Stone: The Story of Amnesty International* (Harmondsworth, 2001) are valuable, but the key essay is by Tom Buchanan, "'The Truth Will Set You Free': The Making of Amnesty International," *Journal of Contemporary History* 37, 4 (2002): 575–94.

Though I argue that only the circumvention of United Nations processes allowed for the public emergence of human rights in the 1970s, those processes remain a wonderful subject for further investigation. In particular, there is the largely unexplored internal history of the small group of human rights functionaries who were the body's permanent employees, like John Humphrey and his deputies Egon Schwelb and Kamleshwar Das, and later figures like Marc Schreiber, Theo van Boven, and Bertrand Ramcharan. Compare Roger S. Clark, "Human Rights Strategies of the 1960s within the United Nations: A Tribute to the Late Kamleshwar Das," *Human Rights Quarterly* 21, 2 (May 1999): 308–41; and Ramcharan, *The Quest for Protection: A Human Rights Journey at the United Nations* (Geneva, n.d.), esp. chap. 5. For several of these figures' own optimistic reading of the tea-leaves in the mid-1970s, see Schreiber, "La pratique récente des Nations Unies dans le domaine de la protection des droits de l'homme," *Recueil des cours de l'Académie du droit international* 145 (1975): 297–398; Ramcharan, ed., *Human Rights: Thirty Years after the Universal Declaration* (The Hague, 1979); as well as van Boven, "Politisation et droits de l'homme," in Gérard Blanc et al., *Les organisations internationales: entre l'innovation et stagnation* (Lausanne, 1985).

The decade of the 1970s is now an exciting period to study, though not yet in human rights history. See, e.g., Philip Jenkins, *Decade of Nightmares: The End of the Sixties and the Birth of 1980s America* (New York, 2006); Edgar Wolfrum, *Die 70er Jahre: Republik im Aufbruch* (Darmstadt, 2007); and Philippe Chassaigne, *Les années 1970: fin d'un monde et origine de notre modernité* (Paris, 2008). By and large, American historians now turn to the decade for an understanding of the right not the left. See, e.g., Bruce J. Schulman and Julian Zelizer, eds., *Rightward Bound: Making America Con-*

servative in the 1970s (Cambridge, Mass., 2009). However, Niall Ferguson et al., eds., *The Shock of the Global: The 1970s in Perspective* (Cambridge, Mass., 2010) promises an enterprising transnational approach.

Along with numerous personal memoirs, the place to start on Soviet dissent is the classic overview by Ludmilla Alexeyeva, *Soviet Dissent: Contemporary Movements for National, Religious, and Human Rights,* trans. Carol Pearce and John Glad (Middletown, 1987). See also Jean Chiama and Jean-François Soulet, *Histoire de la dissidence: Oppositions et révoltes en URSS et dans les démocraties populaires de la mort de Staline à nos jours* (Paris, 1982). On Andrei Sakharov, see Peter Dornan, "Andrei Sakharov: The Conscience of a Liberal Scientist," in Rudolf L. Tökés, ed., *Dissent in the USSR: Politics, Ideology, and People* (Baltimore, 1975), alongside more recent biographies. For a popular history of the Moscow Helsinki group, see Paul Goldberg, *The Final Act* (New York, 1988). A forthcoming study by Benjamin Nathans of the origins and character of Soviet dissidence will renovate the field from the ground up.

On the origins of Latin American human rights networks, Vania Markarian, *Left in Transformation: Uruguayan Exiles and the Latin American Human Rights Networks, 1967–1984* (New York, 2005) is the best study in English on all countries. In contrast, the majority of treatments assume a "human rights revolution" prior to, rather than created by, Latin American and other responses in the 1970s. See, e.g., Thomas C. Wright, *State Terrorism in Latin America: Chile, Argentina, and International Human Rights* (Lanham, 2007). On post-1976 Argentina, see Iain Guest, *Behind the Disappearances: Argentina's Dirty War against Human Rights and the United Nations* (Philadelphia, 1990).

For early legal sources on Inter-American System of Human Rights, by far the most illuminating treatments of the subject can be found in José Cabranes's essays, "Human Rights and Non-Intervention in the Inter-American System," *Michigan Law Review* 65, 6 (April 1967): 1147–82; and "The Protection of Human Rights by the Organization of American States," *American Journal of International Law* 62, 4 (October 1968): 889–908. See also Karal Vasak, *La commission interaméricaine des droits de l'homme* (Paris, 1968); Anna P. Schreiber, *The Inter-American Commission on Human Rights* (Leyden, 1970); A. H. Robertson, *Human Rights in the World* (Manchester, 1972); Thomas Buergenthal, "The Revised OAS Charter and the Protection of Human Rights," *American Journal of International Law* 69, 4 (October

1975): 828–32; and Héctor Gros Espiell, "Le système interaméricain comme régime régional des droits de l'homme," *Recueil des cours* 145, 2 (1975): 1–55. For an extremely skeptical treatment of the Convention for failing to restrict itself to feasible political and civil rights, see Buergenthal, "The American Convention of Human Rights: Illusions and Hopes," *Buffalo Law Review* 21, 1 (Fall 1971): 121–36. More recently, see Klaas Dykmann, *Philanthropic Endeavors or the Exploitation of an Ideal? The Human Rights Policy of the Organization of American States in Latin America (1970–1991)* (Frankfurt, 2004).

Academics in the 1970s certainly noticed the efflorescence of new NGO mobilization, especially around the Soviet dissidents and Latin American repression. Consider Ferdinand Mesch, "Human Rights, Chile, and International Organizations," *DePaul Law Review* 24 (1974–75): 999–1022; and Philip L. Ray, Jr. and J. Sherrod Taylor, "The Role of Non-Governmental Organizations in Implementing Human Rights in Latin America," *Georgia Journal of International and Comparative Law* 7 (1977): 477–506; David Weissbrodt, "The Role of International Non-Governmental Organizations in the Implementation of Human Rights," *Texas International Law Journal* 12 (1977): 293–320; Laurie Wiseberg and David Scoble, "Human Rights NGOs: Notes towards a Comparative Analysis," *Revue de droits de l'homme* 9, 4 (1976): 611–44; and Wiseberg and Scoble, "Monitoring Human Rights Violations: The Role of Nongovernmental Organizations," in Donald P. Kommers and Gilburt D. Loescher, eds., *Human Rights and American Foreign Policy* (Notre Dame, 1979).

There is a recent flurry of activity in the study of the Conference on Security and Cooperation in Europe. See Vojtech Mastny, *Helsinki, Human Rights, and European Security: Analysis and Documentation* (Durham, 1986); Thomas Maresca, *To Helsinki: The Conference on Security and Cooperation in Europe, 1973–1975*, new ed. (Durham, 1987); and now Andreas Wenger et al., eds., *Origins of the European Security System: The Helsinki Process Revisited, 1968–1975* (New York, 2008); Thomas Fischer, "'A Mustard Seed Grows into a Bushy Plant': The Finnish CSCE Initiative of 5 May 1969," *Cold War History* 9, 2 (May 2009): 177–201; and especially Jussi M. Hanhimäki, "Conservative Goals, Revolutionary Outcomes: The Paradox of Détente," *Cold War History* 8, 4 (November 2008): 503–12; compare Richard Davy, "Helsinki Myths: Setting the Record Straight on the Final Act of the CSCE, 1975," *Cold War History* 9, 1 (February 2009): 1–22. For narratives of the Helsinki process that followed, most of which take their stories to be about the triumph of norms or even the ending of the Cold War, see Korey, *The Promises We Keep: Human Rights, the Helsinki Process, and American Foreign Policy* (New York, 1993); Daniel C. Thomas, *The Helsinki Effect: International Norms, Human Rights, and the Demise of Communism* (Princeton, 2001); and Sarah B. Snyder, *The Helsinki Network: Transnational Human Rights Activism in the Late Cold War* (forthcoming).

On the 1970s revolt of the U.S. Congress in the area of foreign affairs—of which the pioneering hearings on human rights were a minor feature—see Thomas M. Franck and Robert Weisband, *Foreign Policy by Congress* (New York, 1979); David P. Forsythe, *Human Rights and U.S. Foreign Policy: Congress Reconsidered* (Gainesville, 1988); and, more recently, Robert David Johnson, *Congress and the Cold War* (New York, 2006), and David Schmitz, *The United States and Right-Wing Dictatorships, 1965–1989* (New York, 2006), chap. 4. Scholars are just beginning to seek the prehistory of Jimmy Carter's January 1977 embrace of human rights. I owe guidance to Simon Stevens, "Jimmy Carter's Presidential Campaign and the Search for a New Foreign Policy" (M.Phil. thesis, University of Cambridge, 2008), while Daniel Sargent, "From Internationalism to Globalism: The United States and the Transformation of International Politics in the 1970s" (Ph.D. diss. Harvard University, 2008) proposes a more ambitious framework. On Carter's presidency itself, Gaddis Smith, *Morality, Reason, and Power: American Diplomacy in the Carter Years* (New York, 1986) remains the most thought-provoking work.

For international law, Martti Koskenniemi's *The Gentle Civilizer of Nations: The Rise and Fall of International Law* (Cambridge, 2002) is the indispensable starting point for all reflection on the modern discipline, and certainly was for my own foray into the period after 1945 in this book. For the "decolonization of international law"—which in spite of much interest in the imperial context of legal thought in earlier eras has received minimal attention—consider B. V. A. Röling, *International Law in an Expanded World* (Amsterdam, 1960); Wolfgang Friedmann, "The Position of Underdeveloped Countries and the Universality of International Law," *Columbia Journal of Transnational Law* 1/2 (1961–3): 78–86; Georges M. Abi-Saab, "The Newly Independent States and the Rule of International Law: An Outline," *Howard Law Journal* 8, 2 (Spring 1962): 95–121; C. Wilfred Jenks, ed., *International Law in a Changing World* (Dobbs Ferry, 1963); Richard A. Falk, "The New States and International Legal Order," *Recueil des cours* 118 (1966): 1–

103; R. P. Anand, *New States and International Law* (Delhi, 1972); and Abi-Saab, "The Third World and the Future of the International Legal Order," *Revue égyptienne de droit international* 27 (1973): 27–66.

Analyses of human rights in theory and practice since the 1970s are, of course, too legion to even begin listing. But two journals of the contemporary era surely provide the best place to gain orientation: *Revue de droits de l'homme,* which appeared starting in 1968; and *Universal Human Rights,* which began in 1979, changing its name to *Human Rights Quarterly* after two years.

Acknowledgments

Though it provides much new information, this book is mainly an attempt to synthesize and reconceive what is known so far in a field as perplexing as it is exciting. For this reason, I owe a debt of gratitude most of all to the fellow historians of human rights whose research I have so often borrowed, if sometimes for very different ends than they may have intended.

For their published volumes or conference papers, e-mailed suggestions or verbal disagreements, I would like to offer heartfelt thanks to Carol Anderson, Gary J. Bass, Manu Bhagavan, Elizabeth Borgwardt, Mark P. Bradley, Roland Burke, G. Daniel Cohen, Michael Geyer, Mary Ann Glendon, Lasse Heerten, Stefan-Ludwig Hoffmann, Lynn Hunt, Barbara Keys, Fabian Klose, Paul Gordon Lauren, Mikael Rask Madsen, A. Dirk Moses, Benjamin Nathans, Devin Pendas, Daniel Sargent, Mira Siegelberg, Bradley Simpson, Brian Simpson, Sarah Snyder, Charles Walton, Keith David Watenpaugh, Eric Weitz, Lora Wildenthal, and Jay Winter. These scholars have been pioneers in the construction of a new field.

Many others invited presentations on one or another aspect of this topic at annual conferences of the American Council of Learned Societies, the American Historical Association, and the Society for French Historical Studies, as well as at events at the Columbia University Center for International History, the Duke University School of Law, the École des Hautes Études en Sciences Sociales, Harvard University, the Left Forum, the New York University Institute for Public Knowledge, Queen's University (Ontario), Rice University, the University of Chicago, the University of Pennsylvania, the University of South Carolina, the University of Wisconsin-Madison, the Yale Law School (twice!), and the Zentrum für zeithistorische

Forschung. I would like to thank all my hosts and interlocutors on these occasions.

A number of colleagues and friends offered help on one or another chapter or the whole manuscript. David Bates, Jeffrey Collins, and especially Andrew Jainchill helped with the first chapter, which Jerrold Seigel also generously read in more primitive form. Eric Foner responded to queries about that newfangled thing American history, while Jan-Werner Müller reflected on old Europe's history and thought. Pablo Piccato advised on Latin American affairs. Peter Holquist, next door in Fuld Hall during our year off, drank my kool-aid (or at least said he did). One of my oldest friends, Paul Hanebrink, commented on the intersection of religion and politics. I have learned many things from Julian Bourg about 1968 and its aftermath. Teaching the history of the law of war with John Fabian Witt was a treat, and helped me decide it was, until recently, a separate topic. Supervising an independent study for Columbia graduate students Simon Stevens and Stephen Wertheim allowed me to argue my views with precocious experts, who also showed me their research and offered me their remarks on my writing. Participating on the committee of Marco Duranti's Yale University dissertation afforded me a number of valuable insights into the 1940s, which helped me revise my chapter on the subject.

A few essential contacts aided me even more. The longstanding or newer complicity of my friends on the editorial collective of *Humanity*, a journal launch intersecting the topic of this book, proved extremely valuable: Nehal Bhuta, Nils Gilman, Nicolas Guilhot, Joseph Slaughter, and Miriam Ticktin deserve my thanks. Editorial attention at *The Nation* from John Palattella and Adam Shatz was a great help, not least for the invitation to write the book review that actually launched this project. Most of all, I benefited from Jan Eckel's providential visit to New York as I was writing the book; he honored me by telling me honestly how my reckless intuition fit (or not) with his more sober reflection, and he reminded me of Borges's piece. Heroically, Mark P. Bradley and Paul W. Kahn, in reviews for the press and in numerous interactions, offered wise observations on my messy first draft, which materially affected how I finalized the manuscript.

Though they allowed me to go my own way on this project, I am not sure how I could repay my debt to my Columbia University history colleagues, notably in the European wing. It has been by far the greatest privilege of my career to witness at close hand a dream team of senior historians at work there: I am thankful to Volker Berghahn, Victoria de Grazia, Mark Mazower, Susan Pedersen, and Michael Stanislawski for their examples and their support. Mark Mazower deserves special thanks for allowing me to commandeer his Center for International History on several occasions to organize events related to my work on this book, and then for counsel and reassurance on a late draft. I am also very grateful to Elazar Barkan and Michael Stanislawski for involving me in Columbia's undergraduate program in human rights.

Though I have been thinking about this topic for the best part of a decade—with apologies to my law school teachers and later the students in my history of human rights classes—I wrote this book essentially during 2008–2009 at the Institute for Advanced Study, where the School of Historical Studies hosted me. Support for this sabbatical was provided by the outstanding generosity of the American Council of Learned Societies Frederick Burkhardt fellowship program for recently tenured scholars and the John Simon Guggenheim Memorial Foundation fellowship program. For extraordinary beneficence, I must thank Columbia University for its H. F. Gerry Lenfest Distinguished Faculty Award, as well as Alan Brinkley and Nicholas B. Dirks for their special kindness. The Jacques Maritain Center at Notre Dame University also provided a week's visiting grant.

I wish I could name all the library and interlibrary staff on whom I depended to amass my materials. At the American Jewish Committee archives, Charlotte Bonelli and her team opened holdings to me and digitized documents for me on demand. Jordan Hirsch provided a fine memo on the campaign on behalf of Soviet Jewry for me. At IAS, Maria Tuya provided valuable support, and Marian Zelazny all kinds of help. The Columbia history department and law school allowed me to hire always essential research assistants: Ariell Cacciola, Toby Harper, and—during especially crucial summers—Charles Clavey and Bryan Kim Butler. In the final, frantic months of drafting, Bryan's assistance was as indispensable as it was professional, and I owe him and the law school summer institute a great deal. Lastly, I was fortunate that James Chappel could provide advice on how to finalize the text, without which the results—especially in the first chapter—would look even worse. At the eleventh hour, Tanisha M. Fazal converted my graph into the correct format.

Sometimes inadvertently, a number of people I mention, or their relatives, provided fascinating autobiographical reflections or useful information. These include Arthur Danto, Cathy Fitzpatrick, Louis Henkin, Donald Kommers, Jeri Laber, Howard Moskowitz, Bertrand Ramcharan, and Thomas Scanlon.

I am profoundly grateful to Joyce Seltzer at Harvard University Press for her longstanding interest in this book, from before I had written a word up to these last ones. Katherine Brick provided superb copyediting, and I owe much to Amelia Atlas, Jeannette Estruth, Graciela Galup, and Kristin Sperber for their help too.

I could not get away without thanking my friends and family most of all, including my sister for lavishing me with irony in pretty much every medium she and I discover. Alisa Berger, my wife, deserves my deepest thanks for creating the life together, and providing the love, that made this book possible. Together with our girls, Lily and Madeleine, she is my utopia—last and first.

Index